Contents

Acknowledgements

To my long-suffering family, John, Kate, Stewart and Patrick for your love, support, encouragement and tolerance. To Mary, Jan and all the team at Heinemann for your unfailing support.

The author and publishers would like to thank the following for permission to reproduce photographs:

John Birdsall Photography – pages 12, 133, 146, 179, 212, 318
Colorsport – page 25
Mary Evans Picture Library – page 31
Gareth Boden – pages 59, 71, 142, 169, 223
Robert Harding Picture Library – page 104
Science Photo Library – page 141
Tony Stone Images – page 166
John Walmsley – page 314

Dedication

To all those who share in providing care.

Introduction

This revised edition of *NVQ Level 2 Care* comes at a time of change in the sector. So much has happened since the book was first written, both in terms of new legislation, guidelines and policies and in the way that issues are approached and addressed, that some changes were absolutely essential. Inevitably, however, this is a period of uncertainty as we await the completion of the new National Occupational Standards and the resulting NVQs.

You will notice some changes in terminology throughout the book, which reflect current usage. You will notice that the term 'service user' has replaced 'client', although 'client' still appears in the Unit and Element titles. This is because, of course, these titles will not change until the new standards appear. As far as possible, the changes in this edition reflect the present climate of opinion and emerging thinking, but change is a constant feature of the sector so there will almost certainly be new initiatives and guidelines of which everyone in the care sector needs to be aware.

The new standards will reflect the changes in the profession, such as the emphasis on quality services, the focus on tackling exclusion, and the influence of the culture of rights and responsibilities. There has been a huge increase, too, in understanding in all parts of the sector, and a recognition of the satisfaction that comes from working alongside service users as partners and directors of their own care, rather than as passive receivers of services.

However, much of what we do in the care sector will remain the same; the basic principles of caring, treating people with dignity and respect, ensuring choice and promoting independence will continue, and the skills of good communication remain as vital as ever.

Very large numbers of candidates have undertaken NVQ qualifications over the five-year life of the previous edition of this book; their skills, knowledge and understanding are a wonderful recommendation for the sector and should reassure those who use the services, or have loved ones who are in need of care or likely to become so.

This new edition provides further, up-to-date guidance and background knowledge to support not only your qualification, but your day-to-day work in providing caring services.

Unit 01 Foster people's equality, diversity and rights

This unit forms the basis of your NVQ. It deals with how you can work in a way which will recognise the rights of people to be treated equally and to be valued as individuals. The elements in this unit should form the basis for how you work, regardless of the tasks you are carrying out. The unit is divided into three elements which cover rights and responsibilities, equality and diversity, and confidentiality. Each of these is equally important and will affect how you work. All of the work you do should be governed by the basic principles in this unit.

Foster people's rights and responsibilities

What you need to learn

- The rights your service users have
- how to support your service users in the exercise of their rights
- how to balance rights and responsibilities

The rights your service users have

Rights and responsibilities are a huge subject. There are international conferences, government summits and libraries full of learned books about rights. In order to look at rights in terms of how they affect the people you work with and provide care for, it is helpful to discuss them under the following headings:

- Basic human rights
- Rights provided by law
- Rights under charters, guidelines and policies.

What are responsibilities? They are the other side of the coin to rights – most of our responsibilities are about protecting, improving or not infringing other people's rights. Responsibilities are the balance for rights, and it is impossible to consider one without the other.

1 Basic human rights

In 1948 the United Nations Universal Declaration of Human Rights identified a set of basic rights which everyone should have. The Declaration sets out to promote and encourage acceptance of personal, civil, political, economic, social and cultural rights, which are only limited by the need to respect the rights and freedoms of others and the needs of morality, public order and general welfare. The thirty rights cited in the Declaration include:

- the right to life, liberty and security of person
- the right to freedom from arbitrary arrest, i.e. you cannot be arrested without good reason
- the right to a fair trial
- the right to be presumed innocent until proven guilty
- the right to freedom of movement and residence, i.e. you can live where you like
- freedom of thought, conscience, religion, opinion and expression, i.e. you can think, write and say what you like as long as it does not threaten others
- the right to freedom of association and peaceful assembly, i.e. you can meet with others as you choose
- the right to social security, work, rest and a standard of living adequate for health and well-being.

For many people throughout the world, these are rights they can only hope for, and not rights they currently enjoy. The United Nations has a Commission on Human Rights which works to promote the world-wide acceptance of these basic rights and to identify abuses and violations of human rights throughout the world. Organisations like Amnesty International play a large role in highlighting abuses of human rights and campaigning against governments that ignore human rights.

Check it out

Look at the rights proclaimed in the Universal Declaration of Human Rights. Which of the rights are particularly important in the care field? Think about what they are and why they matter. Consider ways in which they make a difference in your workplace.

2 Rights provided by law

The Human Rights Act received the royal assent on 9 November 1998 and the majority of its provisions came into force on 2 October 2000. The effects of the Act are far-reaching and bring within UK jurisdiction the rights which were previously contained within the European charter of human rights and which could be pursued only in the European Court of Human Rights in Strasbourg.

The Human Rights Act means that residents of the United Kingdom – this Act applies in England, Scotland, Wales and Northern Ireland – will now be entitled to seek redress (through the courts) in the United Kingdom if they believe that their human rights have been infringed.

Organisations subject to the Human Rights Act 1998	
Residential homes or nursing homes Voluntary organisations	These perform functions which would otherwise be performed by a local authority
Charities Public service	This could include the privatised utilities, such as gas, electric and water companies, which will be affected by the provisions of this Act

It is likely that anyone who works in health or care will be working within the provisions of the Human Rights Act. This Act is all about respect for, and the promotion and fostering of, the rights of individual people through all the functions of a public authority, or any organisation which is carrying out the role of a public authority. Under the Act everyone who works in a setting which is covered by the Act will have to interpret the legislation with which they work in a way which is compatible with the Human Rights Act. The workers will be required to act in accordance with the Human Rights Act. Under the Act the rights which are guaranteed are the following.

1 The right to life. Public authorities must not cause the death of any person and they have a positive obligation to protect life. There are particular situations where the Act defines a limited number of circumstances where it is not a contravention of the Act to take someone's life. But this only applies where the force used is no more than absolutely necessary, such as defending a person from attack or to effect a lawful arrest.

2 The right to freedom from torture and inhuman or degrading treatment or punishment. Torture is identified as the most serious kind of ill-treatment. Inhuman or degrading treatment is less severe than torture and may include physical assaults, inhuman detention conditions or corporal punishment. The ill-treatment relates to both mental and physical suffering. One of the factors which is taken into account under this right is the severity and duration of the torture, inhuman or degrading treatment and the vulnerability of the victim.

3 The right to freedom from slavery, servitude and forced or compulsory labour. Slavery means that a person is owned by somebody else like a piece of property. Servitude is defined as a person not being owned by someone else but being in enforced service to them and unable to leave. There are some exceptions to this right, for example work which may be being carried out as part of a prison sentence.

4 The right to liberty and security of person. People have a right not to be arrested or detained except when the detention is authorised by law. This part of the Act does not just apply to police arrests but covers all aspects of detention, including for medical or psychiatric reasons. There are clearly defined circumstances under which people can be detained, such as after conviction by a court or where there are sufficient grounds to believe that they may have committed a crime.

5 The right to a fair and a public trial within a reasonable time. This right covers all criminal and most civil cases as well as tribunals and some internal hearings. People have a right to be presumed innocent until proven guilty and to be given adequate time and facilities to prepare their defence. The Act gives everyone a right to a trial in public so that justice can never be carried out behind closed doors.

6 The right to freedom from retrospective criminal law and no punishment without law. This right means that people cannot be convicted for an act which was not a criminal offence at the time it was committed, not can they face a punishment which was not in force when the act happened.

7 The right to respect for private and family life, home and correspondence. This is one of the very far-reaching parts of the Human Rights Act. Public authorities may only interfere in someone's private life when they have the legal authority to do so. This covers matters such as the disclosure of private information, monitoring of telephone calls and e-mail, carrying out searches, and entering a person's home. It also covers issues such as the right of families to live together or the right not to suffer from environmental hazard.

8 The right to freedom of thought, conscience and religion. Under this right people can hold whatever thoughts, positions of conscience or religious beliefs they wish. They are guaranteed the right to manifest their religion or belief in worship, teaching, practice and observance.

9 The right to freedom of expression. Freedom of expression includes what is said in conversation or speeches, what is published in books, articles or leaflets, what is broadcast and what is presented as art or placed on the Internet. In fact, any means of communication.

10 The right to freedom of assembly and association. This includes the right of people to demonstrate peacefully and to join or choose not to join trade unions.

11 The right to marry and found a family. This part of the Act is particularly relevant to rules and policies concerning adoption and fostering. Public authorities will have to ensure that their policies in this regard, for example policies to do with age or race of applicants to become adoptive parents, are not contravening the Act.

12 The prohibition of discrimination in the enjoyment of convention rights. The Act recognises that not all differences in treatment are discriminatory; those that are discriminating are defined as those which have no objective or reasonable justification. For example, if a registry office was to provide information about how to undertake a civil marriage in English only, then it is possible for this to be taken as affecting the human rights of someone who was unable to speak English and therefore unable to access the information they need. This could be said to be denying them the means to fulfil their human right to marry. This would probably be viewed as discriminatory because there is no objective or reasonable justification for failing to provide information in other languages. Take another case, that of a young person excluded from school and therefore unable to exercise his or her human right to receive an education. If it could be proved the person was excluded because of disruptive behaviour and not because of race or socio-economic circumstances, then this would not be discriminatory.

13 The right to peaceful enjoyment of possessions and protection of property. The Act defines many possessions as property, not just houses or cars, but things like shares, licences and goodwill. In some circumstances the right to engage in a profession can be regarded as a property right. Under the Act no one can be deprived of their property except where the action is permitted by law.

14 The right of access to an education. The right of access to education must be balanced against the resources available. This right may be relevant to the exclusion of disruptive pupils from schools, and may also prove to be very relevant for children with special needs.

15 The right of free elections. This part of the Act is about elections to whatever legislative bodies are relevant. They must be free and fair and be held at reasonable intervals. It is also likely to raise issues of participation and access and making sure that people with disabilities or those who are ill are still able to participate.

16 The right not to be subjected to the death penalty. This provision abolishes the death penalty.

What does the Human Rights Act mean in practice at work?

Under the Human Rights Act all other legislation, including Acts of Parliament or Regulations, must be read, understood and used in a way which is compatible with the requirements of the Human Rights Act. Government advice is that this is a very strong provision and you must make every effort to interpret the legislation that you work with in a way which is compatible with the Human Rights Act. This means that if there are two possible interpretations of a provision under an Act, such as the Mental Health Act, the Children Act, or the Community Care Act, one which is compatible with the Human Rights Act and one which is not, then the one that is compatible must be followed.

Government guidance lays down that all public authorities have a positive obligation to ensure that respect for human rights is at the core of their day-to-day work. This guidance covers all aspects of activities, including:

- drafting rules and regulations and policies
- internal staff and personnel issues
- administration
- decision making
- implementing policy and working with members of the public.

Check it out

Think about how the laws underpinning the policies and procedures in your workplace could be used better to build a culture of rights and responsibilities. This could be a useful area of discussion at a staff meeting or in a meeting with your line manager.

REMEMBER

- Acts of Parliament don't change attitudes.
- Discrimination may be unlawful, but people still have the right to think, write and speak as they wish. *But* does anyone have a 'right' to view another person as inferior because of his or her race? Would it infringe a person's rights to take steps against him/her because of this view?

Discrimination

Discrimination is a denial of rights. Discrimination can be based on race, gender, disability or sexual orientation. Element O1.2 deals fully with the issue of discrimination; in this element you will look at the main laws which protect people from discrimination and so help to support their rights.

The main Acts of Parliament which are to do with rights are:

- the Race Relations Act 1976
- the Equal Pay Act 1970
- the Sex Discrimination Act 1975
- the Disability Discrimination Act 1995.

Race Relations Act 1976

This Act prohibits all forms of racial discrimination, whether in employment, housing or services. It also makes it an offence to incite (encourage) racial hatred. The Act covers all discrimination whether it is about colour, nationality or race, and forbids both direct and indirect discrimination.

Direct discrimination occurs when someone is stopped from doing something because of their race as, for example, in the two adverts shown below.

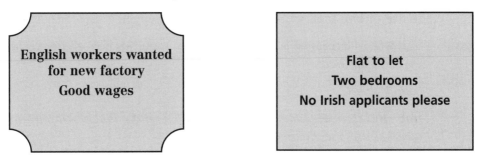

English workers wanted for new factory Good wages

Flat to let Two bedrooms No Irish applicants please

Both of those adverts are blatantly racist and would not be seen anywhere today, but 50 years ago such adverts were commonplace.

Indirect discrimination is more subtle. This can work by imposing conditions which some people would find impossible to meet, as in the advert below, for example.

Bricklayer required Must speak fluent English

This is indirect discrimination because it may exclude people who are fairly recent immigrants. There can be no justification for this requirement because the work does not require use of language or contact with the public.

Another example might be a sheltered housing scheme which has a rule about tenants not being allowed to cook highly-spiced food because of the smell. It would be breaking the law, because Asian food tends to be highly spiced whereas English food does not. This would discriminate against Asian tenants being able to cook their native food.

People's rights to housing and provision of services are also supported by the Act.

Sounds great…

but – *redress is difficult to obtain. Support is given to people bringing cases under the Act by the Commission for Racial Equality, but proving discrimination is notoriously difficult.*

DID YOU KNOW?
Women comprise 50 per cent of the world population, do 90 per cent of the world's work, earn 10 per cent of the world's income and own 1 per cent of the world's wealth. (UNESCO)

The Equal Pay Act 1970

The Equal Pay Act 1970 (amended 1983) is designed to legislate against gender discrimination. It provides a woman with the right to be employed on the same terms and conditions as a man doing an equivalent job, or work of equal value. For example, it has been judged in a court of law that a female canteen cook's work is of equal value to that of a male joiner, painter and sanitation engineer.

This type of legislation is common in many countries now, so the situation for women's pay has improved.

Sounds great…

but – *it is often the kind of work which women do, much of it part-time or low-paid, which causes the difference in average pay.*

but – *of course, the work which women do at home is unpaid!*

DID YOU KNOW?
Average male wages in the UK are still about one-third higher than women's. In the past 30 years that figure has improved by only around 17 per cent. In 1965, women's average wage was half that of men.

Sex Discrimination Act 1975

This Act is designed to provide equal rights to men and women in respect of employment, goods, services and facilities. It prevents discrimination either directly or indirectly which would prevent women from being employed or receiving a service in the same way as men. The Equal Opportunities Commission supports the working of the law, by supporting cases, investigating abuses and promoting equality.

In a similar way to the Race Relations Act, the Sex Discrimination Act can be used by women who, for example, have been repeatedly passed over for promotion at work, even though men who are less qualified have achieved success. There have been several well-publicised cases in public services like the police and fire services.

Women have a right to be admitted to all public places on the same basis as men. This has meant that there are no longer any 'men only' bars – unless they are in private clubs, such as golf clubs.

Men can also use the Act if they have been unfairly discriminated against. For example, the fact that most baby-changing facilities are located in women's public lavatories means that a man who has the care of a baby will have difficulty finding a suitable place to change the baby.

The Act deals with both direct and indirect discrimination. For example, a woman could take an employer to court if a job was advertised like the one below.

Height is not a reasonable requirement in order to do the job, so because far more women are below 5 ft 10 in than men, the advert discriminates against women.

It would also be discriminatory against men if it advertised for people under 5 ft 4 in!

In the provision of services, if, for instance, a primary care group decided no longer to provide treatment for people with osteoporosis, a challenge could be made on the grounds that it is primarily women who suffer from the condition and therefore the decision would discriminate unfairly against women. Similarly, if the group decided not to treat people with prostate problems, the decision could be open to challenge by men.

Sounds great…

but – *like racial discrimination, sex discrimination is difficult to prove.*

CASE STUDY

The A family live in the Midlands. Mr A is from Pakistan, he is very strict in his Muslim beliefs, and the tradition in the area he comes from is that all young men and women are expected to have their marriages arranged by their families. Mr A's daughter M is 16 years old, she was born in the UK, speaks with a local accent, and has friends, both Muslim and non-Muslim in the area. However, her father has now decided that it is time that she was married. He has arranged for her to be married to a distant relative from the family's home town in Pakistan. M is not happy at the prospect, and wants to meet someone in the UK. She is reluctant to go to Pakistan, where she has never been before.

1 What are Mr A's rights? What are his responsibilities?
2 What are M's rights?
3 Does M have responsibilities?
4 What decisions could be made?
5 Do any laws affect this situation?

Disability Discrimination Act 1995

This Act is designed to provide new rights for people with disabilities in:

- employment
- housing
- access to education and transport
- obtaining goods and services.

The Act defines disability as a condition which makes it difficult for someone to carry out normal day-to-day activities. The disability can be physical, sensory or psychological but, to be covered by the Act, it must be substantial and have a long-term effect. (This means that the disability must last, or be expected to last, for at least 12 months.)

Under the Act employers must not treat a disabled person less favourably than an able-bodied person. An employer must examine the changes that need to be made to the workplace, or to how the work is carried out, in order to make it possible for someone with a disability to do the job.

Access for people with disabilities to education and transport means that schools and colleges will have to produce details of how any student will be able to access courses, regardless of disability. All new taxis, buses, trains and coaches have to be accessible for disabled people.

Landlords are not allowed to discriminate against anyone with a disability when letting a property, or to charge a higher rent than they would for a non-disabled person.

Shops, restaurants and anyone who provides a service have to ensure that disabled people are able to make use of the service and are not charged more than a non-disabled person. They have to make it easier for disabled people to use their services by providing any adaptations needed or by arranging for other ways of using the service, for example, by providing a mail order catalogue.

Sounds great...

but – *most of the provisions are only 'if it is reasonable to do so'.*

Reasonable? for whom?

but – *one of the considerations which people can take into account when considering if it is 'reasonable' to change things for disabled people is the cost – so, if it would cost too much to put in a ramp, the shop can justify not doing so.*

but – *there is no overall body, like the Equal Opportunities Commission or Commission for Racial Equality, who will assist disabled people to take up cases of discrimination and defend their rights. Disabled people have to bring their own cases to court, or to industrial tribunals. The Act does provide for the establishment of a National Disability Council and a Northern Ireland Disability Council, but these bodies are only to advise the government on how to improve matters for disabled people; they cannot investigate individual claims of discrimination.*

DID YOU KNOW?

There are over 6.5 million disabled people in the UK – and 31 per cent of these are currently employed.

Only 17 per cent of disabled people were born with their disability.

Particular laws for particular people

Apart from the laws which provide rights for everyone, there are other laws which are likely to affect the particular group of individuals you work with. These laws are not only about providing people with rights, they can also be about restricting rights, when it is in someone's interests to do so.

Mental Health Act 1983

This Act affects people with mental health problems or a learning disability. It provides for compulsorily restricting people to hospital when they are considered to be ill, or to prison if they have committed criminal offences. This is a severe restriction on people's liberty and they have rights to appeal against such detentions. Appeals are heard by special tribunals, and it is easy to see the dilemma which could exist between the rights of an individual and responsibility towards the community.

CASE STUDY

K was convicted ten years ago of sexually abusing two children. He was diagnosed as suffering from a mental illness, and so was committed to a secure hospital under the Mental Health Act rather than being sent to prison. This type of sentence does not carry a particular length of time, but is referred to as HMP (at Her Majesty's pleasure). This essentially means that the person will remain in a special hospital until there is sufficient evidence put before a tribunal for a decision to be made that he or she no longer represents a risk.

K is now in his late fifties and all the psychiatric specialists are of the opinion that his illness is now 'burnt out' and he does not represent a threat to the community. His future is about to be considered by a tribunal who have the power to allow him to be released. K is a pleasant man, who is very 'slow' in his responses. He is completely unaggressive and is very eager to please. He will do exactly as instructed, and has spent the past three years helping in the hospital kitchens. He cannot cope with complicated tasks, but can do simple jobs which do not involve much memory.

However, the local community where he lived and assaulted the children has heard about the possibility of release. There is a great deal of concern, and a local campaign has begun which claims that the tribunal have a responsibility to consider the safety of the local community. There have been threats that K will be the subject of a vigilante campaign if he is released, and the implication is that he may be harmed or forced to leave the area.

1 Whose rights should be considered in this situation?
2 Is there a responsibility on the tribunal and the psychiatrists to consider the community?
3 Whose rights are most important?
4 How could this be resolved?

The Children Act 1989

This Act provides children with the right to be protected from 'significant harm'. The definition of significant harm is decided by the courts at the request of social services departments. The harm could be being inflicted by parents, or by the children themselves if they are 'beyond control' and involved in crime, drugs or prostitution.

This is also the first Act which identifies 'parental responsibility' rather than 'parental rights' and so, for the first time, children are not treated as property over which 'rights' can be exercised.

This Act also ensures that nurseries and residential schools have to reach certain standards, and ensures that they are regularly inspected.

It gives rights to children who have been looked after by social services departments to be supported, to be assisted to become independent and to have access to information about their lives and their own histories.

CASE STUDY

C is 15 years old. She is at a police station refusing to return home. She says that she does not get on with her parents because they are too strict and do not give her any freedom. C wants to be able to go to clubs and go out with boys, which her parents will not allow. She says that she would rather live in a children's home because there she will be allowed more freedom. She is friendly with K, a girl at her school who lives in a small children's home. C feels that K goes out and has boyfriends and can do more or less what she likes. She says that if the police or social workers send her home to her parents, then she will run away. Her parents want her to return home, and her father has arrived at the police station insisting that he is taking her home.

1 What rights does C have?
2 What rights do her parents have?
3 Do social services have any responsibility for C's safety?
4 How can this be resolved?

NHS and Community Care Act 1990

This act gives older and disabled people rights in respect of the services they should be provided with by their social services department.

All social services departments have to publish plans about how they will run the provision of services. These plans must include the criteria which will be used to define how services will be provided for particular needs. Everyone has a right to see the

All people who are in need of community care have the legal right to have their needs assessed and to have services provided.

plans, and to be consulted if they belong to a group which represents people who are likely to use the services.

All people who are in need of community care have the right to have their needs assessed and to have services provided in accordance with the published criteria. People also have a right to complain if the service is not provided.

This is a wide-ranging Act which has provided disabled and older people with more rights than they previously enjoyed, although many social services departments are struggling to provide the services with a limited amount of funding.

CASE STUDY

Mrs B is 93 years old. She is bedridden, has a heart condition, emphysema and severe arthritis and requires round-the-clock care. She is unable to care for herself at all; she is unable to get out of bed without help and is extremely frail. If she were left alone she would be in grave danger of falling or she might need help with using her oxygen supply. Mrs B is not in the slightest bit confused and is very clear that she does not wish to leave her home and go into residential or nursing home care. The local NHS trust will not keep her in hospital as she does not have any acute medical needs that cannot be met in the community.

Her needs assessment has defined that she needs 24-hour care. This is presently provided by a team of carers who work for a local private care agency. The cost is several times more than the cost of providing the equivalent care in a residential setting. The local social services department is presently having to refuse services to some people because of a shortage of cash. This has been explained to Mrs B in an attempt to persuade her to agree to residential care, but she remains adamant that she wants to remain in her own home.

1   Does Mrs B have rights to insist on staying at home?
2   What are the responsibilities of social services to Mrs B? And to others in need?
3   Should Mrs B's rights be more important than the responsibilities to the rest of the community?

3 Rights under charters, guidelines and policies

These are rights which do not have the force of law, but which are designed to improve the services people receive.

The document called 'Your Guide to the NHS', published in 2000, sets out what people can expect from the National Health Service. It covers issues such as people's rights to receive care from a GP, how long they can reasonably be expected to wait for a hospital appointment, and how long before urgent and non-urgent treatment. However, it is different from the Patient's Charter which it replaced because it also identifies the responsibilities of patients (see page 18). The guide includes information on how patients can use services and how they can complain if necessary.

Even though this is set out as a guidance document, the government has made it clear that this is the way in which the Health Service is expected to operate. This means that the performance of all NHS trusts is measured against this guidance.

Charters exist for other services, such as the Passenger's Charter, which lays down standards which can be expected for rail travel.

The key role of charters is to make the expected standards public, so there can be no argument that service users are being unreasonable in their demands, or their expectations are too high. If people know what they have a right to expect, then they can take steps to complain and have things put right if the standards are not met.

Check it out

The organisation you work for is likely to have policies and statements about how it works. Find out what they are, and see how you feel your workplace measures up to its stated aims, mission statements and public charters.

How to support your service users in the exercise of their rights

One of the most useful and important things you can do for someone is to give them information. Knowledge is power, and giving someone information empowers them. Working as a carer means that you are often going to be working with people who are vulnerable and who have no confidence or power. You will be able to support them very effectively by helping them to stand up for their rights. Many people you work with will be unaware of the information they need, because:

- they are unaware that the information exists
- they do not know how to find it
- there are physical barriers to accessing information
- there are emotional barriers to seeking information.

DID YOU KNOW?

Age Concern receives around 16,000 requests for information in a six-month period. When the figures were last analysed, there were found to be around 25 per cent of queries about health and social care, only slightly less about consumer issues (including wills), 10 per cent about financing residential care, and about 20 per cent respectively about income and housing.

If you are going to provide people with information, there are certain basic rules you must observe. There is no point in providing information which is out-of-date or inaccurate, or in giving people the right information at the wrong time.

Keys to good practice

✓ Make sure that your information is up-to-date. You may have to contact quite a few places to make sure you have the most accurate information possible. Check the dates on any leaflets you have and contact the producer of the leaflet to check that it has not been replaced.

✓ Go to the most direct source, wherever possible. For example, for information about benefits, contact the Benefits Agency. If you need to know about Community Care services, contact social services.

✓ Advice services such as the Citizens Advice Bureau are excellent and provide a wide range of information. Make use also of the specialist organisations which represent specific groups, such as Age Concern or Scope.

✓ You will need to check that the information you are providing has local, regional and national elements, if relevant. For instance, if you are providing information about Age Concern's services for older people, it is important to provide the local contact as well as national contact points.

✓ The information you provide must be in a format that can be used by the person it is for. For example, there is little value in providing an ordinary leaflet to an individual with impaired sight. You will need to obtain large print, taped or braille versions depending on the way in which the individual prefers to take in information.

✓ You will also need to consider language and provide information in a language which the individual can easily understand. Information is of no value if it is misunderstood.

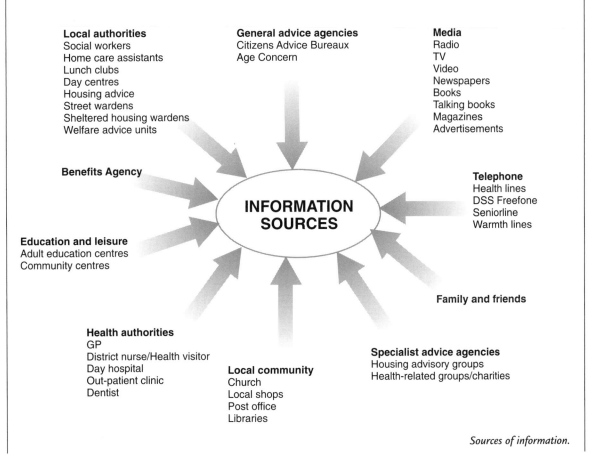

Sources of information.

✓ It is important that you provide information at an appropriate time when the individual can make use of it. For example, a man who has just had a leg amputated, following an accident, will not be ready to receive information about the latest design in wheelchairs or how to join in sports for the disabled. He may be interested in 12 months' time, but initially he is going to need information about support groups and practical information about how artificial limbs work, and how to manage to use the toilet!

✓ The information you provide must be relevant and useful. For example, if an individual wants to make a complaint to the Benefits Agency, you will need to find out what the complaints procedure is and provide the relevant information/forms to be completed. A general leaflet about the services of the Benefits Agency would not be as helpful.

Helping people who cannot help themselves

There may be occasions when you have identified a person's rights and given him or her the information needed. However, the individual may not be able to exercise those rights effectively. There can be many reasons why people miss out on their rights:

● Their rights may be infringed by someone else.
● There may be physical barriers.
● There may be emotional barriers.

Where people cannot exercise their own rights, it is sometimes important that someone acts on their behalf. If it is within your work role to do so, you could act in a formal or informal way to assist.

Acting to help someone exercise his or her rights in a formal way may involve you speaking on that person's behalf to another agency, for example the Benefits Agency. Before you undertake this role you must check with your manager that it is appropriate for you to do so.

You also need to be very sure that you are not assisting someone to exercise his or her rights because you think that it is right or because you are angered by the injustice. It must be because the individual, possibly based on information you have provided, wants to exercise his or her rights. The key when acting on behalf of another is to consult and to constantly ensure that you are doing what he or she wants.

CASE STUDY

Mrs S lives alone on just her state pension. She has never claimed any income support although there is no doubt she would be entitled to it. She struggles to survive on her pension and, by the time she has paid all her bills and fed the cat, there is little left for herself. She eats very little and is reluctant to turn the heating on. Despite being given all the relevant information by her home care assistant, Mrs S will not claim any further benefits. She always says 'I shall be fine, there's others worse off than me. Let it go to those who need it.'

1 What are Mrs S's rights?
2 Should action be taken on her behalf?
3 Would the situation be different if she had a son with a learning disability who lived with her? Would her rights still be the same? Would her responsibilities still be the same?
4 What would your responsibilities be if you were a carer for Mrs S?

You may also need to defend people's rights in a more informal way during your normal work. For example, people have a right to privacy, and you may need to act to deal with someone who constantly infringes upon that by discussing other people's circumstances in public. You will have to balance the rights of one person against another, and decide whose rights are being eroded. You may decide that a right to privacy is more important than the right to free speech. That may be appropriate in your workplace, but does the same principle apply to politicians and the way they are discussed in the media?

Check it out

An individual's right to rest may be being infringed by someone who shouts all night. How would you balance the rights of one person not to be disturbed against the rights of another not to be given medication which is only for the benefit of others?

The role of acting as an advocate for the rights of others is seldom straightforward and you should never assume that any situation has only one angle of approach.

On occasions you may need to contact others to act as advocates for an individual. Sometimes this may be a formal advocate, such as a solicitor or another professional; at other times it may be a friend or relative. It is important, if it is feasible, to ask the individual who he or she wishes to act on his or her behalf, and to ensure that the individual's rights are not further infringed by having decisions made for him or her.

You will need to record any actions you take to promote a person's rights in his or her personal file. Remember that the records may be referred to by someone else in the future, so make accurate, relevant and complete notes. Make careful notes of information you supply to the individual, any discussions or actions you undertake on his or her behalf, and the outcome of these. The keeping of records is covered in more detail in Element O1.3.

How to balance rights and responsibilities

It is often difficult for people to exercise their rights while ensuring that others' rights are respected. A person may have the right to live as he or she wishes, but what about the rest of the community?

CASE STUDY

G is 53 years old. She has lived alone in a large house since her mother died ten years ago. She behaves in a strange way, often walking along the road and talking to herself. She does not acknowledge any of the neighbours, apart from shouting at local children if they venture into her very overgrown garden. She appears very dirty and dresses in the same clothes for months on end. G seems to collect old newspapers and her house is crammed with rubbish. She has 18 cats, five dogs, several ducks, ten chickens and a goat. All the animals are well fed and cared for, but they create a considerable amount of noise and smell.

G has been assessed by a psychiatrist in the past and is not mentally ill. The people in the local community want her to leave. They say that she causes problems with the animals, that the house is a health hazard, she frightens the children and her house is so dilapidated it makes the whole road look scruffy.

1 What rights does G have?
2 What rights do the rest of the community have?
3 Does G have any responsibility to the community she lives in?
4 Do they have any responsibility towards her?
5 How could this be resolved?

Responsibility is a word which has meanings at many levels – it is often used to refer to someone assuming responsibilities as they grow up: buying a house, getting married, having children. All of these things bring responsibilities, but it could be argued that these responsibilities conflict with rights.

For example, looking after children is a great responsibility. It also means that people no longer have the right to please themselves about going out, or spending money as they please, because their responsibilities towards their children come before their rights to satisfy their own desires. Most people accept this willingly and take delight in providing care for their children, but some situations are not so clear cut.

Check it out

Does a person's responsibility to care for an elderly parent outweigh his or her rights to earn a living and have a social life? Discuss this with your colleagues.

The National Health Service clearly identifies the responsibilities of patients. While people have a right to expect a certain level of service from the NHS, it is clear that the health of the nation is a two-way partnership and that everyone has a responsibility to contribute. Patient responsibilities are the following:

- Do what you can to look after your own health, and follow advice on a healthy lifestyle.
- Care for yourself when appropriate. (For example, you can treat yourself at home for common ailments such as coughs, colds and sore throats.)
- Give blood if you are able, and carry an organ donor card or special needs card or bracelet.
- Keep your appointment or let the GP, dentist, clinic or hospital know as soon as possible if you cannot make it. Book routine appointments in plenty of time.
- Listen carefully to advice on your treatment and medication. Tell the doctor about any treatments you are already taking.
- Return any equipment that is no longer needed.
- Pay NHS prescription charges and any other charges promptly when they are due and claim financial benefits or exemptions from these charges correctly. Treat NHS staff, fellow patients, carers and visitors politely, and with respect. We will not accept violence, racial, sexual or verbal harassment.

The dilemma of balancing rights and responsibilities is one most people working in care deal with on a daily basis. Think about your right to go home! You have a time at which you finish your shift or your day, but there are many occasions when it is not that simple. An emergency may have arisen, perhaps someone has fallen, or there may have been a death, or someone has just started to talk to you for the first time. You could be dealing with a relative who is very distressed. Any of these situations, and many more, can mean that you balance your right to finish work on time against the responsibilities you hold towards the individual needing your help, and his or her right to be helped. You also have to consider the rights of your family and the responsibilities you have towards them – you may have children to be picked up from school, meals to be cooked, social engagements; perhaps older relatives of your own needing care or support.

Whatever decision you reach, it will not be easy and you may feel you have let someone down.

REMEMBER

- People can only enforce rights provided by law.
- Information is the key to people being able to exercise their rights.
- Responsibilities are the other side of the coin to rights.
- There is always more than one way of looking at any situation.

Element 01.2 # Foster equality and diversity of people

What you need to learn

● How people are discriminated against
● How to reduce the impact of discrimination
● How to recognise your own prejudices
● The effects of stereotyping

How people are discriminated against

There are many ways in which people are subjected to discrimination: lack of employment opportunities, limited access to services, poor educational opportunities, exclusion from social groups. It is important that you are able to recognise the different forms of discrimination, if you are to take action to promote equality.

Racial discrimination

This can be in a very direct form, such as abuse being shouted in the street, violence and physical abuse. Large numbers of black and Asian people are subjected to these types of attack. This is clear racial harassment and is a criminal offence under the Race Relations Act.

It can also be less easily identified, for example in employment where people with 'foreign' sounding names, or addresses in a particular part of a town, are not invited for interview. There is now an increasingly common practice amongst good employers of using a detachable information section on job application forms for personal details of the candidates. This personal information can then be kept confidential by the personnel department, and only the part of the application form containing information about the candidate's experience and qualifications is given to the people drawing up shortlists – the results have sometimes been surprising!

Racial discrimination affects not only black and Asian people. Many people who have come to this country seeking refuge from wars and conflicts are subjected to racial abuse and prejudice which affect their day-to-day lives.

Find out the percentage of people living in your local area who are from minority ethnic groups. Look at the number of people from these groups who are employed in your workplace. Are the percentages the same? For example, if 5 per cent of the people in your town are from minority ethnic groups, are there 5 per cent in your workforce? Look at the difference, and think about what the reasons may be.

Gender discrimination

Women are generally on the receiving end of gender discrimination, although it can apply to men, particularly those in employment caring for young children. It is usually in terms of employment that women suffer disadvantages. They will be passed over for promotion, or not considered for some jobs, because they are women. It is also common for some companies to make such a high level of demand in terms of the hours of work, and the ability to stay late or arrive early, that many women with family commitments are unable to meet the requirements of top jobs. It is still true that, although men also have family commitments, it is more likely to be women who take time off work when children are ill, or appointments connected with health or education have to be made.

Women are also more likely to be subjected to harassment in the workplace, sexual innuendo or unwelcome advances from male colleagues.

Look at the number of men and women who work for your employer. Does the proportion of women and men in senior management match the proportion of men and women employed? For example, you may find that 95 per cent of home-care assistants are women, but only 20 per cent of senior-manager posts are held by women.

DID YOU KNOW?

Less than 12 per cent of primary school teachers are men. Over 40 per cent of primary school headteachers are men.

Discrimination against people with disabilities

In its most obvious forms, discrimination can be abuse and name calling, and even physical attacks. People with a disability can be very vulnerable to abuse, as they may lack the ability to retaliate, or to chase after abusers, or to see what is happening. Unfortunately, there are criminals who are only too willing to take advantage. At a broader level, there is massive discrimination against all kinds of people because of their disabilities. Historically, local and national governments have not allocated the necessary resources to allow people with disabilities to have proper access to public buildings and transport. Current legislation will improve matters, but very slowly.

Employers are concerned about offering employment to people with disabilities, believing that they will be unable to cope, or will be off sick much of the time.

> **REMEMBER**
> Being disabled is not the same as being ill. Most disabled people are perfectly well. They are no more likely to have time off work ill than anyone else.

Discrimination against people with mental health problems

This is very difficult to counteract. There is still a great fear of mental health problems, largely because, in the past, people with such problems were considered to be 'mad' and were shut away in mental hospitals (or institutions), often for the whole of their lives. The general public, therefore, had little to do with people who suffered with mental health problems, and, as a result, tended to misunderstand and fear them.

It is only in the past 20 years, as those massive institutions have closed down, and the emphasis has been on caring for people in the community, that many people have had contact with those who suffer mental health problems.

Check it out

How many times in a day do you hear, or use, phrases like 'she's a looney', 'you must be mad', 'he's not right in the head'? Having mental health problems is still regarded as something which can be used as an insult.

You may have read reports in the papers, or heard on the news, about cases where there have been proposals to locate hostels for people with mental health problems in local communities. The reaction from local people is usually one of fierce opposition, based on fear and ignorance.

If this is the level of opposition to a facility being provided in a community, imagine the difficulty people with mental health problems face in trying to get a job.

> **DID YOU KNOW?**
> One woman in nine and one man in 12 will experience mental health problems at some point in their lives. Yet it is still viewed as a secret and shameful thing, which people fear.

People with a learning disability

Like people with other disabilities, many people with a learning disability are subjected to verbal or physical abuse. They face major problems in finding employment, because of fear and a lack of understanding about how well they can function, if given tasks within their capabilities.

Local communities tend to react in a similar way to proposals for residential accommodation. There is still much fear and ignorance about learning disability.

People with learning disabilities simply function at a different level. If they are given tasks which are appropriate for them, they will carry them out very well. You might not function very well if you were asked to take over as Managing Director of ICI, or as the Professor of Nuclear Physics at Cambridge University!

Older people

Older people are generally undervalued by our 'western' society. Most Asian and Chinese cultures recognise that older people are to be respected and valued for their experience and wisdom. They have a role within the family and the community.

Older people in the UK are likely to be dismissed as being 'past it', 'wrinkly' or 'crumbly', and are viewed as having nothing useful to contribute.

It is often difficult for people over 50 to find work, despite being very experienced and skilled. However, there are now some companies, notably supermarket and DIY chains, who are employing 'pensioners'. They feel that they are more conscientious, have more skills to contribute and are more reliable than younger workers.

Sexual orientation

Many people are subjected to both verbal and physical abuse because of their sexual orientation. Gay men, particularly, are likely to be subjected to violence.

In certain professions it is not possible for people openly to express their sexual orientation because, despite statements from employers which state that they welcome applications from all, most parents are unlikely to welcome an openly gay teacher or care worker. Many in nursing and midwifery have to be discreet about declaring a lesbian or gay partner because of the likely responses of patients and their relatives.

A Parliamentary Bill proposed in 1996 would have offered protection to lesbians and gay men, in a similar way to other discrimination legislation. However, it did not get past a first reading in the House of Commons, and there are no indications at present that it will be revived.

How to reduce the impact of discrimination

How can you foster and encourage equality, which seems to be about everyone being treated the same, alongside diversity, which is about everyone being different?

The short answer is 'with great difficulty'. However, it is not as impossible as it appears. The first key concept to understand is that what you are being asked to do is to foster 'equality' – and that is not necessarily the same thing as treating everyone the same. Confused?

Try thinking about a race. Everyone would agree that generally, for a race to be fair, all the competitors must be on the start line and start together.

Before people have a chance to take part in the race, they have to reach the starting line. Yet many people in our society need considerable help to reach the starting line so that they can compete fairly.

If you are to help people to reach the starting line, you have to be able to see what additional support they are going to need. This is called 'positive action'. It is not the same thing as 'positive discrimination', which is illegal. Positive discrimination involves acting more favourably towards someone because of their perceived disadvantage. Positive action is about ensuring that people are able to enter into fair competition with others.

At the 1997 general election, there were some 'women-only' shortlists for parliamentary candidates. This is a form of 'positive action' which has resulted in a vast increase in the number of women MPs. In turn, this means that women MPs have the chance to begin at the same point as their male colleagues when it comes to being in posts of responsibility. Previously, so few women were selected as candidates to become MPs that even fewer were successfully elected or given government posts, which meant the waste of a wide range of skills and talents. This results in the 'self-fulfilling prophecy' that women are not really 'cut out' for politics.

Even though the 'women-only' shortlists were not repeated in the 2001 elections, the scene had been set for more women to enter politics and views had changed sufficiently to ensure that in the National Assembly for Wales and the Scottish Parliament over 40 per cent of members elected were women.

A competitor in the London Marathon wheelchair event.

It is easy to apply the same principles to a job. Someone who has impaired vision or is in a wheelchair can do a job just as well, if not better, than someone who is able-bodied, provided that he or she is allowed the opportunity. That means removing physical barriers like steps, or narrow doorways, and installing equipment which allows someone with impaired vision to 'read' documents.

Steps you can take to reduce discrimination

- Think about language. The words and expressions you use are important.
  - Do not use words which degrade people with problems or disabilities, e.g. words that are used as an insult.
  - Avoid language which is racist or could cause offence, and think about expressions such as 'play the white man' which suggests that white people are somehow superior.
  - Older people should not be referred to as 'grannies' or 'wrinklies'. It is not acceptable to call an older person 'pop' or 'grandad' unless you are invited to do so.
  - Avoid using offensive terms to describe homosexuals. Always try to find out the terms which people find acceptable. These are generally 'gay' and 'lesbian'.
  - There are many words and expressions which help to reinforce discrimination against women. Think before using 'like a fishwife' or 'he's a right old woman'.

Encourage people you provide care for to achieve their full potential.

- Do not assume that older people are only capable of quiet activities which do not involve too much excitement.
- Avoid the temptation to over-protect and thus encourage dependence.
- Support people in challenging barriers which stand in their way. If you work with people with disabilities, try to think of ways you can show employers what people are capable of achieving.

- Try to work with the local community. If you work in a facility which is surrounded by neighbours, make sure that they get to know both service users and staff. Knowledge removes the fear which lies behind prejudice.
- Encourage people to behave assertively and to develop confidence in their own abilities.
- Refuse to accept behaviour which you know is discriminatory.
- Do not participate in racist or sexist jokes and explain that you are not amused by 'sick' jokes about people with disabilities or problems.
- If you are uncertain what to do in a particular situation, discuss the problem with your supervisor.

How to recognise your own prejudices

One of the hardest things to do is to acknowledge your own prejudices and how they affect what you do. Prejudices are a result of your own beliefs and values, and may often be in conflict with situations you work in. There is nothing wrong with having your own beliefs and values. Everyone has them, and they are a vital part of making you the person you are, but you must be aware of them, and how they may affect what you do at work.

Think about the basic principles which apply in your life. For example, you may have a basic belief that you should always be honest. Then think about what that could mean for the way you work – might you find it hard to be pleasant to someone who was found to have lied extensively? You may believe that abortion is wrong. Could you deal sympathetically with a woman who had had an abortion? You may have been brought up to take great care of people with disabilities and believe that they should be looked after and protected. How would you cope in an environment which encouraged people with disabilities to take risks and promoted their independence?

Check it out

Make a list of the things you believe in as values, and a second list of how they could affect your work. Then, examine whether they do affect your work – you may need the views of a trusted colleague or your supervisor to help you with this. This exercise is very hard, and it will take a long time to do. It is often better done over a period of time. As you become more aware of your own actions, you will notice how they have the potential to affect your work.

Once you are aware of your own beliefs and values, and have recognised how important they are, you must think about how to accept the beliefs and values of others. The individuals you work with are all different, and so it is important to recognise and accept that diversity.

In the previous element, you looked at the rights which people can exercise under the law. This element is concerned with understanding the varied nature of human beings and how to ensure that the differences are valued and acknowledged.

Many workplaces now have policies which are about 'Managing Diversity' rather than 'Equal Opportunities'. This is because many people have realised that until diversity is recognised and valued, there is no realistic possibility of any policy about equal opportunities being really effective.

CASE STUDY

Woodhey Towers is a block of flats in a large local authority housing estate on the outskirts of a northern city. Families who are seeking asylum from the conflicts in Kosovo have been re-housed in the block, which was scheduled for demolition as no local families wanted to live in it. Many of the Kosovan families have very little English, and most have been through a terrifying ordeal and have seen their homes destroyed and relatives killed. Among the refugees are three teachers, two doctors, several nurses, a man who used to own a very successful packaging business, two computer analysts and a football coach.

Many people in the local community are very hostile to the idea of having this group of refugees living in the area and have organised protests outside the flats. Abuse has been shouted in the streets and the children have been bullied in school. There is a support worker for the families in the flats and she is trying to develop links between them and the local community. She begins in the local women's centre where two of the Kosovan nurses who can speak good English offer to help out with a first-aid course. The football coach has been asked to help out the local team, which is short of staff, and it is hoped that the people with computer skills will be able to support the cyber session at the youth club.

1 What feelings do you think the refugees would have about going into the local community in these ways?
2 Why do you think the community has been hostile?
3 Do you think local people would be surprised at the skills the refugees have? Why?
4 What other ways can you think of in which this group of refugees could be helped to become part of the local community?

Check it out

1 This exercise is best done with a group of colleagues, but you can do it on your own – it just takes longer! Generate some ideas for a list of all the cultures and nationalities you can think of. Write them down. Next to each one, write something that the culture has given to the world. For example, the Egyptians gave mathematics, the Chinese developed some wonderful medicines, and so on.

Next, think about people from the groups you care for. Note down the special angle of understanding each group can bring to society. For instance, someone who is visually impaired will always judge people on how they behave, not on how they look. Older people can often bring a different perspective to a situation based on years of experience and understanding.

2 In your own workplace, find out about the policy for ensuring equal opportunities, or for managing diversity. Make sure you read the policy. Consider whether you think it is being implemented.

The effects of stereotyping

All apples are red – as a statement that is clearly silly. Of course they are not – some are green, some are yellow. It is the same with people – everyone is different. However, there is a tendency to make sweeping statements (generalisations) which we believe apply to everyone who comes into a particular group. In Chapter 2 (Unit CL1) you will look in depth at stereotyping and the effects it has on how people are treated. You need to begin to understand it now because this is central to ensuring that people get a chance for equality.

The effect of the media

One of the major reasons why stereotyping continues is that this type of labelling of groups of people is reinforced by the media, whether it is newspapers, television or films. Young people, particularly those who are black and live in cities, are often portrayed as violent and involved in crime and drugs. Irish people are either shown as being stupid, lazy and drunk or as people involved in terrorism. Attractive women are all slim and young with perfect hair and make-up. Older people are confused and dependent, with little to offer society.

Not only does labelling and stereotyping affect how you judge people, it also affects how they see themselves (their self-image). A young black person, for example, may feel that he has no choice but to be 'hard' and hang around in a gang, because that is what he has grown to see as his role. He is so used to seeing himself portrayed in that way, that he is not aware of any alternatives.

Similarly, older people may decide that they now have to be 'looked after' because they are over a certain age and have now become dependent. There are so few positive images of older people that it is easy to see how people can come to believe that there is no other way to live.

Check it out

Complete the following sentences.

Policemen are _____

Teenagers are _____

Nurses are _____

Politicians never _____

West Indians are all _____

Asians always _____

Men all _____

Women are _____

Americans are _____

You can probably think of plenty of other statements that you make as generalisations about others. Note them down, then think about how all these generalisations could affect the way you work.

Avoiding stereotyping at work

Take the time and trouble to find out what personal beliefs and values apply to each individual you work with. Think about all the aspects of their lives: diet, clothing, worship, language, relationships with others, bathing. It is your responsibility to find out – not for the individual to have to tell you. It will be helpful for you, and for other workers, if this sort of information is recorded in the individual's personal record.

For example, you may need to know that many Muslims will only accept medical treatment from someone of the same gender, that you will need to enable them to wash in running water, not a bowl, that they do not eat pork, and any other meat must have been killed and prepared in a particular way – Halal.

If you are providing care for someone who is an Orthodox Jew, you need to be aware that they will not eat food unless it has been prepared in a specific way – the Kosher way. They do not eat pork. The Jewish Sabbath is a Saturday and Jewish beliefs forbid certain activities on that day.

Although you may hold a different set of values and beliefs from those of the individuals you are caring for, you do not have the right to impose your beliefs upon others. There may, in fact, be occasions when you will have to act as an advocate for their beliefs, even if you do not personally subscribe to them.

CASE STUDY

Mr P is a Jehovah's Witness. He lives alone and has no relations. He has friends in his local religious community, but he is not active in the life of the church any more because of his mobility problems. Mr P is very close to his home-care assistant who has known him for a long time. She is not a Jehovah's Witness, but she and Mr P have had many discussions over the years and she is well aware of his views.

He suddenly collapsed at home one day and was found by the home-care assistant. He was rushed to hospital and needed emergency surgery. He was unconscious by the time he reached hospital and doctors were of the opinion that he would die if he were not operated on.

1   Should the home-care assistant advise doctors of Mr P's beliefs?
2   Should she act on his behalf to prevent the administration of a blood transfusion?
3   What would you do if you were Mr P's home-care assistant?
4   Is it different when someone like Mr P is unconscious and cannot speak for himself?

REMEMBER

The most terrifying films and the scariest fairground rides are those where you do not know what is going to happen next, or you do not know exactly what you are afraid of. It is always not knowing and feeling unsure that makes you more likely to reject something new and different. Once you have information, it is much easier to welcome and value the variety that others can bring.

✓ The wide range of different beliefs and values which you are likely to come into contact with, if you work in a care setting, are part of a rich and diverse series of cultures from all parts of the world.

✓ The best way to appreciate what others have to offer is to find out about them. Ask questions. People will usually be happy to tell you about themselves and their beliefs.

✓ The other key is to be open to hearing what others have to say – do not be so sure that your values and beliefs and the way you live are the only ways of doing things.

✓ Think about the great assets which have come to the UK from people moving here from other cultures, including music, food and entertainment, and different approaches to work or relaxation or medicine. Similarly, far more people travel abroad now than 30 years ago, and you are more likely to have the chance to experience other people's ways of life for yourself and to exchange information about your own.

TEST YOURSELF

1 What would you do if someone told a racist joke:

  a   laugh because it's only fun?
  b   say nothing but feel awkward?
  c   say that you find the joke offensive?

  Explain your answer.

2 Name three groups who are discriminated against.

3 What forms does the discrimination take?

4 How would you attempt to reduce the discrimination in those three instances?

5 What is stereotyping? Give an example.

Element O1.3 | Maintain the confidentiality of information

What you need to learn

● What is meant by confidentiality
● How you can maintain confidentiality
● Looking after information
● When you need to break confidentiality

What is meant by confidentiality

The single most important requirement for anyone who works in a care setting is to be trustworthy. Most individuals want that above all else. It is no use having the kindest doctor in the world if you discover that she has been chatting to your next door neighbour about how bad your haemorrhoids are! You will have to make confidentiality part of your life.

Confidentiality means not giving any information to anyone unless there is a reason to do so. This sounds very straightforward, and in theory it is, but you need to know what this means in practice.

DID YOU KNOW?

Everyone has one friend to whom they can talk in absolute confidence! The problem is that often your friend will have another confidential friend – it does not take long for information to travel if everyone tells just one person.

How you can maintain confidentiality

The most common way in which workers breach confidentiality is by chatting about work with friends or family. It is very tempting to discuss the day's events with your family or with friends over a drink or a meal. This is fine, as it is often therapeutic to discuss a stressful day, or get things into perspective. But you must make it a rule never to mention names.

You never know who's listening!

CARELESS TALK COSTS LIVES

If you always say 'There was this man today...' or 'You won't believe what one of our patients did today...', that is all it takes. Get into the habit of using other characteristics to describe people who appear in your conversation regularly, for example, 'You remember the woman with the very loud voice I told you about last week...'.

When you are out with a group of colleagues, the risks are even greater that you will be tempted to discuss individuals by name. Clearly, your colleagues are already all aware of the individuals, but there is always the likelihood of being overheard in a public place like a pub or restaurant. Again, it is easy to deal with. You just have to make sure that you refer to individuals in a way in which they cannot be identified. The easiest way is to use initials.

It will soon become second nature, and you will find yourself glancing around to make sure you cannot be overheard and referring to individuals by their initials in case conferences and planning meetings!

You also need to be sure that you do not discuss a person you care for with another that you care for. You may not think that you would ever do this but it is so easy to do, with the best of intentions.

Imagine the scene. Someone says 'Ethel doesn't look too good today' and your well-meant response is 'No, she doesn't. She's had a bit of an upset with her son. She'd probably be really glad of some company later, if you've got the time'. This is the type of response which can cause great distress and, above all, distrust. If the lady you have spoken to later says to Ethel, 'Sue said you were a bit down because of the upset with your son', Ethel is not going to know how much you have said. As far as she knows, you could have given her the whole life history to the lady who enquired. The most damaging consequence of this breach of confidentiality is the loss of trust. This can have damaging effects on an individual's self-esteem, confidence and general well-being.

The best way to respond to that comment would be 'Don't you think so? Well, perhaps she might be glad of some company later if you've got the time'.

Check it out

Think of a time when you have told someone something in confidence and later discovered that they had told other people. Try to recall how you felt about it. You may have felt angry or betrayed. Perhaps you were embarrassed and did not want to face anyone. Note down a few of the ways you felt.

Policies of the organisation

Every health and caring organisation will have a policy on confidentiality and the disclosure of information. You must be sure that you know what both policies are in your workplace.

The basic rule is that all information an individual gives, or that is given on his or her behalf, to an organisation is confidential and cannot be disclosed to anyone without the consent of the individual.

Passing on information with consent

There are, however, circumstances in which it may be necessary to pass on information.

In many cases, the passing of information is routine and related to the care of the individual. For example, medical information may be passed to a hospital, to a residential home or to a private care agency. It must be made clear to the individual that this information will be passed on in order to ensure that he or she receives the best possible care.

The key is that only information which is required for the purpose is passed on. For example, it is not necessary to tell the hearing aid clinic that Mr S's son is currently serving a prison sentence. However, if he became seriously ill and the hospital wanted to contact his next of kin, that information would need to be passed on.

Each organisation should have a policy which states clearly the circumstances in which information can be disclosed. According to government guidelines (Confidentiality of Personal Information 1988) the policy should state:

- who are the members of senior management designated to deal with decisions about disclosing information
- what to do when urgent action is required
- what safeguards are in place to make sure that the information will be used only for the purpose for which it is required
- arrangements for obtaining manual records and computer records
- arrangements for reviewing the procedure.

People who need to know

It can be difficult when people claim to have a right or an interest in seeing an individual's records. Of course, there are always some people who do need to know, either because they are directly involved in providing care for the individual or because they are involved in some other support role. However, not everyone needs to know everything, so it is important that information is given on a 'need to know' basis. In other words, people are told what they need to know in order to carry out their role.

Relatives will often claim that they have a 'right to know'. The most famous example of this was Victoria Gillick, who went to court in order to try to gain access to her daughter's medical records. She claimed that she had the right to know if her daughter had been given the contraceptive pill. Her GP had refused to tell her and she took the case all the way to the House of Lords, but the ruling was not changed and she was not given access to her daughter's records. The rules remain the same. Even for close relatives, the information is not available unless the individual agrees.

It is difficult, however, if you are faced with angry or distressed relatives who believe that you have information they are entitled to. One situation you could encounter is where a daughter, for example, believes that she has the right to be told about medical information in respect of her parent. Another example is where someone is trying to find out a person's whereabouts. The best response is to be clear and assertive, but to demonstrate that you understand that it is difficult for them. Do not try to 'pass the buck' and give people the idea that they can find out from someone else. There is nothing more frustrating than being passed from one person to another without anyone being prepared to tell you anything. It is important to be clear and say something like, 'I'm sorry. I know you must be worried, but I can't discuss any information unless your mother agrees', or 'I'm sorry, I can't give out any information about where J is living now. But if you would like to leave me a name and contact details, I will pass on the message and she can contact you'.

Proof of identity

You should always check that people are who they claim to be. It is not unknown for newspaper reporters, unwanted visitors or even a nosey neighbour to claim that they are relatives or professionals from another agency. If basic precautions are not taken to confirm their identity, then they may be able to find out a great deal of confidential information.

Checklist

In person: if you do not know the person who is claiming to have a right to be given information, you should:

● find out whether he or she is known to any of your colleagues
● ask for proof of identity – if he or she claims to be from another agency involved in

providing care, he or she will have an official ID (identity card); otherwise ask for driving licence, bank cards, etc.

On the telephone: unless you recognise the voice of the person, you should:
- offer to take his or her telephone number and call him/her back after you have checked
- if various members of the family or friends are likely to be telephoning about a particular service user, you could arrange a 'password'.

REMEMBER
- Generally you should only give the information with consent.
- Only give people the information they need to know to do their job.
- Information should be relevant to the purpose for which it is required.
- Check the identity of the person to whom you give information.
- Make sure that you do not give information carelessly.

CASE STUDY

Mr R is 59 years old. He is a resident in a nursing home, and he is now very ill. He has Huntington's disease, which is a disease causing dementia, loss of mobility, and loss of speech. It is incurable and untreatable, and it is hereditary. Mr R was divorced many years ago when his children were very young and he has had no contact with his family for over 30 years. A young man who says he is his son comes to the nursing home in great distress. He is aware, through his mother, that his paternal grandfather died 'insane' and he has now heard about his father being in a nursing home. He is terrified that his father has a hereditary disease and that he also may have it. He also has young children and is desperate to know if they are at risk.

1 What can you tell Mr R's son?
2 Does he have a right to know?
3 What do you think should happen?
4 Whose rights are your concern?

Looking after information

Once something is written down or entered on a computer, it becomes a permanent record. For this reason, you must be very careful what you do with any files, charts, notes or other written records. They must always be stored somewhere locked and safe. People should be very careful with files which leave the workplace. There are many stories about files being stolen from cars or left on buses!

Records kept on computers must also be kept safe and protected. Your workplace will have policies relating to records on computers, which will include access being restricted by a password, and the computer system being protected against the possibility of people 'hacking' into it.

Since the Access to Personal Files Act 1987, individuals can see their personal files. This means that people can see their medical records, or social services files, from the date of the Act. Obviously, people are only entitled to see information about themselves, and they cannot see any part of their record which relates to someone else.

The information which you write in files should be clear and useful. Do not include irrelevant information, and write only about the individual concerned. Anything you write should be true and able to be justified, as the two examples below show.

Computer records must be surrounded by proper security.

Name: A. Person

Mr P settling back well after discharge from hosp. Fairly quiet and withdrawn today. Son to visit in Am. Report from hosp included in file, prognosis not good. Not able to get him to talk today, for further time tomorrow.

Name: J. Soap

Joe visited new flat today. Very positive and looking forward to move. No access problems, delighted with purpose-built kitchen and bathroom. Further visit from OT needed to check on any aids required. Confirmed with housing assoc. that Joe wants tenancy. Will send tenancy agreement, should start on 1st.

Need to check: housing benefit, OT visit, notify change of address to Benefits Agency, PACT team, etc., shopping trip with Joe for any household items.

The purpose of a file is to reflect an accurate and up-to-date picture of an individual's situation, and to provide an historical record which can be referred to at some point in the future. Some of it may be required to be disclosed to other agencies. Always think about what you write. Make sure it is ACES:

Accurate
Clear
Easy to read
Shareable.

All information, however it is stored, is subject to the rules laid down in the Data Protection Act 1998, which covers medical records, social service records, credit information, local authority information – in fact, anything which is personal data (facts and opinions about an individual).

The principles of data protection

Anyone processing personal data must comply with the eight enforceable principles of good practice. These say that data must be:

- fairly and lawfully processed
- processed for limited purposes
- adequate, relevant and not excessive
- accurate
- not kept longer than necessary
- processed in accordance with the data subject's rights
- kept secure
- not transferred to countries without adequate protection.

When you need to break confidentiality

Passing on information without consent

There are several reasons why decisions about disclosing information without consent may need to be made, and the individual should be informed about what has been disclosed at the earliest possible opportunity. The one exception to this is where information is given in order to assist an investigation into suspected child abuse. In that case, the individual should not be told of any information which has been disclosed until this has been agreed by those carrying out the investigation.

Information may be required by a tribunal, a court or by the ombudsman. Ideally this should be done with the service user's consent, but it will have to be provided regardless of whether the consent is given.

You may have to consider the protection of the community, if there is a matter of public health at stake. You may be aware that someone has an infectious illness, or is a carrier of such an illness and is putting people at risk. For example, if someone was infected with salmonella, but still insisted on going to work in a restaurant kitchen, you would have a duty to inform the appropriate authorities. There are other situations where you may need to give information to the police. If a serious crime is being investigated, the police can ask for information to be given. There is no definition of 'serious', but it is generally accepted as involving:

- serious harm to the security of the state or to public order
- serious interference with a legal case or investigation
- death
- serious injury
- substantial financial gain or financial loss.

Not only can information only be requested in respect of a serious offence, it has to be asked for by a senior-ranking officer, of at least the rank of superintendent.

This means that if the local constable asks if you know whether Mr J has a history of mental health problems, this is not information you are free to discuss.

There may also be times when it is helpful to give information to the media. For example, an elderly confused man, who wanders regularly, may have gone missing for far longer than usual. A description given out on the local radio and in the local paper may help to locate him before he comes to any serious harm.

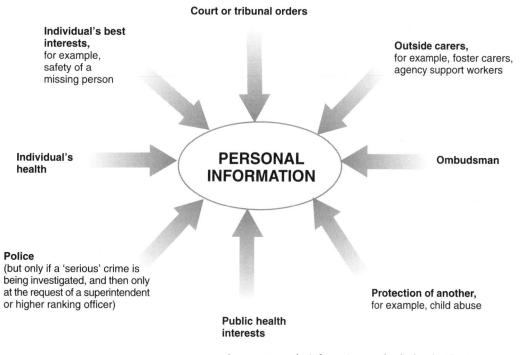

Some reasons why information may be disclosed without consent.

There are other occasions when it is necessary to pass on information which has been given to you in confidence, or which an individual might expect you to keep confidential. One of the most difficult situations is where a child discloses to you that he or she is being abused. The best practice is to try not to get yourself in the position of agreeing to keep a secret.

Keys to good practice

✓ If you have been given information by a child concerning abuse, you have to pass on the information to your line manager, or whoever is named in the alerting procedures. This is not a matter of choice; even if the child refuses to agree, you have a duty to override his or her wishes. There are no circumstances in which disclosures of abuse of children must be kept confidential.

✓ The situation with an adult, perhaps an older person, who is being abused is different. You can only try to persuade him or her to allow you to pass on the information.

✓ You may be faced with information which indicates that someone intends to harm himself or herself. In that situation, you would be justified in breaking a confidence to prevent harm.

✓ If an individual is threatening to harm someone else, you should pass on the information immediately to your line manager, who will inform the police. It is not appropriate to contact the threatened person directly.

CASE STUDY

Mrs E was in labour, and it was decided that she needed an emergency caesarean section to deliver her baby safely. Her husband was present and everything was explained to him. He was worried, but understood the reason for the surgery. Mrs E signed the consent form for surgery and was hurriedly wheeled down to theatre. Mr E walked beside her to theatre and noticed that there was a stamp on the front of the case notes saying 'High Risk'. He tried to ask one of the staff what this meant just as they were going into the theatre. She said, 'Hang on a second love, I'll be with you in minute. I've just got to put on an extra pair of gloves because of your wife being HIV positive.' Mr E had no idea that his wife was HIV positive.

1 Who was at fault?
2 Should Mr E have been told of his wife's HIV status before this stage?
3 How could this have been prevented?
4 How do you think both of them will be feeling?
5 What lessons can you learn from this?

TEST YOURSELF

1 What is the law which governs computer records?

2 Name three of the principles of data protection.

3 What does ACES stand for?

4 Why do records have to be locked away?

5 What are the circumstances in which you can give information to the police?

6 Name three other occasions where you may give information to others.

7 What are the simple steps you can take to make sure that you do not unintentionally give out confidential information?

O1 UNIT TEST

1 People are not discriminated against in the UK because there are laws to stop it. True or false?

2 What are the drawbacks to the laws about discrimination?

3 Do the words people use have important effects on equality?

4 What is diversity?

5 How could you work to encourage a recognition of diversity in your workplace?

6 Is it ever acceptable to break confidentiality?

7 Name three organisations who may be given confidential information.

8 Identify the circumstances in which you may need to break confidentiality.

Promote effective communication and relationships

In this chapter you will look at how to deal with people in a way which takes account of their individuality. When time is short and demands are high, it is often easier to treat everyone in a group in the same way, to make plans for a whole group of people or to assume that what is good for one person will be good for all. You will learn how to avoid this.

Relationships are a part of communication and communication is a part of relationships. The two are linked so closely, that it is difficult to deal with one without the other. Working in a care setting means that you work with other human beings. Being able to make relationships and to communicate with them is a very basic requirement for doing your job. Each person you care for is an individual – completely different and unique. This may sound obvious but it is so important that it is worth repeating.

You will learn how to avoid making judgments about people which are based not on knowledge and understanding of that person, but on generally accepted stereotypes, often with little truth behind them.

The work you have chosen will involve you in relationships with other people all the time. Working in caring is different from other jobs. It is not only about having good working relationships with colleagues, although good teamwork is essential; it is also about the relationships you will make with the individuals you are caring for, and it is about understanding other relationships they have, with their friends and relatives.

ement CL1.1   Develop relationships with people which value them as individuals

What you need to learn
- How to treat people as individuals
- Knowing yourself and your prejudices
- Behaviour which fails to value people
- How to challenge unacceptable behaviour

How to treat people as individuals

One in a million

One of the most effective ways you have of helping people is by recognising them as individuals. Learn never to make assumptions about people in groups.

Think about the number of ways in which people can be identified – they can be described by age, gender, eye colour, place of residence, job, and so on. This will remind you of the number of different aspects there are to any one individual.

The problem with 'labelling' people into particular groups for particular purposes is that it is very rarely accurate. It may be very convenient when planning care to decide that 'all individuals will want…' or 'this age group will benefit from…', but the number of individuals contained within any group means that any planning that starts with a generalisation is doomed to be unsatisfactory.

Check it out

Think of a way to describe yourself, starting with the most general – 'I am a woman' or 'I am a man'. So are many other people, so that does not describe you. 'I have brown hair' – so do a great many others. Continue thinking of ways to describe yourself, getting closer all the time to finding a description which is unique to you (i.e. which describes you, and no one else). Each time you think of another way to describe yourself, it will eliminate more and more people from the group, until finally you may (depending on how well you know yourself) come up with a description which applies to no one else but you.

Each time you are tempted to treat people as one of a group, remember how long this task took and how many descriptions you listed before you found a unique reference to you. Remember that everyone you deal with is unique – an individual.

You will say 'I'm not prejudiced'. Most people do, but the reality is that everyone has prejudices. They come from all kinds of previous experiences. You may be afraid of dogs because you were once bitten. Not every dog you meet is going to bite you, but that will not stop you judging all dogs from one experience. The way you have been brought up and the attitudes you grew up with will shape the kind of person you turn out to be.

What are stereotypes?

Prejudice is what makes people think in stereotypes and, equally, stereotypes support prejudice. Stereotypes are an easy way of thinking about the world. Stereotypes would suggest that all people over 65 are frail and walk with a stick, that all black young people who live in inner cities are on drugs, that all fat people are lazy, or that all families have a mother, father and two children. These stereotypes, or ways of looking at the world, are often reinforced by the media or by advertising. Television programmes will often portray violent, criminal characters as young and black.

Check it out

Next time you watch television note down the number of adverts for cars which show trendy, good-looking young business people with a wealthy lifestyle. The advertisers attempt to convince us that buying that particular brand of car will make us good-looking and trendy and give us the kind of lifestyle portrayed.

1   How many people do you know with those particular makes of car who are anything like the people in the adverts?
2   How many do you know who wish they were?

What effect do stereotypes have?

The effect of stereotypes is to make us jump to conclusions about people. How many times have you felt uneasy seeing a young man with a shaved head walking towards you? You know nothing about him, but the way he looks has made you form an opinion about him. If you have a picture in your mind of a social worker or a policeman, think about how much that is influenced by the media – do they really all look like that?

1 What do you think each of these people does for a living?

2 What kind of place does each of them live in?

3 Why have you given the answers you have?

Accents can often evoke prejudice. Try to be aware of what regional accents mean – think about these stereotypes:

People from...	are known as...	are thought to be...
Liverpool	Scousers	work-shy, scroungers, funny
Birmingham	Brummies	slow, not very bright, boring
London	Cockneys	wheeler dealers, not trustworthy, clever
Glasgow	Glaswegians	aggressive, looking for a fight, drinkers
Newcastle	Geordies	warm, friendly, tough, 'salt of the earth'

The next time you find yourself making a judgement about somebody's character based on an accent, stop and think. Try to avoid a stereotype.

'Have you heard the one about...?'

Telling jokes at the expense of particular groups of people is similarly displaying prejudices. Stereotypes about people being mean or stupid because of their nationality fail to treat people as individuals and fail to recognise that there are individuals everywhere and that all people are different.

Check it out

Stop yourself every time you make a generalisation and look at the prejudice. Think about why you think the way you do, and do something about it. The next time you hear yourself saying 'Social workers never understand what is really needed', 'GPs always take ages to visit' or 'Our residents wouldn't be interested in that', stop and think what you are really doing.

It is probably quite correct that some social workers won't understand, maybe even all those you have met so far! But that does not necessarily apply to them all.

Perhaps most of your residents would not be interested in whatever was being suggested – a trip to the art gallery? a bike ride? or a naughty underwear party? – but you cannot make that assumption. You need to ask.

Treating people as individuals

You should always consult the individual before you carry out any procedure, and explain everything you do. Even if the procedure is part of his or her plan of care and has been done many times before, you should never take a person's agreement for granted.

Everyone should be offered choices wherever possible. This may be about when, where or how their care is provided. In circumstances where a choice is not possible, either because of an individual's circumstances or a lack of resources, this should be explained.

These are examples of the kinds of choice you may be able to offer to people when you provide care:

Care service	Choices
Personal hygiene	Bath, shower or bed bath Assistance or no assistance Morning, afternoon or evening Temperature of water Toiletries
Food	Menu Dining table or tray Timing Assistance In company or alone

Clearly, the range of choices will vary depending on the circumstances, but the principle remains the same – that people should not have care imposed on them without being able to be actively involved in the decisions about how and when care is delivered.

Part of valuing people as individuals is having respect for all of the people you deal with. Respect is usually something which develops as you form relationships. When you provide care for someone, you will get to know and talk to him or her, and a relationship will grow. This is not easy with all individuals you care for. When there appears to be no two-way communication, you may find that forming a relationship is difficult. If you work with people who do not appear to relate to you, perhaps because they are very confused, because they have a very low level of functioning or even because they are not conscious, then it is easy to forget that they are still individuals and need to be treated as such.

Keys to good practice

✓ Make sure that any service which you provide for someone is with their agreement. People have a right to choose the care which they receive and the way in which they receive it.

✓ You must make sure that each person you care for is treated in the same way, regardless of his or her ability to respond to you. This means talking to people who do not seem to understand you, and to people who may appear not to respond. You should explain everything you are doing and go through the details of any procedures you are carrying out.

REMEMBER

● Everyone has the right to make choices about care.
● All people are different.

If you accept these points, you will never be guilty of making generalisations or making prejudiced judgements about people again.

If only it were that simple! Of course, you cannot suddenly stop doing and thinking things which you have been doing and thinking all your life, but you can develop an awareness of what you are doing and start to ask yourself questions about why you have acted in the way you have.

Once you realise how your own background and beliefs alter the way you think about people, you can begin to recognise the differences and see the value of other cultures and beliefs. It is inevitable that, by thinking carefully about what has influenced you, you will also consider what has influenced others with whom you come into contact.

You need to talk to people, whether they are colleagues or service users, about aspects of their culture or lifestyle you do not understand. As a care professional, it is your responsibility to make sure that you have considered the culture, beliefs and lifestyle of someone for whom you are providing care. It is not acceptable to expect that they will adapt to your set of cultural beliefs and expectations.

The diversity of the human race is what makes living in our society such a rich and varied experience. If you try to welcome this diversity, rather than resist, condemn or belittle the things you do not understand, you will find that your relationships with colleagues and service users will be much more rewarding and the quality of your care practice will be greatly improved.

CASE STUDY

T is in her mid-30s and has a busy job in an international finance company. She is from a Chinese family who have lived in a large city and run a restaurant for the past 40 years. Her parents have now retired from the restaurant and have both suffered from ill-health in the past year. They are too frail to continue caring for themselves without support. T's brothers are busy running the family business and T has decided to stop working in order to care for her parents. Her English friends and work colleagues are horrified that she is prepared to give up such a good career to do this. The local social services department has offered to provide domiciliary care for T's parents, but the family have refused, explaining that it will not be necessary. T is having difficulty making her non-Chinese friends, colleagues and even social services understand her view that she is willing to do this for her parents and that their welfare is a greater priority than her career.

1 Can you see where the key differences are between the attitude of T and the attitudes of many western families?
2 Would you encourage T to give up her job? If so – why? If not – why not?
3 What should the role of social services be in this situation?

REMEMBER
- Stereotypes can influence how you think about someone.
- Don't rush to make judgements about people.
- Don't make assumptions.
- Everyone is entitled to his or her own beliefs and culture. If you don't know about somebody's way if life – ask.

Knowing yourself and your prejudices

'To see ourselves as others see us'

It is vital, if you are to help anyone effectively, that you understand how you affect any situation. Human beings do not react in the same way to everyone. You have doubtless experienced meeting someone who makes you feel relaxed and at ease – you find it easy to talk to them and feel as if you had known them for a long time. Equally, there are other people you meet and find it much harder to talk to – they make you feel nervous, or unsure; you can't think of anything to say and feel generally uncomfortable. You are still the same person, but you have reacted in a totally different way to two different people. This is called interaction and describes what takes place between human beings. To be a good practitioner in caring, you have to learn to understand how people react to you and the way in which your own beliefs, background and prejudices will influence and alter the outcome of an interaction.

It is essential that you understand about interaction if you are working in caring. It is not always easy to understand how it works. It may help if you think about it as a fairground mirror – all of the reflections look different, some are short and fat, some long and thin, some are wavy and curved; it all depends on the mirror. You are still the same, but the mirror makes everything appear different. It is the same with people. The same person will behave in a different way – interact – depending on the person they are talking to.

Check it out

Try this out for yourself at work. Pick two different people and tell them both the same thing. For example, you could ask to leave early on the next shift, explain why a particular person needs a change in their plan of care, or explain where the new delivery of equipment is – in fact, anything at all. Note down how you carried out the task with each person and how you felt. Make sure you note the differences in your behaviour and feelings. Try to work out how, and why, each of them made you feel different.

Working in caring makes huge demands on people. The most important attribute you bring to the job is your own personality. This is why it is so important that you know yourself, and know what you bring to the job. You will have to learn to recognise your own prejudices and what effect they will have in the workplace.

Learning about yourself is not an easy task. Everyone thinks they know themselves so well – or do they? Often you never take the time to examine your own behaviour in depth. It is often a shock when someone else points out something you are doing, or a way you have of behaving, which you had not realised before.

Keys to good practice

✓ If you intend to be effective as a carer, then you will need to spend some time looking at your own behaviour and try to look in the mirror of others' reactions. You will never really know how you look in a physical way to others because you can only ever see a mirror image of yourself. If you think about looking at the world through a mirror, you will realise that it always looks slightly different from how you see it first-hand. However, you can judge how your actions and behaviour affect others by using them as your 'mirror' and being sensitive to their reactions.

Mirror, mirror on the wall...

✓ If you are talking to someone and he or she suddenly seems to close down the conversation, or appear unsure, try to think back to the point at which the atmosphere changed. Be honest with yourself. Did you react to something he or she said? What did you say? Was it a little thoughtless? Did you laugh? Maybe he or she thought you were laughing at him/her? Or did he or she begin to back away when you looked at your watch, or spoke briefly to someone else who wanted your attention?

✓ Do some individuals seem to find it easier to talk to you than others? Do you find it easier to talk to some individuals than others? Of course, there are bound to be some people you like more than others, but when you are working as a professional carer it is not enough just to acknowledge that. You have to know 'why' in order make sure that it does not result in individuals being treated differently.

✓ Only you can work at examining your own behaviour. If you have a manager or colleague to work with you, that is a great help, but essentially, no one can do it for you. You will need to be able to ask yourself a series of questions, and be prepared to answer them: Which people do you find it hard to deal with? Can you work better with women than men? Do you find it hard to talk to young people? or to older people? or to people of a particular social class? or to people of particular races? or to anyone with a different accent?

✓ Do you find that you have less patience with some people? Can you identify which people? Is there a pattern? You may not always like the answers you come up with, but until you can work out how you behave towards others and why, you will never be able to make any adjustments to your responses.

✓ You will need to look at your own culture and beliefs. You may have grown up surrounded by people who believed that it was unthinkable to owe a penny to anyone, so you may find it difficult to offer empathy and support to someone who is desperate because he or she is in massive debt. If you have lived in a culture which holds older family members in high regard and accords them respect, you may find it hard to relate to the family of someone who hardly ever visits and does not appear interested in his or her welfare. Nevertheless, in your role as a carer you have to be aware of how your own background may influence you and to ensure that you include that factor in the analysis of any situation.

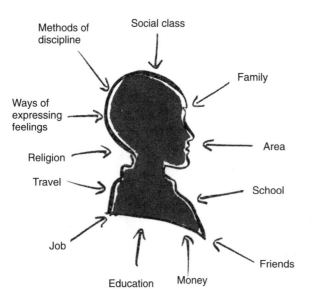

Influences on who you are.

✓ Don't be too hard on yourself. Acknowledging your own prejudices is to go more than halfway to overcoming them. Just being able to understand why you behave in the way you do is more than most people achieve in a lifetime! So don't worry if it takes a while before you feel that you are really thinking about what you do and how you affect others. It may seem unlikely, but knowing how people respond to you and making allowances for that will, eventually, become second nature.

TEST YOURSELF

1. How can your personality affect how you work?

2. Why do you need to know about yourself?

3. Stereotypes are:
   a. ways of measuring what music people listen to
   b. generalised beliefs about people
   c. differences between people.

4. People react in the same way, regardless of whom they speak to. True or false?

5. Is there any point in talking to someone who clearly doesn't understand you? Give reasons for your answer.

Behaviour which fails to value people

Practising a policy of equal opportunities in the workplace is one part of recognising and welcoming diversity. There are several pieces of legislation which address equal opportunities for various groups, and they are covered in depth in Chapter 1 (Unit O1), but whether or not any of those principles are put into practice is influenced by how much people are valued as individuals in any care setting.

There is little point in having legislation unless it is generally observed, and any breaches of the law are dealt with. Legislation gives rights to certain groups of people which should ensure that they are not discriminated against, but individual workers have to be prepared to defend and uphold those rights for themselves and others.

However, valuing people and welcoming the fact that everyone is diverse is about more than just upholding the law, although that is very important. Workers must be prepared to recognise when someone is subjected to behaviour which infringes upon their rights.

Generally you can define behaviour as unacceptable if:

- it is outside what you would normally see in that situation
- it does not take into account the needs or views of others
- people are afraid or intimidated
- people are undermined or made to feel guilty
- the behaviour is likely to cause distress or unhappiness to others.

Examples of unacceptable behaviour include:

- threatening violence
- subjecting someone to unwelcome sexual harassment
- playing loud music in a quiet area, or late at night
- verbal abuse, racist or sexist taunts
- spreading malicious gossip about someone
- attempting to isolate someone.

All of these types of behaviour are oppressive to others and need to be challenged. You can probably think of many other situations in your own workplace which have caused unhappiness. You may have had to deal with difficult situations, or have seen others deal with them, or perhaps you have wished that you had done something to challenge oppressive behaviour.

You may come across unacceptable and oppressive behaviour in your colleagues or other professionals in your workplace. Behaviour which is actually abusive is dealt with in Chapter 4 (Unit Z1). While you may see or hear a colleague behaving in a way which is not abusive as such, it may be oppressive and unacceptable. This can take various forms such as:

- speaking about service users in a derogatory way
- speaking to service users in a rude or dismissive way
- humiliating service users
- undermining people's self-esteem and confidence
- bullying or intimidation
- patronising and talking down to people
- removing people's right to exercise choice
- failing to recognise and treat people as individuals
- not respecting people's culture, values and beliefs.

In short, the types of behaviour which are unacceptable from workers in care settings are those which simply fail to meet the standards required of good quality practitioners. Any care worker who fails to remember that all people they care for are individuals and that all people have a right to be valued and accepted, is likely to fall into behaving in an oppressive or inappropriate way.

Check it out

Ask three colleagues in your workplace to state one behaviour that they would find unacceptable in (a) a service user and (b) a colleague. Compare the six answers and see if they have anything in common. Find out from your supervisor about the type of behaviour that is challenged in your workplace, and that which is allowed.

How to challenge unacceptable behaviour

Steps to dealing with difficult situations

Step 1 Consider all the people involved in the situation

If you have some knowledge of an individual's background, culture and beliefs, it may be easier to see why he or she is behaving in a particular way. This does not make it acceptable, just easier to understand. For example, men in some cultures, such as in Arab countries, are far more likely to touch other men (hugging and kissing as a sign of friendship), than men from the UK, where such physical contact (except between footballers!) is not generally acceptable. An individual who has been in a position of wealth or power may be used to giving people instructions and expecting to have immediate attention, and may be quite rude if it does not happen. This type of attitude is obviously not going to be tolerated, but approaching the situation with some understanding allows people to maintain their dignity whilst adapting their behaviour.

Step 2 Be aware of everyone's needs

If you are in a work situation, it can be complicated by the fact that the person whose oppressive behaviour you are challenging may also be one of your service users. In this case, it is important to ensure that you challenge the behaviour without becoming aggressive or intimidating yourself, and that you do not undermine the individual.

Step 3 Decide on the best approach

How you decide to deal with an incident of unacceptable behaviour will depend on:

- whether the behaviour is violent or non-violent – if the behaviour is violent, what the potential dangers of the situation are, who may be in danger and what needs to be done to help those in danger
- who is involved, how well you know them and know how to deal with them
- whether you need help, and who is available to help you
- whether the cause is obvious and the solution is easy to deal with.

Clearly, you will need to weigh up the situation quickly, in order to deal with it promptly. You will, no doubt, feel under pressure, as this is a stressful situation to be in, whether you are experienced or not. Try to remain calm and think clearly.

Step 4 Deal with non-violent behaviour

If the behaviour you have to deal with is not physical aggression or violence, then you will need to deal with it by ensuring that you make the challenge in a situation which provides privacy and dignity. You should challenge without becoming aggressive, remain calm and quietly state what you consider to be unacceptable about their behaviour. Do not try to approach it from various angles, or drop hints. Be clear about the problem and what you want to happen.

For example, 'Bill, you have been playing your radio very loudly until quite late each night. Other residents are finding it difficult to get to sleep. I would like you to stop playing it so loudly if you want to have it on late.' You may well have to negotiate with Bill about times, and the provision of headphones, but do not be drawn into an argument and do not be sidetracked into irrelevant discussions. For example:

Bill: 'Who's been complaining? No one's complained to me. Who is it?'

You: 'Bill, this is about your radio being too loud. The issue is not about who complained, but about the fact that it is upsetting residents and I want you to stop doing it.'

By the end of this discussion, Bill should be very clear about what is being required of him and be in no doubt that his behaviour will have to change.

Step 5 Attempt to calm a potentially violent situation

It is always better to avoid a violent situation than to respond to one, so you need to be aware of the signals which may indicate that violence could erupt. Be on the lookout for verbal aggression; raised volume and pitch of voice; threatening and aggressive gestures; pacing; quick, darting eye movements; prolonged eye contact.

Try to respond in ways least likely to provoke further aggression:

- Use listening skills, and appear confident (but not cocky).
- Keep your voice calm and at a level pitch.
- Do not argue.
- Do not get drawn into prolonged eye contact.
- Attempt to defuse the situation with empathy and understanding. For example, 'I realise you must be upset if you believe that George said that about you. I can see that you're very angry. Tell me about what happened.'

Be prepared to try a different approach if you find you are not getting anywhere. Always make sure that an aggressor has a way out with dignity, both physically and emotionally.

DID YOU KNOW?

There is a technique which is recommended for use in situations which become violent. It is called 'Breakaway' and is approved by the Home Office for use in all types of care settings. It provides you with methods for dealing with a physical threat or attack without causing injury. Ask your employer to arrange for you to attend a course with an approved trainer.

Step 6 Deal with aggressive or violent behaviour

Be aware of the situation you are in and take some common-sense precautions: make sure that you know where the exits are, move so that the aggressor is not between you and the exit; notice if there is anything which could be used as a weapon, and try to move away from it; make sure that the aggressor has enough personal space, and do not crowd him or her.

If you are faced with a violent situation, you should try to remain calm (even though that is easier said than done!) and not resort to violence or aggression yourself.

It is often the case that a simple technique like holding up a hand in front of you, as if you were directing traffic, and shouting 'Stop' may deflect an attacker, or stop him or her long enough for you to get away. You should remove yourself from the situation as speedily as possible.

If there are other, vulnerable people at risk, you must decide whether you can summon help more effectively from outside or inside the situation.

If you decide to remain, you must summon help at once. You should do one of the following:

- Press a panic alarm or buzzer, if one is provided.
- Shout 'help!' very loudly and continuously.
- Send someone for help.
- Call the police, or security, or shout for someone else to do so.

Do not try to be a hero – that is not your job.

Check it out

Your workplace should have a policy on dealing with aggression and violence. Ask to see it and make sure that you read it carefully.

REMEMBER
- Everyone is different and will react differently to each situation.
- You are the factor that makes the difference.
- Learn to know yourself before you think you can know about others.
- Each person should be valued as a unique individual.

TEST YOURSELF
1 What kinds of behaviour fail to value others?
2 What are stereotypes?
3 What is the problem with thinking in stereotypes?
4 How does society reinforce stereotypes?
5 Why do you have to challenge oppressive behaviour?
6 How should you deal with aggressive behaviour?

ment CL1.2 Establish and maintain effective communication with people

What you need to learn
- Ways in which people communicate
- Barriers to communication
- How to listen
- How to communicate clearly

Ways in which people communicate

This element is about how people reach out to each other. Communication is much more than talking. It is about how people respond to each other in many different ways: touch, facial expression, body movements, dress, position – and this is before you start on written communication, telephone, cyberspace, message in a bottle or pigeon!

REMEMBER

You are the most important tool you have for doing your job. Carers do not have carefully engineered machinery or complex technology – your own ability to relate to others and to understand them is the key you need!

More than talking

Any relationship comes about through communication. In order to be an effective care worker, you must learn to be a good communicator. But communication is about much more than talking to people!

People communicate through:

- speaking
- body language
- dress
- facial expression
- position
- gestures.

You will have to know how to recognise what is being communicated to you, and to be able to communicate with others without always having to use words.

Check it out

Do this with a friend or colleague.

1 Write the names of several emotions (such as anger, joy, sadness, disappointment, fear) on pieces of paper.

2 One of you should pick up a piece of paper. Your task is to communicate the emotion written on the paper to your partner, without saying anything.

3 Your partner then has to decide what the emotion is and say why.

4 Then change places and repeat the exercise. Take it in turns, until all the pieces of paper have been used. Make sure that you list all the things which made you aware of the emotion being expressed.

5 Discuss with your partner what you have discovered about communication as a result of this exercise.

Keys to good practice

When you carried out the last exercise, you will have found out that there are many things which told you what your partner was trying to communicate. It is not only the expression on people's faces which tells you about how they feel, but it is also the way they use the rest of their bodies. This area of human behaviour is referred to as non-verbal communication. It is very important for developing the ability to understand what people are feeling. If you understand the importance of non-verbal communication, you will be able to use it to improve your own skills when you communicate with someone.

Recognising the signals

Look at a person's facial expression. Much of what you will see will be in his or her eyes, but the eyebrows and mouth also contribute.

Notice whether someone is looking at you, or at the floor, or at a point over your shoulder. Lack of eye contact should give a first indication that all may not be well. It may be that they are not feeling confident. They may be unhappy, or feel uneasy about talking to you. You will need to follow this up.

Look at how a person sits. Is he or she relaxed and comfortable, sitting well back in the chair, or tense and perched on the edge of the seat? Is he or she slumped in the chair with the head down? Posture can indicate a great deal about how somebody is feeling. People who are feeling well and cheerful tend to hold their heads up, and sit in a relaxed and comfortable way. An individual who is tense and nervous, who feels unsure and worried is likely to reflect that in the way he or she sits or stands.

Observe hands and gestures carefully. Someone twisting his or her hands, or playing with hair or clothes is a signal of tension and worry. Frequent little shrugs of the shoulders or spreading of the hands may indicate a feeling of helplessness or hopelessness.

CASE STUDY

Mrs B is very confused. She has little recognition of time or place and only knows her daughter, who has cared for her for many years. As she became increasingly frail and began to fall regularly, she finally stopped eating or drinking and her daughter had to arrange for her admission to hospital for assessment. She is in a large psycho-geriatric ward. Many of the patients are aggressive and disinhibited in their behaviour. Mrs B is quiet, gentle and confused, and she has no idea where she is. She does not know anyone, and she keeps asking to go home.

1   What would you expect Mrs B's body language to be?
2   What would you look for in her facial expression?
3   As her carer, how do you think you might make her feel better?
4   How would you communicate with her?
5   How might you help her daughter?

DID YOU KNOW?

Research shows that people pay far more attention to facial expressions and tone of voice than they do to spoken words. For example, in one study, words contributed only 7 per cent towards the impression of whether or not someone was liked, tone of voice contributed 38 per cent and facial expression 55 per cent. The study also found that if there was a contradiction between facial expression and words, people believed the facial expression.

Giving out the signals

Being aware of your own body language is just as important as understanding the person you are talking to.

Keys to good practice

✓ Make sure that you maintain eye contact with the person you are talking to, although you should avoid staring! Looking away occasionally is normal, but if you find yourself looking around the room, or watching others, then you are failing to give people the attention they deserve.

✓ Be aware of what you are doing and try to think why you are losing attention.

✓ Sit where you can be comfortably seen. Don't sit where someone has to turn in order to look at you.

✓ Sit a comfortable distance away – not so far that any sense of closeness is lost, but not so close that you 'invade their space'.

✓ Make sure that you are showing by your gestures that you are listening and interested in what they are saying – sitting half-turned away gives the message that you are not fully committed to what is being said.

✓ Folded arms or crossed legs can indicate that you are 'closed' rather than 'open' to what someone is expressing.

✓ Nodding your head will indicate that you are receptive and interested – but be careful not to overdo it and look like a nodding dog!

✓ Lean towards someone to show that you are interested in what he or she is saying. You can use leaning forward quite effectively at times when you want to emphasise your interest or support. Then move backwards a little at times when the content is a little lighter.

✓ Using touch to communicate your caring and concern is often useful and appropriate. Many individuals find it comforting to have their hand held or stroked, or to have an arm around their shoulders.

✓ Be aware of a person's body language, which should tell you if he or she finds touch acceptable or not.

✓ Always err on the side of caution if you are unsure about what is acceptable in another culture. Later in this chapter, and in many other places throughout the book, you will look at issues about cultures in which touch is unacceptable.

✓ Think about age and gender in relation to touch. An older woman may be happy to have her hand held by a female carer, but may be uncomfortable with such a response from a man.

✓ Ensure that you are touching someone because you think it will comfort him or her, and not because you feel helpless and can't think of anything to say.

Check it out

Do this with at least one other person – two or three is even better.

1 Think of an incident or situation which is quite important and significant to you. Stand still in the middle of a room and begin to tell your partner about your significant incident.

2 Your partner should start at the edge of the room and slowly move closer and closer to you.

3 At the point where you feel comfortable talking to your partner, say 'Stop'. Mark this point and measure the distance from where you are standing.

4 Continue. At the point where you feel that your partner is too close, say 'Stop'. Mark this point and measure the distance from where you are standing.

5 Change places and repeat the exercise.

You may find that you and your partner(s) will have different distances at which you feel comfortable, but it is likely to be in the range of 3–5ft.

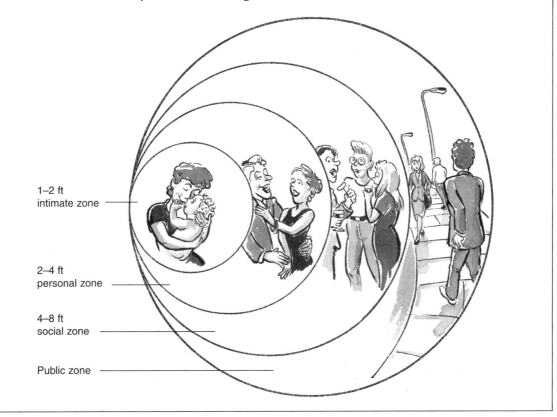

1–2 ft
intimate zone

2–4 ft
personal zone

4–8 ft
social zone

Public zone

REMEMBER

- You can often learn as much by observing as by listening.
- Learn to 'listen with your eyes'.
- Your body sends out as many messages as the person you are talking to.
- Be aware of the messages you give to others.

Barriers to communication

Not getting through?

There are many factors which can get in the way of good communication. You will need to understand how to recognise these and to learn what you can do to overcome them. Until you do this, your communication will always be less effective than it could be. It is easy to assume that everyone can communicate, and that any failure to respond to you is because of someone's unwillingness rather than inability. There are as many reasons why people find communication difficult as there are ways to make it easier.

Checklist
Practical difficulties ✓
Cultural difficulties ✓
What words mean ✗
Physical barriers ✓

Thinking about the obstacles

Never assume that you can be heard and understood and that you can be responded to, without first thinking about the individual and his or her situation. Check first to ensure you are giving the communication the best possible chance of success by dealing with as many barriers as possible.

Practical difficulties

If you need to communicate with someone who has a known disability, such as hearing loss, impaired vision, mobility problems or speech impairment, you must consider the implications for your communication.

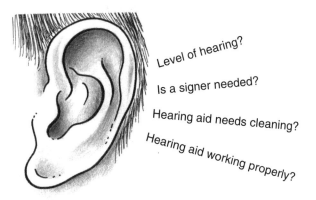

Level of hearing?

Is a signer needed?

Hearing aid needs cleaning?

Hearing aid working properly?

If someone is profoundly deaf, you will need to establish what sort of assistance he or she needs. If he or she communicates by signing, you will need to have a sign language interpreter available. Do not assume that you can do this yourself – it is highly skilled and people train for a long time to do this. If someone uses a hearing aid, consider that it may not be operating efficiently if you seem to be having communication problems.

Consider the level of someone's hearing. Many people are hard of hearing, but this may not be a profound hearing loss. It can mean that they have difficulty hearing where there is background noise and other people talking.

Facial expressions may seem inappropriate

Hand and arm gestures may not be possible

Body posture may not give out the messages you would expect.

If someone has a physical disability, you will need to consider whether this is likely to affect his or her non-verbal communication. Also, his or her body language may not be what you would expect.

CASE STUDY

Mr T lives alone. For many years he had been well known in the neighbourhood. He was never particularly chatty, but always said a polite 'Good Morning' on his way to the shops, and had a smile and a kind word for the children. His wife died about 15 years ago. They had only had one son, and he was killed in the war. Recently, however, Mr T's health has begun to deteriorate. He has had a bad winter with a chest infection and a nasty fall in the snow. This has seemed to shake his confidence, and he has accepted the offer of a home-care assistant twice each week.

Neighbours began to notice that Mr T no longer spoke to them, and he failed to acknowledge the children. His outings to the shops became less frequent. Jean, his home-care assistant, was worried that he hardly responded to her cheerful chat as she worked. She realised that Mr T's hearing was deteriorating. After medical investigations, Mr T was provided with a hearing aid. He began to be much more like his old self – he spoke to people again, smiled at the children and enjoyed his visits to the shops.

1 How do you think Mr T felt when he began to have problems hearing people?
2 Why do you think he reacted in the way he did?
3 What other factors might Jean have thought were causing Mr T's deterioration?
4 How are people likely to have reacted to Mr T?

Individuals who have visual impairment to any significant degree will need to be addressed with thought and care. Do not rely on your facial expressions to communicate your interest and concern – use words and touch where appropriate. Remember to obtain any information they may need in a format they can use. Think about large-print books, braille or audio tapes. If you need any further information, the Royal National Institute for the Blind (RNIB) will be able to advise you about local sources of supplies.

Make sure that you know what language an individual is comfortable with – do not assume it is the same as yours without making certain! Find out if you need to provide any translation facilities, or written information in another language. If translation is needed, your team leader or manager should be able to help you to arrange it. Your local social services department will have a list of interpreters, as will the police or the consulate or embassy of their country. Many organisations provide information about where specialised assistance can be obtained.

> **DID YOU KNOW?**
> The Benefits Agency produces a catalogue of its leaflets, posters and information. This lists which items are available in other languages, braille, large print or on audio tape. Many other agencies and organisations do the same. Always make sure you ask if information is available in the format your service user needs. Being given information in an accessible format is far better than having to receive it 'secondhand'.

Cultural difficulties

You will need to be aware of cultural differences between you and the person you are talking to. For example, using first names or touching someone to whom you are not related, or a very close friend, can be viewed as disrespectful in some cultures. Talking familiarly to someone of a different gender or age group can be unacceptable in some cultures. For example, some young Muslim women do not talk at all to men to whom they are not related.

Many older men and women consider it disrespectful to address people by their first names. You will often find older people with neighbours they have known for 50 years, who still call each other 'Mrs Baker' or 'Mrs Wood'.

> **REMEMBER**
> The golden rule when you are communicating with someone from a different culture is to *find out*. Do not assume that you can approach everyone in the same way. It is your responsibility to find out the way to approach someone.

What words mean

Be aware that the words you use can mean different things to different people and generations – words like 'cool', 'chip' or 'gay'. Be aware of particular local words which are used in your part of the country, which may not mean the same to someone from another area.

Think carefully about the subject under discussion. Some people from particular cultures, or people of particular generations, may find some subjects very sensitive and difficult to discuss. These days, it is not unusual amongst a younger age group to discuss personal income levels. However, people of older generations may consider such information to be highly personal.

Physical barriers

Communication can be hindered by physical and environmental factors. This may seem obvious, but they need to be considered when planning communication.

Always provide a private situation if you have personal matters to discuss. It is rarely the case that the best which can be arranged is to pull the curtains around a bed.

You need to think about the surroundings. People find it difficult to talk in noisy, crowded places. A communal lounge with a television and other people is not going to produce good communication.

Remember the temperature – make sure that it is comfortable. Think about lighting. Is it too dark or too bright? Is the sun in someone's eyes? Make sure that you do not sit with your face in shadow. It is very disconcerting not to be able to see someone's face when talking to him or her – remember the previous section on non-verbal communication.

TEST YOURSELF

1 What factors would you consider if you had to communicate with someone who had had a stroke?

2 What major means of communication may be missing as the result of a disability?

3 Who would you ask if you needed a signer?

4 Who would you ask if you needed a foreign language interpreter?

5 List three physical factors you would consider when planning good communication.

REMEMBER

- Never take communication for granted.
- Not everyone communicates in the same way.
- It is your responsibility to ensure that the individual is able to communicate.
- As far as possible, plan ahead and think what you will need to take into account.

How to listen

So far you have looked at some of the factors which assist effective communication, and some of the barriers which can hinder it. Now it is time to look at the key areas of listening and talking. You may think that this comes naturally to most people. Not so. You can learn some basic skills which will improve your communication significantly.

> ## REMEMBER
> - To hear what someone is really telling you, you have to be a good listener.
> - To help someone understand what you are saying and tell you what he or she wants to say, you have to be a good communicator.

Active listening

Active listening is about doing much more than simply hearing the words which an individual is speaking. It is the way you encourage someone to talk to you, the way you let him or her know that you are interested, concerned and supportive, and the way you allow him or her the space, time and attention to express feelings and concerns.

Check it out

This really needs to be done with a friend or colleague. Begin to tell your partner about something simple and straightforward – about your holiday, what you did last Saturday, a planned shopping trip – anything at all. Your partner's job is to look around the room, to look at you but not nod or make any sound, to examine his or her nails – in short to fail to respond to you in any way. You should stop talking when you feel uncomfortable. Then change places. During this exercise you will begin to see how difficult it is to keep talking when you do not get a positive response.

The way in which you listen to someone can make all the difference to how easy he or she finds it to talk to you. When someone is talking to you, keep encouraging him or her by responding – nodding and 'mm' or 'I see' are often all that is needed. There is nothing worse than talking to someone who gives you no response.

Sometimes people find it difficult to express what they want to say and need some encouragement. You can help by repeating back to them what they have been saying, not in a 'parrot style', but in an encouraging way, such as:

Service user: 'My family are very busy, I don't see them much, they all have important jobs…' [silence].

You: 'So your children don't have much time to come here because they all work so hard…'

Paraphrasing what someone has told you can also be a useful way of showing that you have understood what he or she is saying. In paraphrasing you take what someone has been saying and repeat it in a slightly different way.

This can be used effectively to clarify what someone has said. For example, if an individual has just told you about feelings ranging from sadness and anger to relief at coming into residential care, a reply of something like 'so your feelings are very mixed – that's very understandable' demonstrates that you have heard what he or she said and also offers reassurance that this reaction is normal and only to be expected.

How to communicate clearly

How you talk to someone matters a great deal. You can ask 'open' or 'closed' questions. Which questions you use makes a difference to the response you will get:

- Closed questions are those which allow people to answer 'Yes' or 'No'. For example, 'Are you worried about the tests tomorrow?' This may get only a one-word response. If you then want to find out any more, you have to ask another question. If you are not careful, individuals can then end up feeling like they are on 'Twenty Questions'.
- Open questions are those which do not allow a one-word response. So, if you rephrase the previous question it becomes 'How do you feel about tomorrow's tests?' The difference is obvious, and there is a far greater chance that the person you are talking to will feel able to express his or her feelings.

Advice

There will be occasions when you are asked to give advice. Sometimes this is appropriate. If, for example, someone asked whether he or she would be able to carry on claiming a particular benefit whilst in residential care, it would be pretty silly to say 'Well, do you think that you will continue to need that benefit?' Clearly, there are three possible answers: 'Yes', 'No' or 'I'm not sure, but I'll find out'. These sorts of request for factual advice are quite different from a situation where someone is dealing with personal or emotional issues.

What you say

Make sure that you are not the one doing all the talking. Be careful not to tell someone what you think and keep giving your opinions. Telling someone 'If I were you I would…' is not good practice and is not good communication.

Do not ever say 'That's silly' or 'Oh you shouldn't feel like that'. That effectively dismisses people's feelings or tells them that they have no right to feel that way.

How you say it

Think about the speed and volume of what you say. We often fail to realise how quickly we speak. It can often be difficult for someone who has some impairment of hearing or poor eyesight to catch what you say, if you speak too fast.

Think about your accent, and the individual you are talking to. Local accents can be difficult to understand, if they are unfamiliar.

You may not know how strong your own accent is. Try making a tape recording and listening to yourself. Or ask a friend or colleague to advise you honestly about the strength of your accent and the speed at which you talk.

Volume is also important. There is no need to shout – it simply distorts what you say and plays havoc with your facial expression! You should, however, make sure that you speak clearly and at a reasonable level. Generally, speaking too softly can make it hard for you to be understood.

There are some occasions when you may have to balance the volume of what you say with the need to maintain someone's privacy. It may be worth having to repeat yourself a few times, if it helps to keep a discussion private.

Stages of an interaction

As you spend time in communication with someone, the nature of the interaction will go through changes.

- *Stage 1:* Introduction, light, general. At first, communication may be light and general with very little content of any significance. This is the stage at which both parties decide if they want to continue the discussion, and how comfortable they feel. Body language and non-verbal communication are very important at this stage.
- *Stage 2:* Main contact, significant information. The middle of any interaction is likely to contain the 'meat' and this is where you will need to use active listening skills to ensure that the interaction is beneficial.
- *Stage 3:* Reflect, wind up, end positively. People often have the greatest difficulty in knowing how to end an interaction. Ending in a positive way where all participants are left feeling that they have benefited from the interaction is very important. You may find that you have to end an interaction because of time restrictions, or you may feel that enough has been covered – the other person may need a rest, or you may need a break!

At the end of an interaction you should always try to reflect on the areas you have covered, and try to offer a positive and encouraging ending, for example, 'I'm glad you have talked about how unhappy you have been feeling. Now we can try to work at making things better.'

Even if the content of an interaction has been fairly negative, you should encourage the individual to see the fact that the interaction has taken place as being positive in itself.

If you get called away before you have had a chance to properly 'wind up' an interaction with an individual, make a point of returning to end things in a positive way. If you say 'I'll be back in a minute', make sure that you do go back.

Written communication

Written communication may not be something you do very frequently. You may not write many formal letters, but as a care worker you will have to write information in records which could prove to be of vital importance.

The golden rule of good communication is to consider its purpose. If you are completing a care plan or record for an individual, then that information needs to be there in order to inform the next carer who takes over.

Think about the sort of information you would need to know. What things are important when handing over care?

You need to record accurately any distress or worries you have tried to deal with, any physical signs of illness or accidents. You may need to record fluid balances or calorie intake charts. It may be important to record visitors, or any medical interventions. The purposes of records and the systems will be dealt with in detail in Chapter 6 (Unit CU5), but the importance in this context is the usefulness of what you write in terms of communication.

Written communication is useless unless it is legible. There is no point in scribbling something unreadable in someone's notes. It is actually worse than not writing anything, because colleagues waste time trying to decipher what is there, and have to deal with the concerns raised by the fact that there was clearly something worth recording, but they have no idea what it was.

You also need to convey the message in a clear and concise way. People do not want to spend time reading a lengthy report when the main points could have been expressed in a paragraph. Equally, you need to make sure that the relevant points are there. Often bullet points can be useful in recording information clearly and concisely. Look at the examples below.

Mrs P had a bad night.

Too little information

Mrs P had a bad night. It began when I found her crying about 10 p.m. She said she had been thinking about her husband. I thought she seemed a bit hot, so I made her a cup of tea and got her to sit in the lounge for a while before she went to bed. After about half an hour, I managed to get her to go to her room and I went with her . . .

Too much irrelevant information

Mrs P had a bad night because:
a) she was distressed about her husband
b) she wandered out of her room about 2 a.m. crying again
c) unable to settle despite further cocoa
d) wandered into Mr W's room at 5.30 believing he was her husband
She will need to be closely observed today. Any further confused episodes should be logged.

Clear, helpful. Gives a short picture of problems overnight, and suggests action for next day.

Records should be accurate, clear and concise.

CL1 UNIT TEST

1   Why is it important to recognise people as individuals?

2   Name some of the effects of treating people as stereotypes in a caring situation.

3   List some examples of unacceptable behaviour and say how you would challenge each.

4   What should be your first steps in dealing with aggressive behaviour?

5   Name three possible barriers to communication. How would you deal with each of them?

6   How would you communicate with someone who has profound hearing loss?

7   What factors would you take into account when communicating with someone with a physical disability?

8   What environmental factors do you need to consider when planning communication?

9   What is the difference between an open question and a closed question? Name situations where you would use each type of question.

10   How should you end an interaction?

Promote, monitor and maintain health, safety and security in the workplace

This chapter is about the way you can contribute to making your workplace a safe, secure and healthy place for people who need care. Workplace, in this unit, means a home environment or any other facility which provides a health or care service. In the first element you will need to learn about what needs to be done to ensure a safe workplace environment. In the second element you will be looking at how you may need to adapt the way you work and become more safety conscious. The third element in this unit is about how to respond in an emergency.

Element CU1.1 Monitor and maintain the safety and security of the work environment

What you need to learn
- How to maintain safety
- How to maintain security
- The legal framework
- Dealing with hazardous waste

How to maintain safety

What is safety?

It sounds very simple and straightforward: make sure that the place in which you work is safe and secure. However, when you start to think about it – safe for whom? from whom? safe from tripping over things? or safe from hazardous fumes? safe from infection? safe from intruders? safe from work-related injuries? You can begin to see that this is a wide and complex subject. It may help if you think about safety and security in respect of the areas of responsibility shown in the table.

Responsibilities for safety and security in the workplace

Employer's responsibilities	Employee's responsibilities	Shared responsibilities
Planning safety and security Providing information about safety and security Updating systems and procedures	Using the systems and procedures correctly Reporting flaws or gaps in the systems or procedures when in use	Safety of individuals being cared for Safety of the environment

Safety of the environment

You share the responsibility with your employer for the safety of all the people in your care. There are many hazards which can cause injury to people, even more so if they are old, ill or disabled. You need to be aware of:

- *environmental hazards,* such as:
  - wet or slippery floors
  - cluttered passageways or corridors
  - re-arranged furniture
  - worn carpets or rugs
  - electrical flexes

- *hazards to do with equipment and materials,* such as:
  - faulty brakes on beds
  - worn or faulty electrical or gas appliances
  - worn or damaged lifting equipment
  - worn or damaged mobility aids
  - incorrectly labelled substances, such as cleaning fluids
  - leaking or damaged containers
  - faulty waste disposal equipment

- *hazards connected with people,* such as:
  - visitors to the building
  - handling procedures
  - intruders
  - violent and aggressive behaviour.

Your responsibility to contribute to a safe environment is more than simply being aware of these potential hazards. You must take steps to check and deal with any sources of risk.

You can fulfil your role in two ways:

- by dealing directly with the hazard, which means that you have taken individual responsibility. This will probably apply to obvious hazards such as:
  - trailing flexes – roll them up and store them safely
  - wet floors – dry them as far as possible and put out warning signs
  - cluttered doorways and corridors – remove objects and store them safely or dispose of them appropriately. If items are heavy, use assistance or mechanical aids
  - visitors to the building – challenge anyone you do not recognise. 'Can I help you?' is usually sufficient to establish whether a person has a good reason to be there or not
  - fire – by following the correct procedures to raise the alarm and assist with evacuation

- by informing your manager, which means that it becomes an organisational responsibility. This applies to hazards which are beyond your role and competence to deal with, such as:
  - faulty equipment – fires, kettles, computers, etc.
  - worn floor coverings

- loose or damaged fittings
- obstructions too heavy for you to move safely
- damaged or faulty aids – hoists, bed brakes, bathing aids, etc.
- people acting suspiciously on the premises
- fire.

Manual handling

Handling and moving service users is dealt with in detail in Chapter 11 (Unit Z7), but the implications for the safety of both the care worker and the service user are examined in this unit.

DID YOU KNOW?

Lifting and handling individuals is the single largest cause of injuries at work in health and care settings. One in four workers take time off because of a back injury sustained at work.

The Manual Handling Operations Regulations 1993 require employers to avoid all manual handling where there is a risk of injury 'so far as it is reasonably practical'. Everyone from the European Commission to the Royal College of Nurses has issued policies and directives about avoiding lifting. Make sure you check out the policies in use in your workplace and that you understand them.

There is almost no situation in which manual lifting and handling could be considered acceptable.

REMEMBER

- Always use lifting and handling aids.
- There is no such thing as a safe lift.
- Use the aids which your employer is obliged to provide.

On the rare occasions when it is still absolutely necessary for manual lifting to be done, the employer has to make a 'risk assessment' and put procedures in place to reduce the risk of injury to the employee. This could involve ensuring that sufficient staff are available to lift or handle someone safely, which can often mean that four people are needed.

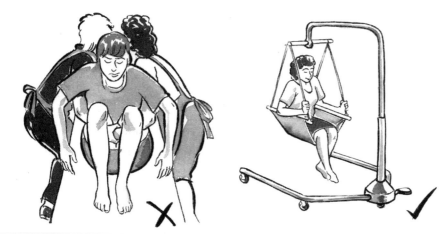

Use the aids which your employer is obliged to provide.

Your employer should arrange for you to attend a lifting and handling course. You must attend one each year, so that you are up-to-date with the safest possible practices.

Fire safety

Your workplace will have procedures which must be followed in the case of an emergency. All workplaces must display information about what action to take in case of fire. The fire procedure is likely to be similar to the one shown below.

Fire Safety Procedure

1   Raise the alarm.

2   Inform telephonist or dial 999.

3   Ensure that everyone is safe and out of the danger area.

4   If it is safe to do so, attack fire with correct extinguisher.

5   Go to fire assembly point (this will be stated on the fire procedure notice).

6   Do not return to the building for any reason.

- Make sure that you know where the fire extinguishers or fire blankets are in your workplace, and that you know where the fire exits are.
- Your employer will have installed fire doors to comply with regulations – *never* prop them open.

- Your employer should provide fire lectures each year. You must attend and make sure that you are up-to-date with the procedures to be followed.

The Fire Precautions (Workplace) (Amendment) Regulations 1999 require that all workplaces should be inspected by the fire authority to check means of escape, firefighting equipment and warnings, and that a fire certificate must be issued. A breach of a fire regulations could lead to a prosecution of the employer, the responsible manager, or other staff members.

Which for what?

There are specific fire extinguishers for fighting different types of fire. It is important that you know this. You do not have to memorise them as each one has clear instructions on it, but you do need to be aware that there are different types and make sure that you read the instructions before use.

> ## DID YOU KNOW?
> All new fire extinguishers are red. Each one has its purpose written on it. Each one also has a patch of the colour previously used for that type of extinguisher.

Extinguisher type and colour	Use for	Danger points	How to use	How it works
Red Water	Wood, cloth, paper, plastics, coal, etc. Fires involving solids.	Do **not** use on burning fat or oil, or on electrical appliances.	Point the jet at the base of the flames and keep it moving across the area of the fire. Ensure that all areas of the fire are out.	Mainly by cooling burning material.
Blue Multi-purpose dry powder	Wood, cloth, paper, plastics, coal etc. Fires involving solids. Liquids such as grease, fats, oil, paint, petrol, etc. but **not** on chip or fat pan fires.	Safe on live electrical equipment, although the fire may re-ignite because this type of extinguisher does not cool the fire very well. Do **not** use on chip or fat pan fires.	Point the jet or discharge horn at the base of the flames and, with a rapid sweeping motion, drive the fire towards the far edge until all the flames are out.	Knocks down flames and, on burning solids, melts to form a skin smothering the fire. Provides some cooling effect.
Blue Standard dry powder	Liquids such as grease, fats, oil, paint, petrol etc. but **not** on chip or fat pan fires.	Safe on live electrical equipment, although does not penetrate the spaces in equipment easily and the fire may re-ignite This type of extinguisher does not cool the fire very well. Do **not** use on chip or fat pan fires.	Point the jet or discharge horn at the base of the flames and, with a rapid sweeping motion, drive the fire towards the far edge until all the flames are out.	Knocks down flames.
Cream AFFF (Aqueous film-forming foam) (multi-purpose)	Wood, cloth, paper, plastics, coal, etc. Fires involving solids. Liquids such as grease, fats, oil, paint, petrol, etc. but **not** on chip or fat pan fires.	Do **not** use on chip or fat pan fires.	For fires involving solids, point the jet at the base of the flames and keep it moving across the area of the fire. Ensure that all areas of the fire are out. For fires involving liquids, do not aim the jet straight into the liquid.	Forms a fire extinguishing film on the surface of a burning liquid. Has a cooling action with a wider extinguishing application than water on solid combustible materials.

Extinguisher type and colour	Use for	Danger points	How to use	How it works
			Where the liquid on fire is in a container, point the jet at the inside edge of the container or on a nearby surface above the burning liquid. Allow the foam to build up and flow across the liquid.	
Cream Foam	Limited number of liquid fires.	Do **not** use on chip or fat pan fires. Check manufacturer's instructions for suitability of use on other fires involving liquids.	Do not aim jet straight straight into the liquid. Where the liquid on fire is in a container, point the jet at the inside edge of the container or on a nearby surface above the burning liquid. Allow the foam to build up and flow across the liquid.	
Black Carbon dioxide CO_2	Liquids such as grease, fats, oil, paint, petrol, etc. but **not** on chip or fat pan fires.	Do **not** use on chip or fat pan fires. This type of extinguisher does not cool the fire very well. Fumes from CO_2 extinguishers can be harmful if used in confined spaces: ventilate the area as soon as the fire has been controlled.	Direct the discharge horn at the base of the flames and keep the jet moving across the area of the fire.	Vaporising liquid gas smothers the flames by displacing oxygen in the air.
Fire blanket	Fires involving both solids and liquids. Particularly good for small fires in clothing and for chip and fat pan fires, provided the blanket **completely** covers the fire.	If the blanket does not completely cover the fire, it will not be extinguished.	Place carefully over the fire. Keep your hands shielded from the fire. Take care not to waft the fire towards you.	Smothers the fire.

Evacuating buildings

You may be involved in evacuating buildings if there is a fire, or for other reasons, such as:

- a bomb scare
- the building has become structurally unsafe
- an explosion
- a leak of dangerous chemicals or fumes.

The evacuation procedure you need to follow will be laid down by your workplace. The information will be the same whatever the emergency is: the same exits will be used and the same assembly point. It is likely to be along the following lines:

- Stay calm, do not shout or run.
- Do not allow others to run.
- Organise people quickly and firmly without panic.
- Direct those who can move themselves and assist those who cannot.
- Use wheelchairs to move people quickly.
- Move the bed with the person in, if necessary.

TEST YOURSELF

1 Name three aspects of safety which you could deal with in your workplace.

2 List the actions you would take in each of the three situations you have identified.

3 Name three areas which your employer is responsible for.

How to maintain security

Most workplaces where care is provided are not under lock and key. This is an inevitable part of ensuring that people have choice and that their rights are respected. However, they also have a right to be secure. Security in a care environment is about:

- security against intruders
- security in respect of their privacy and decisions about unwanted visitors
- security against being abused
- security of property.

Security against intruders

If you work for a large organisation, such as an NHS trust, it may be that all employees are easily identifiable by identity badges with photographs. Some of these even

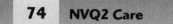

contain a microchip which allows the card to be 'swiped' to gain access to secure parts of the building. This makes it easier to identify people who do not have a right to be on the premises.

In a smaller workplace, there may be a system of issuing visitors' badges to visitors who have reasons to be there, or it may simply rely on the vigilance of the staff.

Keys to good practice

✓ Be aware of everyone you come across. Get into the habit of noticing people and thinking, 'Do I know that person?'
✓ Challenge anyone you do not recognise.
✓ The challenge should be polite. 'Can I help you?' is usually enough to find out if a visitor has a reason to be on the premises.

If a person says that he or she is there to see someone:
✓ Don't give directions – escort him or her.
✓ If the person is a genuine visitor, he or she will be grateful. If not, he or she will disappear pretty quickly!

The more dependent individuals are, the greater the risk. If you work with babies, high-dependency or unconscious patients, people with a severe learning disability or multiple disabilities or people who are very confused, you will have to be extremely vigilant in protecting them from criminals.

REMEMBER
If you find an intruder on the premises, don't tackle him or her – raise the alarm.

Protecting people
If very dependent individuals are living in their own homes, the risks are far greater. You must try to impress on them the importance of finding out who people are before letting them in. If they are able to use it, the 'password' schemes from the utilities (water, gas and electricity companies) are helpful. Information record cards like those provided by the 'Safe as Houses' scheme can be invaluable in providing basic information to anyone who is involved in helping in an emergency.

REMEMBER
- Every time you visit, you may have to explain again what the individual should do when someone knocks on the door.
- Give the individual a card with simple instructions.
- Obtain agreement to speak to the local 'homewatch' scheme and ask that a special eye is kept on visitors.
- Speak to the local police and make them aware that a vulnerable individual is living alone in the house.

People also have a right to choose who they see. This can often be a difficult area to deal with. If there are relatives or friends who wish to visit and an individual does not want to see them, you may have to make this clear. It is difficult to do, but you can only be effective if you are clear and assertive. You should not make excuses or invent reasons why visitors cannot see the person concerned. You could say something like: 'I'm sorry, Mr P has told us that he does not want to see you. I understand that this may be upsetting, but it is his choice. If he does change his mind we will contact you. Would you like to leave your phone number?'

Do not allow yourself to be drawn into passing on messages or attempting to persuade – that is not your role. Your job is to respect the wishes of the person you are caring for. If you are asked to intervene or to pass on a message, you must refuse politely but firmly: 'I'm sorry, that is not something I can do. If your uncle does decide he wants to see you, I will let you know right away. I will tell him you have visited, but I can't do anything else.'

Abuse is dealt with in depth in Chapter 4 (Unit Z1), but it can never be repeated often enough that individuals have a right to be protected from abuse, and you must report immediately any abuse you see or suspect.

Check it out

You need a colleague or friend to try this role play. One of you should be the person who has come to visit and the other the care worker who has to tell him or her that a friend or relative will not see them. Try using different scenarios – angry, upset, aggressive, and so on. Try at least three different scenarios each. By the time you have practised a few times, you may feel better equipped to deal with the situation when it happens in reality.

If you cannot find anyone to work with you, it is possible to do a similar exercise by imagining three or four different scenarios and then writing down the words you would say in each of the situations.

Security of property

Property and valuables belonging to individuals in care settings should be safeguarded. It is likely that your employer will have a property book in which records of all valuables and personal possession are entered.

There may be particular policies within your organisation, but as a general rule you are likely to need to:

- make a record of all possessions on admission
- record valuable items separately
- describe items of jewellery by their colour, for example yellow metal not 'gold'
- ensure that individuals sign for any valuables they are keeping, and that they understand that they are liable for their loss
- inform your manager if an individual is keeping valuables or a significant amount of money.

Find out where the property book is in your workplace, and how it is filled in. Check who has the responsibility to complete it. If you are likely to have to use the book at any time, make sure you know exactly what your role is. Do you have to enter the property in the book, then give it to someone else to deal with the valuables? Do you have to make sure the valuables are safe? Do you have to give the individual a copy of the entry in the book? Ask the questions in advance – don't leave it until you have to do it.

It is always difficult when items go missing in a care setting, particularly if they are valuable. It is important that you check all possibilities before calling the police.

Action stages when property goes missing.

The legal framework

The settings in which you provide care are generally covered by the Health and Safety at Work Act 1974 (HASAWA). This Act has been updated and supplemented by many sets of regulations and guidelines, which extend it, support it or explain it. The regulations most likely to affect your workplace are shown in the diagram on page 78.

The effect of the laws

There are many regulations, laws and guidelines dealing with health and safety. You do not need to know the detail, but you do need to know where your responsibilities begin and end.

The laws place certain responsibilities on both employers and employees. For example, it is up to the employer to provide a safe place in which to work, but the employee also has to show reasonable care for his or her own safety.

Employers have to:

- provide a safe workplace
- ensure that there is safe access to and from the workplace
- provide information on health and safety
- provide health and safety training
- undertake risk assessment for all hazards.

HEALTH & SAFETY AT WORK ACT

Control of Substances Hazardous to Health Regulations 2002 (COSHH)

Reporting of Injuries, Diseases and Dangerous Occurrences Regulations 1995 (RIDDOR)

Manual Handling Regulations 1992

Health and Safety First Aid Regulations 1981

Management of Health and Safety at Work Regulations 1999

The Health and Safety at Work Act is like an umbrella.

Workers must:

- take reasonable care for their own safety and that of others
- co-operate with the employer in respect of health and safety matters
- not intentionally damage any health and safety equipment or materials provided by the employer.

Both the employee and employer are jointly responsible for safeguarding the health and safety of anyone using the premises

Each workplace where there are five or more workers must have a written statement of their health and safety policy. The policy must include:

- a statement of intention to provide a safe workplace
- the name of the person responsible for implementing the policy
- the names of any other individuals responsible for particular health and safety hazards
- a list of identified health and safety hazards and the procedures to be followed in relation to them
- procedures for recording accidents at work
- details for evacuation of the premises.

Check it out

Find out where the health and safety policy is for your workplace and make sure you read it.

Risk assessment

The Management of Health and Safety at Work Regulations 1999 states that employers have to assess any risks which are associated with the workplace and work activities. This means *all* activities, from walking on wet floors to dealing with violence. Having carried out a risk assessment, the employer must then apply *risk control measures*. This means that actions must be taken to reduce the risks, for example, alarm buzzers may need to be installed or extra staff employed, as well as steps like extra training provided for staff or written guidelines produced on how to deal with a particular hazard.

Risks in someone's home

Of course, the situation is somewhat different if you work in an individual's own home. Your employer can still carry out risk assessments and put risk control measures in place, such as a procedure for working in twos in a situation where there is a risk of violence. What cannot be done is to remove environmental hazards such as trailing electrical flexes, rugs with curled up edges, worn patches on stair carpets or old equipment. All you can do is to advise the person whose home it is of the risks, and suggest how things could be improved. You also need to take care!

> ## REMEMBER
>
> - It may be your workplace, but it is the person's home. If you work in an individual's home or long-term residential setting, you have to balance the need for safety with the rights of people to have their living space the way they want it.
>
> - Both you and the individuals receiving care are entitled to expect a safe place in which to live and work, but remember their rights to choose how they want to live.

Control of Substances Hazardous to Health (COSHH)

What are hazardous substances? There are many substances hazardous to health – nicotine, many drugs, even too much alcohol! In this context, however, COSHH applies to substances which have been identified as being toxic, corrosive or irritant. This includes cleaning materials, pesticides, acids, disinfectants and bleaches, and naturally occurring substances such as blood, bacteria, etc. Workplaces may have other hazardous substances which are particular to the nature of the work carried out.

Employers must take the following steps to protect employees from hazardous substances.

Step 1

Find out what hazardous substances are used in your work place and the risks these substances pose to people's health.

Step 2

Decide what precautions are needed before any work starts with hazardous substances.

Step 3

Prevent people being exposed to hazardous substances, but where this is not reasonably practicable, control the exposure.

Step 4

Make sure control measures are used and maintained properly, and that safety procedures are followed.

Step 5

If required, monitor exposure of employees to hazardous substances.

Step 6

Carry out health surveillance where assessment has shown that this is necessary, or COSHH makes specific requirements.

Step 7

If required, prepare plans and procedures to deal with accidents, incidents and emergencies.

Step 8

Make sure employees are properly informed, trained and supervised.
(*Health and Safety Executive, 2002*)

Every workplace must have a COSHH file. This file lists all the hazardous substances used in the workplace. It should detail:

- where they are kept
- how they are labelled
- their effects
- the maximum amount of time it is safe to be exposed to them
- how to deal with an emergency involving one of them.

Hazardous substances are not just things like poisons and radioactive material, they are also substances like cleaning fluids and bleach.

Check it out

Ask to see the COSHH file in your workplace. Make sure you read it and know which substances you use or come into contact with. Check in the file what the maximum exposure limits are. Your employer must include this information in the COSHH file.

If you have to work with hazardous substances, make sure that you take the precautions detailed in the COSHH file – this may be wearing gloves or protective goggles, or it may involve limiting the time you are exposed to the substance or only using it in certain circumstances.

The COSHH file should also give you information about how to store hazardous substances. This will involve using the correct containers as supplied by the manufacturers. All containers must have safety lids and caps, and must be correctly labelled.

Never use the container of one substance for storing another, and *never* change the labels.

These symbols, which warn you of hazardous substances, are always yellow.

The symbols above indicate hazardous substances. They are there for your safety and for the safety of those you care for. Before you use *any* substance, whether it is liquid, powder, spray, cream or aerosol, take the following simple steps:

- Check the container for the hazard symbol.
- If there is a hazard symbol, go to the COSHH file.
- Look up the precautions you need to take with the substance.
- Make sure you follow procedures, which are intended to protect you.

If you are concerned that a substance being used in your workplace is not in the COSHH file, or if you notice incorrect containers or labels being used, report it to your supervisor. Once you have informed your supervisor, it becomes his or her responsibility to act to correct the problem.

Reporting of Injuries, Diseases and Dangerous Occurrences (RIDDOR)

Reporting accidents and ill-health at work is a legal requirement. All accidents, diseases and dangerous occurrences should be reported to the Incident Contact Centre. The Contact Centre was established on 1 April 2001 as a single point of contact for all incidents in the UK. The information is important because it means that risks and causes of accidents, incidents and diseases can be identified. All notifications are passed on to either the local authority Environmental Health department, or the Health and Safety Executive, as appropriate.

Your employer needs to report:

- deaths
- major injuries (see below)
- accidents resulting in more than three days off work
- diseases
- dangerous occurrences.

Reportable major injuries and diseases

The following injuries need to be reported:

- fracture other than to fingers, thumbs or toes
- amputation
- dislocation of the shoulder, hip, knee or spine
- loss of sight (temporary or permanent)
- chemical or hot metal burn to the eye or any penetrating injury to the eye
- injury resulting from an electric shock or electrical burn leading to unconsciousness or requiring resuscitation or admittance to hospital for more than 24 hours
- any other injury which leads to hypothermia (getting too cold), heat-induced illness, or unconsciousness; requires resuscitation; or requires admittance to hospital for more than 24 hours
- unconsciousness caused by asphyxia (suffocation) or exposure to a harmful substance or biological agent
- acute illness requiring medical treatment, or leading to loss of consciousness, arising from absorption of any substance by inhalation, ingestion or through the skin
- acute illness requiring medical treatment where there is reason to believe that this resulted from exposure to a biological agent or its toxins or infected material.

Reportable diseases include:

- certain poisonings
- some skin diseases such as occupational dermatitis, skin cancer, chrome ulcer, oil folliculitis acne
- lung diseases including: occupational asthma, farmer's lung, pneumoconiosis, asbestosis, mesothelioma
- infections such as: leptospirosis, hepatitis, tuberculosis, anthrax, legionellosis (Legionnaires' disease) and tetanus
- other conditions such as: occupational cancer, certain musculoskeletal disorders, decompression illness and hand-arm vibration syndrome.

Dangerous occurrences

If something happens which does not result in a reportable injury, but which clearly could have done, then it may be a dangerous occurrence which must be reported immediately.

Accidents at work

If accidents or injuries occur at work, either to you or to an individual you are caring for, then the details must be recorded. For example, someone may have a fall, or slip on a wet floor. You must record the incident regardless of whether there was an injury.

Your employer should have procedures in place for making a record of accidents, either an accident book or an accident report form. This is not only required by the RIDDOR regulations, but also, if you work in a residential or nursing home, by the Care Standards Commission.

Make sure you know where the accident report forms or the accident book are kept, and who is responsible for recording accidents. It is likely to be your manager.

You must report any accident in which you are involved, or have witnessed, to your manager or supervisor.

Date: 24.3.03   **Time:** 14.30 hrs   **Location:** Main lounge

Description of accident:
PH got out of her chair and began to walk across the lounge with the aid of her stick. She turned her head to continue the conversation she had been having with GK, and as she turned back again she appeared not to have noticed that MP's handbag had been left on the floor. PH tripped over handbag and fell heavily, banging her head on a footstool.

She was very shaken and although she said that she was not hurt, there was a large bump on her head. P appeared pale and shaky. I asked J to fetch a blanket and to call Mrs J, deputy officer in charge. Covered P with a blanket. Mrs J arrived immediately. Dr was sent for after P was examined by Mrs J.

Dr arrived after about 20 mins and said that she was bruised and shaken, but did not seem to have any injuries.

She wanted to go and lie down. She was helped to bed.

Incident was witnessed by six residents who were in the lounge at the time: GK, MP, IL, MC, CR and BQ.

Signed   Name:

-        - - - - - - - - - - - - -

An example of an accident report.

Any medical treatment or assessment which is necessary should be arranged without delay. If an individual has been involved in an accident, you should check if there is anyone he or she would like to be contacted, perhaps a relative or friend. If the accident is serious, and you cannot consult the individual – because he or she is unconscious, for example – the next of kin should be informed as soon as possible.

Complete a report, and ensure that all witnesses to the accident also complete reports. You should include the following in any accident report (see the example on the previous page):

- date, time and place of accident
- person/people involved
- circumstances and details of exactly what you saw
- anything which was said by the individuals involved
- the condition of the individual after the accident
- steps taken to summon help, time of summoning help and time when help arrived
- names of any other people who witnessed the accident
- any equipment involved in the accident.

Check it out

Your manager has asked you to design a new incident/accident report form for your workplace. She has asked you to do this because the current form does not provide enough information. The purpose of the new form is to provide sufficient information to:

- ensure the individual receives the proper medical attention
- provide information for treatment at a later date, in case of delayed reactions
- give information to any inspector who may need to see the records
- identify any gaps or need for improvements in safety procedures
- provide information about the circumstances in case of any future legal action.

Think about how you would design the new report form and what headings you would include. Use the list above as a checklist to make sure you have covered everything you need.

Dealing with hazardous waste

As part of providing a safe working environment, employers have to put procedures in place to deal with waste materials and spillages. There are various types of waste, which must be dealt with in particular ways. These are summarised in the table opposite.

REMEMBER

- Other people will have to deal with the waste after you have placed it in the bags or containers.
- Make sure it is properly labelled and in the correct containers.

Type of waste	Method of disposal
Clinical waste – used dressings	Yellow bags, clearly labelled with contents and location. This waste is incinerated.
Needles, syringes, cannulas ('sharps')	Yellow sharps box. Never put sharps into anything other than a hard plastic box. This is sealed and incinerated.
Body fluids and waste – urine, vomit, blood, sputum, faeces	Cleared and flushed down sluice drain. Area to be cleaned and disinfected.
Soiled linen	Red bags, direct into laundry; bags disintegrate in wash. If handled, gloves must be worn.
Recyclable instruments and equipment	Blue bags, to be returned to the Central Sterilisation Services Department (CSSD) for recycling and sterilising.

Check it out

Look carefully around your workplace. Try to identify six potential hazards, or risky activities. When you have chosen them, check through the Health and Safety Manual and find the risk control measures and provisions made for each of them. If you believe that you have noticed a potential risk which your employer has not covered, you should discuss it with your manager or supervisor immediately.

TEST YOURSELF

1 Look at the picture below. How many possible hazards and risks can you find in the picture?
   a List at least six.
   b Which of these are the responsibility of the employer?
   c Which should you do something about?
2 Name three types of waste and their methods of disposal.
3 What type of manual lifting is encouraged?
4 How should hazardous substances be stored?
5 What are the employer's responsibilities in respect of hazardous substances?
6 What are the employee's responsibilities for hazardous substances?
7 What should you do if you see someone in your workplace whom you do not recognise?

Promote standards of health and safety in working practice

This element is about what you *do* when you are working. In the previous element, you looked at the procedures and policies which have to be put in place to protect workers and people who use the service, and the laws which govern health and safety. Now you need to learn about the steps you should be following to ensure that the laws and policies actually work in practice.

What you need to learn

- How to promote a safe work environment
- How to contribute to infection control
- How to maintain personal safety
- How to move and handle service users safely

How to promote a safe work environment

It is important that you develop an awareness of health and safety risks and that you are always aware of any risks in any situation you are in. If you get into the habit of making a mental checklist, you will find that it helps. The checklist will vary from one workplace to another, but could look like the one below.

Checklist for a safe work environment

Hazards	Check
Environment Floors Carpets and rugs Doorways and corridors Electrical flexes	 Are they dry? Are they worn or curled at the edges? Are they clear of obstacles? Are they trailing?
Equipment Beds Electrical or gas appliances Lifting equipment Mobility aids Substances such as cleaning fluids Containers Waste disposal equipment	 Are the brakes on? Are they high enough? Are they worn? Have they been safety checked? Is it worn or damaged? Are they worn or damaged? Are they correctly labelled? Are they leaking or damaged? Is it faulty?
People Visitors to the building Handling procedures Intruders Violent and aggressive behaviour	 Should they be there? Have they been assessed for risk? Have police been called? Has it been dealt with?

One of the other factors to consider in your checklist may be what your colleagues do about health and safety issues. It is very difficult if you are the only person following good practice. You may be able to encourage others by trying some of the following options:

- always showing a good example yourself
- explaining why you are following procedures
- getting some health and safety leaflets from your trade union or environmental health office and leaving them in the staffroom for people to see
- bringing in any information you can about courses or safety lectures
- asking your supervisor if he or she can arrange a talk on health and safety.

What you wear in the workplace has an important bearing on health and safety. What problems can you see in this picture?

What you wear

You may not think that what you wear has much bearing on health and safety, but it is important. Even if your employer supplies, or insists on you wearing, a uniform, there are still other aspects to the safety of your work outfit.

There may be restrictions on wearing jewellery or carrying things in your pocket which could cause injury. This can also pose a risk to you – you could be stabbed in the chest by a pair of scissors or ball-point pen!

Many workplaces do not allow the wearing of rings with stones. Not only is this a possible source of infection, but they can also scratch people or tear protective gloves.

High-heeled or poorly supporting shoes are a risk to you in terms of foot injuries and very sore feet! They also present a risk to individuals you are helping, because if you overbalance or stumble, so will they.

Keys to good practice

Simple precautions can often be the most effective in reducing the risk. Always look for the risk and take steps to reduce it.

THINK RISK $\rightarrow$ ASSESS $\rightarrow$ REDUCE $\rightarrow$ AVOID

How to contribute to infection control

The very nature of work in a care setting means that great care must be taken to control the spread of infection. You will come into contact with a number of people during your working day – an ideal opportunity for infection to spread. Infection which spreads from one person to another is called 'cross-infection'. If you work in the community, cross-infection is difficult to control. However, if you work in a residential or hospital setting, infection control is essential. There are various steps which you can take in terms of the way you carry out your work (wherever you work), which can help to prevent the spread of infection.

You do not know what viruses or bacteria may be present in any individual, so it is important that you take precautions when dealing with everyone. The precautions are called 'universal precautions' precisely because you need to take them with everyone you deal with.

Wear gloves

When	Why	How
Any occasion when you will have contact with body fluids (including body waste, blood, mucus, sputum, sweat or vomit), or when you have any contact with anyone with a rash, pressure sore, wound, bleeding or any broken skin. You must also wear gloves when you clear up spills of blood or body fluids or have to deal with soiled linen or dressings.	Because gloves act as a protective barrier against infection.	Check gloves before putting them on. Never use gloves with holes or tears. Check that they are not cracked or faded. Pull gloves on, making sure that they fit properly. If you are wearing a gown, pull them over the cuffs. Take them off by pulling from the cuff – this turns the glove inside out. Pull off the second glove whilst still holding the first so that the two gloves are folded together inside out. Dispose of them in the correct waste disposal container and wash your hands.

Wash your hands

When	Why	How
Before and after carrying out any procedure which has involved contact with an individual, or with any body fluids, soiled linen or clinical waste. You must wash your hands even though you have worn gloves. You must also wash your hands before you start and after you finish your shift, before and after eating, after using the toilet and after coughing, sneezing or blowing your nose.	Because hands are a major route to spreading infection. When tests have been carried out on people's hands, an enormous number of bacteria have been found.	In running water, in a basin deep enough to hold the splashes and with either foot pedals or elbow bars rather than taps, because you can re-infect your hands from still water in a basin, or from touching taps with your hands once they have been washed. Use the soaps and disinfectants supplied. Make sure that you wash thoroughly, including between your fingers.

Wear protective clothing

When	Why	How
You should always wear a gown or plastic apron for any procedure which involves bodily contact or is likely to deal with body waste or fluids. An apron is preferable, unless it is likely to be very messy, as gowns can be a little frightening.	Because it will reduce the spread of infection by preventing infection getting on your clothes and spreading to the next person you come into contact with.	The plastic apron should be disposable and thrown away at the end of each procedure. You should use a new apron for each individual you come into contact with.

Tie up hair

Why
Because if it hangs over your face, it is more likely to come into contact with the individual you are working with and could spread infection. It could also become entangled in equipment and cause a serious injury.

Clean equipment

Why	How
Because infection can spread from one person to another on instruments, linen and equipment just as easily as on hands or hair.	By washing large items like trolleys with antiseptic solution. Small instruments must be sterilised. Do not shake soiled linen or dump it on the floor. Keep it held away from you. Place linen in proper bags or hampers for laundering.

Deal with waste

Why	How
Because it can then be processed correctly, and the risk to others working further along the line in the disposal process is reduced as far as possible.	By placing it in the proper bags. Make sure that you know the system in your workplace. It is usually: ● clinical waste – yellow ● soiled linen – red ● recyclable instruments and equipment – blue.

Take special precautions

When	How
There may be occasions when you have to deal with an individual who has a particular type of infection that requires special handling. This can involve things like hepatitis, some types of food poisoning or highly infectious diseases.	Your workplace will have special procedures to follow. They may include such measures as gowning, double gloving or wearing masks. Follow the procedures strictly. They are there for your benefit and for the benefit of the other individuals you care for.

Check it out

Make notes of three ways in which infection can be spread. Then note down three effective ways to reduce the possibility of cross-infection.

How to maintain personal safety

There is always an element of risk in working with people. There is little doubt that there is an increase in the level of personal abuse suffered by workers in the health and care services. There is also the element of personal risk encountered by workers who visit people in the community, and have to deal with homes in poor states of repair and an assortment of domestic animals!

However, there are some steps which you can take to assist with safety.

Keys to good practice

✓ If you work alone in the community, always leave details of where you are going and what time you expect to return. This is important in case of accidents or other emergencies, so that you can be found.
✓ Carry a personal alarm, and use it if necessary.
✓ Ask your employer to provide training in techniques to combat aggression and violence. It is foolish and potentially dangerous to go into risky situations without any training.
✓ Try to defuse potentially aggressive situations by being as calm as possible and by talking quietly and reasonably. But if this is not effective, leave. There is more detail on how to deal with potentially violent situations in Chapters 2 (Unit CL1) and 4 (Z1).
✓ If you work in a residential or hospital setting, raise the alarm if you find you are in a threatening situation.
✓ Do not tackle aggressors, whoever they are – raise the alarm.
✓ Use an alarm or panic button if you have it – otherwise yell – very loudly.

CASE STUDY

K was a home-care assistant on her first visit to a new service user, Mr W. She had been warned that his house was in a poor condition and that he had a large dog. She also knew that he had a history of psychiatric illness and had, in the past, been admitted to hospital compulsorily under the Mental Health Act.

When K arrived on her first morning, the outside of the house was in a very poor state – the garden was overgrown, and it was full of rubbish and old furniture. The front door was half open and she could see that half the floor boards in the hallway appeared to be missing – there were simply joists and a drop into the cellar below. Mr W's dog was in the hallway growling and barking, and Mr W was at the top of the stairs shouting 'Who are you? You won't get me out of here – I'll kill you first!'

1 Q What should K do?
   A Leave! She should leave the house at once and report the situation to her manager.

2 Q When should she go back?
   A Only after a risk assessment has been carried out.

3 Q What sort of risks need to be assessed?
   A a Mr W's mental health and whether any treatment or support is required.
      b The safety of the house. Mr W will have to be consulted about whether he is willing for his house to be made safe and the floorboards repaired.
      c The dog and whether it is likely to present a risk of attack on a visitor to the house.

4 Q If Mr W refuses to allow a risk assessment, or his house to be repaired, should K go back in anyway?
   A No. K's job is to provide care, but not at the risk of her own safety.

5 Q Who should carry out the risk assessment?
   A K's employer.

How to move and handle service users safely

In the previous element you found out about the regulations which govern moving and handling. Chapters 10 (Unit Z6) and 11 (Unit Z7) will give you detailed information about using moving and handling equipment safely.

You will know that your employer is required to carry out a risk assessment of any moving and handling which is necessary and to supply the necessary equipment, and sufficient people, to carry out the move.

All moving and handling should be carried out using appropriate aids and sufficient people. Manual lifting is not something to be undertaken in the normal course of events and you should use mechanical lifting aids and hoists wherever possible.

If you do have to consider lifting, what should you do?

Encourage all individuals to help themselves – you would be surprised how much 'learned helplessness' exists. This is largely brought about by care workers who find it is quicker and easier to do things themselves rather than allowing a person to do it for himself or herself! Does this sound familiar?

It is also essential that the views of the person being moved are taken into account. While your employer, and you, need to make sure that you are not put at risk by moving or lifting, it is also important that the person needing assistance is not caused pain, distress or humiliation by the policies in place. Groups representing disabled people have pointed out that blanket policies which exclude any lifting may infringe the human rights of an individual needing mobility assistance. For example, individuals may in effect be confined to bed unnecessarily and against their will by a lack of lifting assistance.

There is more detailed information in Chapters 10 (Unit Z6) and 11 (Unit Z7) about maintaining mobility and helping people to move themselves.

> **TEST YOURSELF**
> 1 Why are there precautions about the kind of clothing and jewellery you wear?
> 2 Why do you need to wash your hands?
> 3 How should you wash them?
> 4 What are the different ways of disposing of waste?
> 5 What should you do if you find an intruder on the premises?

Element CU1.3 Minimise the risks arising from health emergencies

This element is about first aid, and helping you to understand the actions you should take if a health emergency arises. This is not a substitute for a first aid course, and will only give you an outline of the steps you need to take. Reading this part of this chapter will not qualify you to deal with these emergencies. Unless you have been on a first aid course, you should be careful about what you do, because the wrong action can cause more harm to the casualty. It may be better to summon help.

What you need to learn

- What you can safely do
- How you can help the casualty in a health emergency
- Other ways to help
- How to deal with witnesses' distress – and your own

What you can safely do

Most people have a useful role to play in a health emergency, even if it is not dealing directly with the ill or injured person. It is also vital that someone:

- summons help as quickly as possible
- offers any assistance to the competent person who is dealing with the emergency
- clears the immediate environment and makes it safe – for example, if someone has fallen through a glass door, the glass must be removed as soon as possible before there are any more injuries.
- offers help and support to other people who have witnessed the illness or injury and may have been upset by it. Clearly this can only be dealt with once the ill or injured person is being helped.

REMEMBER

Only attempt what you know you can safely do. Do not attempt something you are not sure of. You could do further damage to the ill or injured person and you could lay yourself and your employer open to being sued. Do not try to do something outside your responsibility or capability – summon help and wait for it to arrive.

How you can help the casualty in a health emergency

It is important that you are aware of the initial steps to take when dealing with the commonest health emergencies. You may be involved with any of these emergencies when you are at work, whether you work in a residential, hospital or community setting. Clearly, there are major differences between the different work situations:

- If you are working in a hospital where skilled assistance is always immediately available, the likelihood of your having to act in an emergency, other than to summon help, is remote.
- In a residential setting, help is likely to be readily available, although it may not necessarily be the professional medical expertise of a hospital.
- In the community you may have to summon help and take action to support a casualty until the help arrives. It is in this setting that you are most likely to need some knowledge of how to respond to a health emergency.

This section gives a guide to the recognition and initial action to be taken in a number of health emergencies:

- severe bleeding
- shock
- cardiac arrest
- loss of consciousness

- epileptic seizure
- fractures and suspected fractures
- poisoning
- choking and difficulty with breathing
- burns and scalds
- electrical injuries.

Severe bleeding

Severe bleeding can be the result of a fall or injury. The most common causes of severe cuts are glass, as the result of a fall into a window or glass door, or knives from accidents in the kitchen.

Symptoms

There will be apparently large quantities of blood from the wound. In some very serious cases, the blood may be pumping out. Even small amounts of blood can be very frightening, both for you and the casualty. Remember that a small amount of blood goes a long way, and things may look worse than they are. However, severe bleeding requires urgent medical attention in hospital. Although people rarely bleed to death, extensive bleeding can cause shock and loss of consciousness.

Aims

- To bring the bleeding under control
- To limit the possibility of infection
- To arrange urgent medical attention

Action

1   You will need to apply pressure to a wound that is bleeding. If possible, use a sterile dressing. If one is not readily available, use any readily available absorbent material, or even your hand. Do not forget the precautions (see 'Protect yourself' below). You will need to apply direct pressure over the wound for ten minutes (this can seem like a very long time) to allow the blood to clot.

2   If there is any object in the wound, such as a piece of glass, *do not* try to remove it. Simply apply pressure to the sides of the wound.

3   Lay the casualty down and raise the affected part if possible.

4   Make the person comfortable and secure.

5   Dial 999 for an ambulance.

Lay the casualty down and raise the affected part.

Protect yourself

You should take steps to protect yourself when you are dealing with casualties who are bleeding. Your skin provides an excellent barrier to infections, but you must take care if you have any broken skin such as a cut, graze or sore. Seek medical advice if blood comes into contact with your mouth, nose or gets into your eyes. Blood-borne viruses (such as HIV or hepatitis) can be passed only if the blood of someone who is already infected comes into contact with broken skin.

- If possible, wear disposable gloves.
- If possible, wash your hands thoroughly in soap and water before and after treatment.
- If this is not possible, cover any areas of broken skin with a waterproof dressing.
- Take care with any needles or broken glass in the area.
- Use a mask for mouth-to-mouth resuscitation if the casualty's nose or mouth is bleeding.

Cardiac arrest

Cardiac arrest occurs when a person's heart stops. Cardiac arrest can happen for various reasons, the most common of which is a heart attack, but a person's heart can also stop as a result of shock, electric shock, a convulsion or other illness or injury.

Symptoms

- No pulse
- No breathing

Aims

- To obtain medical help as a matter of urgency
- It is important to give oxygen, using mouth-to-mouth resuscitation, and to stimulate the heart, using chest compressions. This procedure is called cardio-pulmonary resuscitation – CPR. You will need to attend a first aid course to learn how to resuscitate – you cannot learn how to do this from a book. On the first aid course you will be able to practise on a special dummy.

Action

1 Check whether the person has a pulse and whether he or she is breathing.

2 If not, call for urgent help from the emergency services.

3 Start methods of resuscitation *if* you have been taught how to do it.

4 Keep up resuscitation until help arrives.

(a)   **(b)**

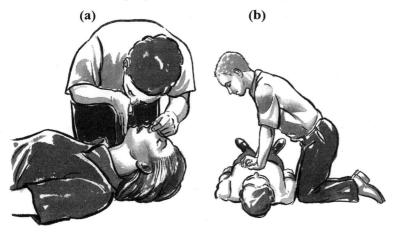

Mouth-to-mouth resuscitation (a) and chest compressions (b).

Shock

Shock occurs because blood is not being pumped around the body efficiently. This can be the result of loss of body fluids through bleeding, burns, severe vomiting or diarrhoea, or a sudden drop in blood pressure or a heart attack.

Symptoms

The signs of shock are easily recognised. The person:

- will look very pale, almost grey
- will be very sweaty, and the skin will be cold and clammy
- will have a very fast pulse
- may feel sick and may vomit
- may be breathing very quickly.

Aims

- To obtain medical help as a matter of urgency
- To improve blood supply to heart, lungs and brain

Action

1 Call for urgent medical assistance.

2 Lay the person down on the floor. Try to raise the feet off the ground to help the blood supply to the important organs.

3 Loosen any tight clothing.

4 Watch the person carefully. Check the pulse and breathing regularly.

5 Keep the person warm and comfortable, but *do not* warm the casualty with direct heat, such as a hot water bottle.

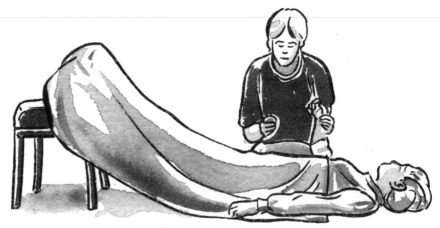

Raise the feet off the ground and keep the casualty warm.

Do not:
- allow casualty to eat or drink
- leave the casualty alone, unless it is essential to do so briefly in order to summon help.

Loss of consciousness

Loss of consciousness can happen for many reasons, from a straightforward faint to unconsciousness following a serious injury or illness.

Symptom

A reduced level of response and awareness. This can range from being vague and 'woozy' to total unconsciousness.

Aims

- To summon expert medical help as a matter of urgency
- To keep the airway open
- To note any information which may help to establish the cause of the unconsciousness

Action

1   Make sure that the person is breathing and has a clear airway.

2   You need to maintain the airway by lifting the chin and tilting the head backwards.

3   Look for any obvious reasons why the person may be unconscious, such as a wound or an ID band telling you of any condition they may have. For example, many people who have medical conditions which may cause unconsciousness, such as epilepsy or diabetes, will wear special bracelets or necklaces giving information about their condition.

Open the airway.

4   Place the casualty in the recovery position (see below), *but not if you suspect a back or neck injury*, until the emergency services arrive.

Do not:
- attempt to give anything by mouth
- attempt to make the casualty sit or stand
- leave the casualty alone, unless it is essential to leave briefly in order to summon help.

The recovery position

Many of the actions you need to take to deal with health emergencies will involve you in placing someone in the recovery position. In this position a casualty has the best chance of keeping a clear airway, not inhaling vomit and remaining as safe as possible until help arrives. This position should not be attempted if you think someone has back or neck injuries, and it may not be possible if there are fractures of limbs.

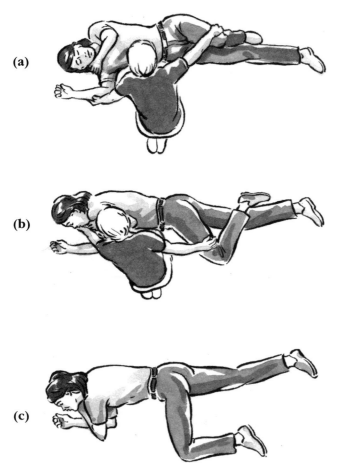

1. Kneel at one side of the casualty, at about waist level.

2. Tilt back the person's head – this opens the airway. With the casualty on his/her back, make sure that limbs are straight.

3. Bend the casualty's near arm as in a wave (so it is at right angles to the body). Pull the arm on the far side over the chest and place the back of the hand against the opposite cheek (**a** in diagram opposite).

4. Use your other hand to roll the casualty towards you by pulling on the far leg, just above the knee (**b** in the diagram). The casualty should now be on his or her side.

5. Once the casualty is rolled over, bend the leg at right angles to the body. Make sure the head is tilted well back to keep the airway open (**c** in diagram).

The recovery position.

Epileptic seizure

Epilepsy is a medical condition that causes disturbances in the brain which result in sufferers becoming unconscious and having involuntary contractions of their muscles. This contraction of the muscles produces the fit or seizure. People who suffer with epilepsy do not have any control over their seizures, and may actually do themselves harm by falling when they have a seizure.

Aims

- To ensure that the person is safe and does not injure himself or herself during the fit
- To offer any help needed following the fit

Action

1. Try to make sure that the area in which the person has fallen is safe.

2. Loosen all clothing.

3. Once the seizure has ended, make sure that the person has a clear airway and place in the recovery position.

4. Make sure that the person is comfortable and safe. Particularly try to prevent head injury.

5 If the fit lasts longer than five minutes, or you are unaware that the casualty is a known epileptic, call an ambulance.

Do not:
- attempt to hold the casualty down, or put anything in the mouth
- move the casualty until he or she is fully conscious, unless there is a risk of injury in the place where he or she has fallen.

Choking and difficulty with breathing (in adults and children over 8 years)

This is caused by something (usually a piece of food) stuck at the back of the throat. It is a situation which needs to be dealt with, as people can quickly stop breathing if the obstruction is not removed.

Symptoms
- Red, congested face at first, later turning grey
- Unable to speak or breathe, may gasp and indicate throat or neck

Aims
- To remove obstruction as quickly as possible
- To summon medical assistance as a matter of urgency if the obstruction cannot be removed

Action

1 Try to get the person to cough. If that is not immediately effective, move on to step 2.

2 Bend the person forwards. Slap sharply on the back between the shoulder blades up to five times (**a** in diagram opposite).

3 If this fails, stand behind the person with your arms around him/her. Join your hands just below the breastbone. One hand should be in a fist and the other holding it (**b** in the diagram).

4 Then sharply pull your joined hands upwards and into the person's body at the same time. The force should expel the obstruction.

5 You should alternate backslaps and abdominal thrusts until you clear the obstruction.

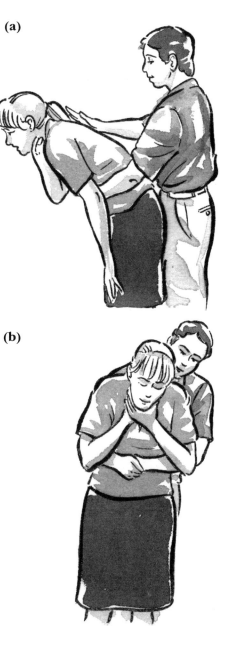

(a)

(b)

Dealing with an adult who is choking.

Fractures and suspected fractures

Fractures are breaks or cracks in bones. They are usually caused by a fall or other type of injury. The casualty will need to go to a hospital as soon as possible to have a fracture diagnosed correctly.

Symptoms

- Acute pain around the site of the injury
- Swelling and discoloration around the affected area
- Limbs or joints may be in odd positions
- Broken bones may protrude through the skin

Action

1 The important thing is to support the affected part. Help the casualty to find the most comfortable position.

2 Support the injured limb in that position with as much padding as necessary – towels, cushions or clothing will do.

3 Take the person to hospital or call an ambulance.

Do not:
- try to bandage or splint the injury
- allow the casualty to have anything to eat or drink.

Support the injured limb.

Burns and scalds

There are several different types of burn; the most usual are burns caused by heat or flame. Scalds are caused by hot liquids. People can be burned by chemicals or by electrical currents.

Symptoms

- Depending on the type and severity of the burn, skin may be red, swollen and tender, blistered and raw or charred
- Usually severe pain and possibly shock

Aims

- To obtain immediate medical assistance if the burn is over a large area (as big as the casualty's hand or more) or is deep
- To send for an ambulance if the burn is severe or extensive. If the burn or scald is over a smaller area, the casualty could be transported to hospital by car
- To stop the burning and reduce pain
- To minimise possibility of infection

Action

1   For major burns, summon immediate medical assistance.

2   Cool down the burn. Keep it flooded with cold water for 10 minutes. If it is a chemical burn, this needs to be done for 20 minutes. Ensure that the contaminated water used to cool a chemical burn is disposed of safely.

3   Remove any jewellery, watches or clothing which are not sticking to the burn.

4   Cover the burn if possible, unless it is a facial burn, with a sterile or, at least, clean dressing. For a burn on a hand or foot, a clean plastic bag will protect it from infection until it can be treated by an expert.

If clothing is on fire, remember the basics: *stop*, *drop*, *wrap* and *roll* the person on the ground.

Do not:

● remove anything which is stuck to a burn
● touch a burn, or use any ointment or cream
● cover facial burns – keep pouring water on until help arrives.

Cool the burn with water.

REMEMBER

If a person's clothing is on fire, STOP – DROP – WRAP – ROLL:

● *Stop* him or her from running around.

● Get him/her to *drop* to the ground – push him/her if you have to and can do so safely.

● *Wrap* him/her in something to smother the flames – a blanket or coat, anything to hand. This is better if it is soaked in water.

● *Roll* him/her on the ground to put out the flames.

Poisoning

People can be poisoned by many substances, drugs, plants, chemicals, fumes or alcohol.

Symptoms

Symptoms will vary depending on the poison.

● The person could be unconscious
● There may be acute abdominal pain
● There may be blistering of the mouth and lips

Aims

- To remove the casualty to a safe area if he/she is at risk, and it is safe for you to move him/her
- To summon medical assistance as a matter of urgency
- To gather any information which will identify the poison
- To maintain a clear airway and breathing until help arrives

Action

1   If the casualty is unconscious, place him/her in the recovery position to ensure that the airway is clear, and that he/she cannot choke on any vomit.

2   Dial 999 for an ambulance.

3   Try to establish what the poison is and how much has been taken. This information could be vital in saving a life.

4   If a conscious casualty has burned mouth or lips, he or she can be given small frequent sips of water or cold milk.

Do not try to make the casualty vomit.

Electrical injuries

Electrocution occurs when an electrical current passes though the body.

Symptoms

Electrocution can cause cardiac arrest and burns where the electrical current entered and left the body.

Aims

- To remove the casualty from the current when you can safely do so
- To obtain medical assistance as a matter of urgency
- To maintain a clear airway and breathing until help arrives
- To treat any burns

Action

There are different procedures to follow depending on whether the injury has been caused by a high or low voltage current.

Injury caused by high voltage current:

This type of injury may be caused by overhead power cables or rail lines, for example.

1   Contact the emergency services immediately.

2   *Do not* touch the person until all electricity has been cut off.

3   If person is unconscious, clear the airway.

4   Treat any other injuries present, such as burns.

5   Place in the recovery position until help arrives.

Injury caused by low voltage current:

This type of injury may be caused by powered kettles, computers, drills, lawnmowers, etc.

1   Break the contact with the current by switching off the electricity at the mains if possible.

2   It is vital to break the contact as soon as possible, *but* if you touch a person who is 'live' (still in contact with the current) you too will be injured. If you are unable to switch off the electricity, then you must stand on something dry which can insulate you, such as a telephone directory, rubber mat or a pile of newspapers, and then move the casualty away from the current as described below.

3   Do not use anything made of metal, or anything wet, to move the casualty from the current. Try to move him/her with a wooden pole or broom-handle, even a chair.

4   Alternatively, drag him/her with a rope or cord or, as a last resort, pull by holding any of the person's dry clothing which is *not* in contact with his/her body.

5   Once the person is no longer in contact with the current, you should follow the same steps as with a high voltage injury.

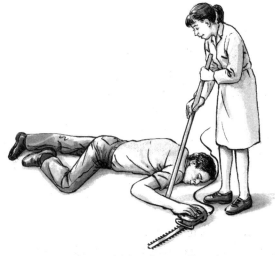

Move the casualty away from the current.

Other ways to help

Summoning assistance

In the majority of cases this will mean telephoning 999 and requesting an ambulance. It will depend on the setting in which you work and clearly is not required if you work in a hospital! But it may mean calling for a colleague with medical qualifications, who will then be able to make an assessment of the need for further assistance. Similarly, if you work in the residential sector, there should be a medically qualified colleague available. If you are the first on the scene at an emergency in the community, you may need to summon an ambulance for urgent assistance.

If you need to call an ambulance, try to keep calm and give clearly all the details you are asked for. Do not attempt to give details until they are asked for – this wastes time. Emergency service operators are trained to find out the necessary information, so let them ask the questions, then answer calmly and clearly.

Follow the action steps outlined in the previous section whilst you are waiting for help to arrive.

Assist the person dealing with the emergency

A second pair of hands is invaluable when dealing with an emergency. If you are assisting someone with first aid or medical expertise, follow all his or her instructions, even if you don't understand why. An emergency situation is not the time for a discussion or debate – that can happen later. You may be needed to help to move a casualty, or to fetch water, blankets or dressings, or to reassure and comfort the casualty during treatment.

Make the area safe

An accident or injury may have occurred in an unsafe area – and it was probably for precisely that reason that the accident occurred there! Sometimes, it may be that the accident has made the area unsafe for others. For example, if someone has tripped over an electric flex, there may be exposed wires or a damaged electric socket. Alternatively, a fall against a window or glass door may have left shards of broken glass in the area, or there may be blood or other body fluids on the floor. You may need to make the area safe by turning off the power, clearing broken glass or dealing with a spillage.

It may be necessary to redirect people away from the area of the accident in order to avoid further casualties.

Maintain the privacy of the casualty

You may need to act to provide some privacy for the casualty by asking onlookers to move away or stand back. If you can erect a temporary screen with coats or blankets, this may help to offer some privacy. It may not matter to the casualty at the time, but he or she has a right to privacy if possible.

Make accurate reports

You may be responsible for making a report on an emergency situation you have witnessed, or for filling in records later. Concentrate on the most important aspects of the incident and record the actions of yourself and others in an accurate, legible and complete manner.

How to deal with witnesses' distress – and your own

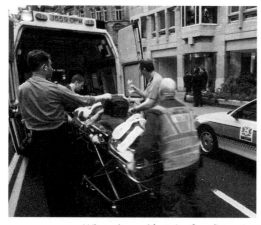

Witnessing accidents is often distressing.

People who have witnessed accidents can often be very distressed by what they have seen. The distress may be as a result of the nature of the injury, or the blood loss. It could be because the casualty is a friend or relative or simply because seeing accidents or injuries is traumatic. Some people can become upset because they feel helpless and do not know how to assist, or they may have been afraid and then feel guilty later.

You will need to reassure people about the casualty and the fact that he or she is being cared for appropriately. However, do not give false reassurance about things you may not be sure of.

You may need to allow individuals to talk about what they saw. One of the commonest effects of witnessing a trauma is that people need to repeat over and over again what they saw.

What about you?

You may feel very distressed by the experience you have gone through. You may find that you need to talk about what has happened, and that you need to look again at the role you played. You may feel that you could have done more, or you may feel angry with yourself for not having a greater knowledge about what to do.

There is a whole range of emotions which you may experience. Chapter 4 (Unit Z1) covers in detail the different ways to cope with these feelings, but you should be able to discuss your feelings with your supervisor and use any support provided by your employer.

If you have followed the basic guidelines in this element, you will have done as much as could be expected of anyone at the scene of an emergency who is not a trained first aider.

TEST YOURSELF

1 You should always attempt first aid because it is always better to do something. True or false?

2 What is the single most important act for an untrained person to do in a health emergency?

3 List three tasks you can carry out at the scene of an emergency which do not necessarily involve first aid.

4 How would you talk to a casualty while you waited for help?

5 What would you say to others who had witnessed the incident?

CU1 UNIT TEST

1 Imagine you are just about to start work in a new day-care facility for older people.

a What kinds of substance would you expect to see in the COSHH file?
b Which tasks would you expect to find in the risk assessment file?
c Would you expect to see any specialised care equipment in the centre?
d What type of equipment?
e What basic precautions will you expect to follow?
f Do you think there will be an expectation about how you dress? What do you think it will be?
g What training courses would you expect to undertake?
h List at least three security precautions you think the setting may take.

2 Now imagine that you are about to start working in a residential home for teenagers. Answer the same questions. Which of your answers are different and which remain the same?

3 Describe two types of health emergency (e.g. a fall) that could occur in a day-care facility for older people. List the steps you would take to assist in each case.

In this chapter you will look at some of the most difficult issues that you will face as a care professional. You need to know how society handles abuse, how to recognise it, and what to do about it. It is a tragic fact that almost all disclosures of abuse are true – and you will have to learn to *think the unthinkable.* If you can learn always to consider the possibility of abuse, always to be aware of potentially abusive situations and always to *listen* and *believe* when you are told of abuse, then you will provide the best possible protection for people in your care.

This chapter refers to 'children and young people', and deals with children between 8 and 18 years. Work with very young children (under 8 years) is not covered by the NVQ Care qualification. If this is the age group you work with, you should look at an NVQ in Early Years Care and Education.

Element Z1.1 | Contribute to minimising the level of abuse in care environments

What you need to learn

- What is meant by abuse in care environments
- How the law affects what you do
- How you can contribute to the minimising of abuse
- How to report and to record information

What is meant by abuse in care environments

What is a care environment?

The obvious answers are residential care and hospitals, but people are cared for in many other situations: children are cared for by their parents, by a childminder, in school or out-of-school club, in a youth group or in foster homes. Vulnerable adults can be cared for in supported living schemes, at home with informal carers or professional carers, with relatives and in day care, as well as in residential or nursing homes.

What is abuse?

Abuse is more than being hit or sexually assaulted. Of course, they are the most violent and obvious forms of abuse, and they may be the ones which are easier to identify. But there are other ways in which people can be abused, as the diagram on the next page shows.

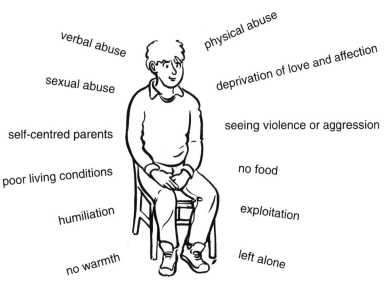

verbal abuse

physical abuse

sexual abuse

deprivation of love and affection

self-centred parents

seeing violence or aggression

poor living conditions

no food

humiliation

exploitation

no warmth

left alone

Ways in which children can be abused.

Children can be abused:

- emotionally, by being deprived of love or physical contact or by being constantly belittled and humiliated
- verbally, by being constantly shouted at
- by having to witness violent or aggressive scenes at home
- by being parented by people who are unable to put their child's needs before their own
- by being physically neglected, by living in filthy conditions
- by being deprived of food, warmth or shelter
- by being left without adult protection, to fend for themselves
- at the hands of other children, by being bullied at school or in the local neighbourhood
- by being exploited for sexual purposes or financial gain
- by those who use or purchase materials for the production of which children were exploited.

REMEMBER

Child abuse can be:

- physical
- sexual
- emotional
- neglect.

DID YOU KNOW?

Childline, the helpline for children, receives 10 attempted calls every minute.

no medical attention

harassment

physical abuse

no food

cold

isolated

financial exploitation

humiliation

Ways in which vulnerable adults can be abused.

Vulnerable adults are also abused. The broad definition of a 'vulnerable adult', according to government guidelines, is a person *'who is or may be in need of community care services by reason of mental or other disability, age or illness; and who is or may be unable to take care of himself or herself, or unable to protect himself or herself against significant harm or exploitation'*.

The guidelines are called 'No Secrets: Guidance on developing and implementing multi-agency policies and procedures to protect vulnerable adults from abuse', and are published by the Department of Health and the Home Office. They define abuse as *'a violation of an individual's human and civil rights by any other person or persons'*.

Abuse may consist of a single act or repeated acts. It may be physical, verbal or psychological, it may be a deliberate act of neglect or a failure to act, or it may occur when a vulnerable person is persuaded to enter into a financial or sexual act to which he or she has not given or cannot give informed consent.

- **Physical abuse** includes hitting, slapping, pushing, kicking, misuse of medication or restraint, or inappropriate sanctions.
- **Sexual abuse** includes rape and sexual assault or sexual acts to which the vulnerable adult has not consented, or could not consent, or was pressured into consenting.
- **Psychological abuse** includes emotional abuse, threats of harm or abandonment, deprivation of contact, humiliation, blaming, controlling, intimidation, coercion, harassment, verbal abuse, isolation or withdrawal from services or supportive networks.
- **Financial or material abuse** includes theft, fraud, exploitation, pressure in connection with wills, property or inheritance or financial transactions, or the misuse or misappropriation of property, possessions or benefits.
- **Neglect and acts of omission** include ignoring medical or physical care needs; failure to provide access to appropriate health, social care or educational services; and the withholding of the necessities of life, such as medication, adequate nutrition and heating.

- **Discriminatory abuse** includes racist and sexist abuse, abuse based on a person's disability, and other forms of harassment, slurs or similar treatment.

Any of these types of abuse may be the result of deliberate intent, negligence or ignorance.

Check it out

How many types of abuse does your workplace have guidelines to deal with? Look at the policy and procedures for dealing with abuse. See how many types of abuse are listed and what the procedures are. Ask your supervisor if you cannot find any information.

Who can abuse?

Abuse can take place at home or in a formal care setting. At home, it could be an informal carer who is the abuser, although it could be a neighbour or regular visitor. It can also be a professional care worker who is carrying out the abuse. This situation can mean that abuse goes undetected for some time because of the unsupervised nature of a carer's visits to someone's home.

In a formal care setting, abuse may be more likely to be noticed, although some of the more subtle forms of abuse, such as humiliation, can sometimes be so commonplace that it is not recognised as abusive behaviour.

Abuse is not only carried out by individuals; groups, or even organisations can also create abusive situations. It has been known that groups of carers in residential settings can abuse individuals in their care. Often people will act in a different way in a group than they would alone. Think about teenage 'gangs' which exist because people are prepared to do things jointly which they would not think to do if they were by themselves.

Abuse in a care setting may not just be at the hands of members of staff. There is also abuse which comes about because of the way in which an establishment is run, where the basis for planning the systems, rules and regulations is not the welfare, rights and dignity of the residents or patients, but the convenience of the staff and management. This is the sort of situation where people can be told when to get up and go to bed, given communal clothing, only allowed medical attention at set times and not allowed to go out. This is referred to as 'institutional abuse'.

CASE STUDY

Julie was 43, and she had worked as a senior support worker in a residential unit for people with a learning disability for the past five years. Julie loved her job and was very committed to the residents in the unit. She was very concerned for the welfare of the people she supported and did everything she could for them. Many of them had been in the unit for many years and Julie knew them well. The unit was not very large and had only a small staff who were able to work very closely with the resident group.

Julie and the other staff were concerned that the residents could easily be taken advantage of, as some were not able to make effective judgments about other people and potentially risky situations.

Regular mealtimes were arranged so that everyone could share the day's experiences and talk together, and bedtimes and getting-up times were also strictly adhered to. The staff found that this was a good way of keeping the residents organised and motivated. Residents did not go out into the local town in the evenings because of the potential safety risk, but the staff would plan evenings of TV watching, choosing programmes which they thought would interest the residents. Sometimes simple games sessions or walks in the local park were arranged.

A new manager was appointed to the unit and Julie and the other staff were very surprised to find that the new manager was horrified by many of these practices, and wanted to make major changes.

1 What changes do you think the manager may have suggested?
2 Why do you think those changes may be needed?
3 Do you consider that Julie and the other staff members were practising in the best way for the residents?
4 Think about, or discuss, whether this situation was abusive.

Up to this point, consideration has been given to abuse by carers, whether parents, informal or professional. But, do not forget that in residential or hospital settings, abuse can occur between residents or patients, and it can also happen between visitors and residents or patients. People can also abuse themselves.

As a carer whose role is to reduce the risk of abuse wherever you can, you need to be very much aware of abuse between individuals you are caring for and to take action whenever you suspect that this is happening. Bear in mind the types of behaviour which are abusive and be alert to any signs of those behaviours.

Visitors can also behave abusively, and if the care team considers that they pose a risk to the health or well-being of an individual, then a plan will be developed for how the visitor should be dealt with. You must ensure that you follow the plan of care, and always check with your supervisor if you are unsure about access.

DID YOU KNOW?

Some of the most difficult places to make secure are hospitals and residential homes. The large number of visitors makes it almost impossible to have a secure system of identifying everyone on the premises at any given time.

The one abuser it is very hard to protect someone from is himself or herself. Individuals who self-harm will be identified in their plan of care, and responses to their behaviour will be recorded. You must ensure that you follow the agreed plan for provision of care for someone who has a history of self-harm. It is usual that an individual who is at risk of harming himself or herself will be closely supported and you may need to contribute towards activities or therapies which have been planned for the individual.

TEST YOURSELF

1   Name three types of abusive behaviour towards children.
2   People can only be abused by individuals. True or false?
3   Name the government guidelines which deal with abuse of older people.
4   Name as many different care environments as you can.

How the law affects what you do

Much of the work in caring is governed by legislation, but the only group where legislation specifically provides for protection from abuse is children. Older people, people with a learning disability, physical disabilities or mental health problems have service provision, restrictions, rights and all sorts of other requirements laid down in law, but no overall legal framework to provide protection from abuse. The laws which cover your work in the field of care are summarised in the table on the next page.

There are, however a number of sets of guidelines, policies and procedures in respect of abuse for service user groups other than children, and you will need to ensure that you familiarise yourself with policies for your area of work and particularly with those policies which apply in your own workplace.

Check it out

Ask your supervisor about the procedures in your workplace for dealing with abuse. There should be a written policy and guidelines to be followed if abuse is suspected. Ask if there are any laws or guidelines which are related to the way you work. Check with experienced colleagues about situations they have dealt with and ask them to tell you about what happened.

Service user group	Laws which govern their care	Protection from abuse?
Children	Children Act 1989	Yes
People with mental health problems	Mental Health Act 1983 (new draft Mental Health Bill June 2002)	No
Adults with a learning disability	Mental Health Act 1983	No
Adults with disabilities	Chronically Sick and Disabled Persons Act 1986 Disability Discrimination Act 1995	No
Older people	National Assistance Act 1948 NHS and Community Care Act 1990	No
All service user groups	Care Standards Act 2000	Yes, through raising standards

Government policies and guidelines

The most influential set of government guidelines which lay down practices for inter-agency co-operation is called 'Working Together to Safeguard Children'. It was published in 1999 and replaced the earlier version. It forms the basis for present child protection work. This guideline ensures that information is shared between agencies and professionals, and that decisions in respect of children are not taken by just one person.

There is a similar set of guidelines published by the government about adults, called 'No Secrets' (see page 108). These guidelines state that older people have specific rights, which include being treated with respect, and being able to live in their home and community without fear of physical or emotional violence or harassment.

The guidance gives local authorities the lead responsibility in co-ordinating the procedures. Each local authority area must have a multi-agency management committee for the protection of vulnerable adults, which will develop policies, protocols and practices. The guidance covers:

- identification of those at risk
- setting up an inter-agency framework
- developing inter-agency policy – procedures for responding in individual cases
- recruitment, training and other staff and management issues.

A government White Paper published in 2001, 'Valuing People: A New Strategy for Learning Disability in the 21st Century', sets out the ways in which services for people with a learning disability will be improved. 'Valuing People' sets out four main principles for service provision for people with a learning disability:

- civil rights
- independence
- choice
- inclusion.

The White Paper also makes it clear that people with a learning disability are entitled to the full protection of the law.

Recent policy approaches to protecting children and vulnerable adults in care environments have concentrated on improving and monitoring the quality of the service provided to them. The principle behind this is that if the overall quality of practice in care is constantly improved, then well-trained staff working to high standards are less likely to abuse service users, and are more likely to identify and deal effectively with any abuse they find.

What does the law say about protecting children?

The Children Act 1989 requires that local authority social services departments provide protection from abuse for children in their area. The Act of Parliament gives powers to social services departments, following the procedures laid down by the Area Child Protection Committee, to take legal steps to ensure the safety of children.

What happens in an emergency?

In an emergency, a social worker, or an NSPCC officer, can apply to a magistrate for an order to look after a child. This is an Emergency Protection Order (known as an EPO). The police are also able to take immediate steps to protect children in an emergency situation. (This is a Police Protection Order, or PPO.) These orders require evidence which shows that there is reasonable cause to believe that a child may suffer 'significant harm'. They are short-term orders, usually for 3–7 days, and are followed by a court hearing where more detailed evidence is produced and the parents are represented.

The three agencies able to take legal steps to protect children.

Not all investigations into abuse are emergencies, and not all involve legal proceedings. Some abusive, or potentially abusive, situations are dealt with by working with the family, usually by agreeing a 'contract' between social services and the family.

What does the law say about protecting vulnerable adults?

The Acts of Parliament which are mainly concerned with provisions for vulnerable adults are the National Assistance Act 1948 and the NHS and Community Care Act 1990. They do not specifically give social services departments a 'duty to protect' but, of course, people are protected by the law. If a vulnerable adult is abused and that abuse is considered to be a criminal offence, then the police will act. It is sometimes thought that because someone is confused, that a prosecution will not be brought – this is not so. All vulnerable adults will have the full protection of the law if any criminal offences are committed.

Some vulnerable adults suffer abuse in residential or hospital settings. These settings are ultimately controlled by legislation. Hospitals have complaints procedures and arrangements for allowing 'whistleblowers' who have concerns about abuse to come forward. Residential homes and nursing homes have to be registered with the National

Care Standards Commissioner, who will investigate allegations of abuse and can ultimately close an unsatisfactory residential home or nursing home.

The Mental Health Act 1983 (and the draft Mental Health Bill) forms the framework for service provision for people with mental health problems and people with a learning disability. There are provisions within this legislation for social services departments to assume responsibility for people who are so 'mentally impaired' that they are not able to be responsible for their own affairs. This is called guardianship. However, like all other vulnerable adults, there is no specific duty to protect people from abuse.

'Valuing People' (see page 112) will form the basis for services to all people with a learning disability and will provide rights, but no specific duty of protection.

While the Chronically Sick and Disabled Persons Act and the Disability Discrimination Act provide disabled people with rights, services and protection from discrimination, they do not provide any means of comprehensive protection from abuse.

As with all vulnerable groups, there is a long and tragic history to the physical and emotional abuse suffered by people with physical disabilities or a learning disability. The public humiliation and abuse of those with mental health problems is still visible today, so it is hardly surprising that abuse on an individual level is still all too commonplace.

What happens in an emergency?

Many social services departments now have procedures in place similar to those for protecting children. There will be an investigation of the alleged or suspected abuse, followed by a case conference where information will be shared between all the professionals concerned and a plan of action worked out. The vulnerable adult concerned and/or a friend or advocate will also be invited to take part in the conference if he or she wishes.

What if a professional carer abuses?

There are special procedures in place for investigating abuse which is inflicted by care workers or foster carers. It is investigated by an outside agency and immediate steps are taken to remove the suspected abuser (often called the 'perpetrator') from contact until the investigation has been completed.

These issues are well publicised at the moment as many cases of systematic and long-term abuse by care workers are coming to light. Later, this chapter will make sure that you know how to deal with a situation where you know of, or suspect, abuse in your workplace.

TEST YOURSELF

1   Which service user group is legally protected from abuse?
2   Is there any protection for other service user groups?
3   What are the laws which affect work with older people?
4   What are the government guidelines called which cover work with child protection?
5   Who are the people involved when an emergency situation concerns an older person?

How you can contribute to the minimising of abuse

One of the key contributions you can make towards limiting abuse is to be aware of where abuse may be happening. It is not easy to accept that abuse is going on, and it is often simpler to find other explanations.

Be prepared to *think the unthinkable*. If you know about the circumstances in which abuse has been found to occur most frequently, then you are better able to respond quickly if you suspect a problem.

It is not possible accurately to predict situations where abuse will take place – a great deal of misery could be saved if it were. It is possible, though, to identify some factors which seem to make it more likely that abuse could occur. This does not mean that abuse will definitely happen – neither should you assume that all people in these circumstances are abusers – but it does mean that you should be aware of the possibility when you are dealing with these situations.

Situations when child abuse can happen

Child abuse can happen in situations where:

- parents are unable to put a child's needs first
- parents or carers need to show dominance over others
- parents or carers have been poorly parented themselves
- parents or carers were abused themselves as children
- families have financial problems (this does not just mean families on low incomes)
- families have a history of poor relationships or of use of violence.

Situations when vulnerable adults may be abused at home

Adults may be abused at home in situations where:

- carers have had to change their lifestyles unwillingly
- the dependent person has communication problems, has had a personality or behaviour change (such as dementia), rejects help or is aggressive
- there is no support from family or professional carers
- carers are becoming dependent on drugs or alcohol
- carers have no privacy
- the dependent person is difficult and inconsiderate.

Check it out

Think about the service users you deal with. Make a list of how many of them fit into the circumstances outlined. Now resolve to keep a particular eye on those service users and watch for any signs that abuse may be happening. Be prepared to *think the unthinkable*.

Situations when abuse can happen in a care setting

Abuse can happen in a care setting when:

- staff are poorly trained or untrained
- there is little or no management supervision or support

- staff work in isolation
- there are inadequate numbers of staff to cope with the workload
- there are inadequate security arrangements
- there is no key worker system and good relationships are not formed between staff and residents.

Check it out

Look at your workplace. Do any of the above points apply? If any of these are the case in your workplace, you need to be aware that people can be put under so much stress that they behave abusively. Remember that abuse is not just about physical cruelty. If none of these things happen in your workplace, then try to imagine what work would be like if they did. Sit down with a colleague, if you can, and discuss what you think the effects of any two of the items in the list would be. If you cannot do this with a colleague, you can do it on your own by making a list.

If you want to be effective in helping to stop abuse you will need to:

- believe that abuse happens
- recognise abusive behaviour
- be aware of when abuse can happen
- understand who abusers can be
- know the policies and procedures for handling abuse
- follow the individual's plan of care
- recognise likely abusive situations
- report any concerns or suspicions.

Your most important contribution will be to be *alert*. For example, an individual's plan of care or your organisational policy should specify ways in which the individual's whereabouts are constantly monitored – and if you are alert to where a vulnerable person is, and who he or she is with, you can do much to help avoid abusive situations.

There are many factors involved in building protection against abuse.

? **TEST YOURSELF**

1 Identify three situations in which children may be abused.

2 There are some different circumstances which could lead to vulnerable adults being abused. What are they?

3 Abuse can happen when people are being cared for. Name the circumstances which make this more likely.

4 What should you do if abuse is suspected?

! **REMEMBER**
Either in a care setting or in an individual's own home, it is important to establish that callers are genuinely entitled to see the individual. Any doubts about rights of access should be cleared up immediately.

How to report and record information

Information about abuse you suspect, or situations you are working with which are 'high risk', must be recorded after being reported to your supervisor. Your supervisor will be responsible for passing on the information, if necessary.

Sometimes your information may need to be included in a service user's plan of care or personal records, particularly if you have noticed a change in the way he or she is cared for, or if his/her behaviour could be an 'early warning' that the care team need to be especially observant. Your workplace may have a special report form for recording 'causes for concern'. If not, you should write your report, making sure you include the following:

- what happened to make you concerned
- who you are concerned about
- whether this links to anything you have noticed previously
- what needs to happen next.

P. was visited by her son this afternoon. She was very quiet over tea, did not join in conversation or joke with anyone. Just said she was tired when asked what was wrong. Went to her room without going into lounge for the 'seconds evening'. Said she thought the clothes were too expensive and she couldn't afford them. Unusual for her. Similar to incident about a month ago when she said she couldn't afford the hairdresser - again after a visit from her son.
Needs to be watched. Is he getting money from her? For discussion at planning meeting.

Discuss your report and your concerns with your supervisor and colleagues.

You must report anything unusual that you notice, even if you think it is too small to be important. It is the small details which make the whole picture. Sometimes, your observations may add to other small things noticed by members of the team, and a picture may start to emerge. Teamwork and good communication are vitally important.

CASE STUDY

One family support worker had a nickname – he was known as 'Cecil', short for Cecil B. de Mille the film director. Cecil was known for regularly phoning the schools, social workers and GP surgeries of the families he visited every time there was any event, incident or change with the families. Cecil always started his conversation with 'I'm just keeping you in the picture' hence, the nickname!

However, with the G family, it was thanks to being 'kept in the picture' by Cecil that the social worker was made aware of the mother's new boyfriend. When his details were checked out, it was discovered that he had lived with another family where the children were on the Child Protection register. When this information was put together with the teacher noticing that one of the children had become much quieter recently, alarm bells began to ring and the children were carefully monitored, both at home and school.

...to keep you in the picture...

1   What was Cecil doing which was important?
2   What might have happened if the information had not been passed on?
3   Why was Cecil in a good position to keep everyone informed?

DID YOU KNOW?

If you were to take one piece from a jigsaw puzzle, it would be very difficult to guess from it what the complete picture is – if not impossible. It would be easy to guess wrongly! You would need quite a few pieces before you could begin to draw a conclusion. The same applies to identifying the true picture in cases of abuse.

REMEMBER

- Care environments are not just in residential homes and hospitals.
- Abuse is about far more than physical or sexual assault.
- Vulnerable adults and children can be abused by carers, other patients or service users or by organisations.
- Children are the only service user group specifically protected by the law.
- You need to be alert to the situations where abuse can occur.
- You must share information.
- You must record information clearly and accurately.

TEST YOURSELF

1 Why is it important to record information?

2 Look back to the case study on page 110. Write a report on this situation, making sure you include the main information points.

3 Make a list of the people in your workplace with whom you would need to share information. Say why each of them is on your list.

4 If you had to name the most important point about information, what would it be?

Element Z1.2 Minimise the effects of abusive behaviour

What you need to learn

- Indications of abuse
- How to respond to disclosure of abuse
- How to deal with abusive behaviour
- The effects of abuse on all those concerned

Indications of abuse

This is not a comprehensive list of all the indicators of abuse. It is not possible to be exhaustive, neither does the existence of one of these signs mean that abuse has definitely occurred. Each is an *indicator*, which needs to be used alongside your other skills, such as observation and listening. It is a further piece of evidence – often the conclusive one – in building a complete picture.

Physical signs of abuse in children

- Bruising, or injuries which the child cannot explain
- Bruises in the shape of objects – belt buckles, soles of shoes, etc.
- Handmarks
- Bruises in lines
- Injuries to the frenulum (the piece of skin below the tongue), or between the upper and lower lips and the gums

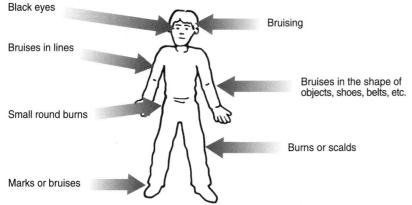

Black eyes

Bruises in lines

Small round burns

Marks or bruises

Bruising

Bruises in the shape of objects, shoes, belts, etc.

Burns or scalds

- Black eyes
- Bruising to ears
- Burns, particularly small round burns which could have come from a cigarette
- Burns or scalds to buttocks and backs of legs
- Burns in lines, like the elements of an electric fire

Physical signs of abuse in children.

Emotional signs of abuse in children

- Sudden change in behaviour, becoming quiet and withdrawn
- Change to overtly sexual behaviour, or an obsession with sexual comments
- Problems sleeping or onset of nightmares
- A sudden unwillingness to change clothes or participate in sports
- Complaints of soreness or infections in the genital/anal area
- Frequent complaints of abdominal pain
- Deterioration of personal hygiene
- Finding excuses not to go home
- Appearing tense or frightened with a particular adult

Physical signs of abuse in adults

- Series of unexplained falls or injuries
- 'Pepperpot' bruising – a covering of small bruises, usually on the chest and caused by poking with a finger or tightening of clothing
- Finger marks
- Bruising in unusual areas, such as inside arms or thighs
- Burns in unusual areas
- Marks to wrists, arms or legs which could show use of physical restraint
- Ulcers or bed sores, rashes caused by wet clothing
- Unusual sexual behaviour
- Recurrent genital infections
- Blood or marks on underclothes

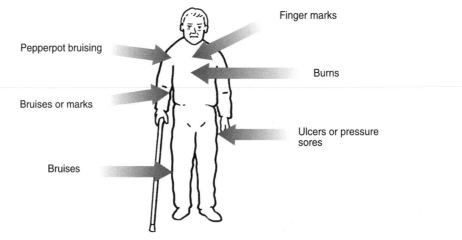

Physical signs of abuse in adults.

Emotional signs of abuse in adults

- Changes in behaviour, becoming withdrawn or anxious
- Unusually expressing feelings of hopelessness and depression
- Change in eating pattern, loss/gain in weight
- Sleep problems
- Fear of making decisions or choices
- Difficulty for care professionals to gain access to individual – be concerned if there is always a reason why the person cannot be seen

- Sudden apparent change in financial circumstances
- Disappearance of bank account records or pension books
- Unusual level of interest by carer or others in finances and assets
- Financial arrangement which the individual has not understood or has not willingly agreed to
- Excessive requests for repeat prescriptions
- Insistence by carer on being present at interviews
- References to the dependent person in a derogatory way by the carer

Check it out

Think of three service users you have worked with in the past month. Look carefully at the list of indications of abuse, and write down any which could apply to the service users you have selected. If there are none, that is fine. If you have noticed any signs, the first thing to do is to report this to your supervisor. Then go back to the previous element and look at the list of circumstances in which abuse is likely to occur. Do any of those fit? If so, you should also discuss this with your supervisor and develop a plan to monitor the situation.

How to respond to disclosure of abuse

If abuse is disclosed to you by someone you are caring for, you should deal with it in the same way whether it is a child or adult. First, you must *listen* and *believe*. Make sure that you communicate, both by words and by body language, that you believe the person.

DID YOU KNOW?

Being abused is terrible, and not being believed makes that abuse ten times worse. Don't be the second abuser – always *listen* and *believe*.

Do not ask any questions which could possibly be leading questions, for example 'and then did he hit you again?' The only questions you should ask should be to prompt the individual to continue his or her disclosure, such as 'and then what happened?'

You may well be asked to promise not to tell anyone – *never make that promise,* as it is not one you can keep. If you are asked 'If I tell you something, will you promise not to tell anyone?' you must always make it clear that you cannot make that promise. You must say something like, 'I can't say that until I know what you are going to tell me'.

Following disclosure, you must make it clear that you have to tell others about what you have been told, but you should also make it clear that the information is confidential within the group of people who need to know in order to protect. The answer to 'I don't want people to know' is to say something like 'The only people who will know are those who will make you safe'.

How to deal with abusive behaviour

Most of the time, your role in dealing with abuse will be the vital one of being aware of the possibility of abuse, reporting and recording any concerns you have, or reporting any disclosure made to you.

However, there may be occasions when you have to intervene in order to prevent an abusive situation developing. The abuse can be physical, verbal or behavioural. This is most likely to happen in a hospital, residential or day-care setting between patients or service users. If you work in the community, you could be in the situation of having to deal with abusive behaviour from a carer. If you do have to act directly to prevent abuse, you need to take the following steps:

- Always prevent a situation if you can. If you know, for example, that two people regularly disagree violently about everything from politics to whether or not it is raining, try to arrange that they are involved in separate activities and, if possible, have seats in separate lounges! Alternatively, you may decide to deal with the situation by talking to them both, and offering to help them to try to resolve their disagreements.
- Deal with abusive behaviour in the same way as aggression – be calm and be clear. Do not get drawn into an argument and do not become aggressive, but make it very clear that abusive behaviour will not be tolerated.
- You should only intervene directly if there is an immediate risk. You will need to use your communication skills to ensure that you handle the situation in a way that does not make things worse and will ensure that you protect the person at risk.
- If there is not an immediate risk, you should report the incident and get assistance as soon as possible.
- If you do have to intervene in an abusive situation, you will need to behave assertively. Do not shout, panic or get into an argument. State firmly and clearly what you want to happen – 'Mary, stop hitting Enid now!' You can deal with the

consequences a little later, but the key action is to stop the abuse – 'Lee, stop calling Mike those names and move away from him now!' There must be no mistake about what has to happen. This is not the time to discuss it, this is the time to stop it – the discussion comes later.

- If you have witnessed, or intervened in, an act of abuse which may constitute a criminal offence, you must *not* remove any possible evidence until the police have examined the scene.

Rules for dealing with abusive behaviour
1 Avoid it if possible.
2 Try to get people talking.
3 Keep calm. Be clear.
4 Be assertive, never aggressive.

Check it out

Think of a situation where you have had to act to stop abuse or likely abuse. Make a note of how you handled it. Could you have dealt with it in a better way? What else could you have done? Would it have turned out differently? If you have never had to act in such a situation, ask an experienced colleague to tell you about an incident he or she has had to deal with.

Then answer the same questions, based on what your colleague has told you. Remember – your colleague may not want to hear the answers you come up with!

Once the immediate risk has been averted, you must then report the incident to your manager, and the correct procedures for dealing with abuse must be followed. You are not in a position to take a decision about what is and what is not serious enough to be followed up. That is a decision which will be taken after discussion with the agencies involved.

Where there are injuries, or the possibility of physical evidence, as in sexual abuse, then a medical examination must be carried out. If an adult has been abused, he or she must consent to an examination before one can be carried out. In the case of a child, the parents must consent, unless they are the suspected abusers.

Recording an incident

It is also important that you write a report of the incident as soon as possible. You may think that you will never forget what you saw or heard, but details do become blurred with time and repetition. Your workplace may have a special form or you may have to write a report. If there is a reason why writing a report is not possible, then you should record your evidence on audio tape. It is not acceptable practice to pass on the information verbally – there must be a record which can be referred to. Your evidence may be needed by the social workers and police officers who will investigate the situation. It may be useful for a doctor who will conduct an examination, or it may be needed for the case conference or for court proceedings.

Check it out

Think about the children's game of Chinese Whispers. The players sit in a circle and a message is whispered from one person to the next around the circle. The last player speaks the message aloud. It has usually changed quite a lot as it has been passed around the circle!

So it is easy to see how verbal information can become distorted, or messages lose their emphasis, as they are retold. Always make sure you record information as soon as you can.

When risk situations occur in the community, you may be in a position to intervene directly or to report to your supervisor and offer suggestions about ways to reduce risks.

No one can guarantee to prevent abuse from happening – human beings have always abused each other in one form or another. However, using the information you have about possible abusive situations, you are now able to work towards preventing abuse by recognising where it can happen.

Try to ensure that people in potentially abusive situations are offered as much support as possible. A carer, whether of a child or an adult, is less likely to resort to abuse if he or she feels supported, acknowledged and appreciated. Showing caring and understanding of a person's situation can often defuse potential explosions. A care worker could express this by saying, 'It must be so hard caring for your mother. The demands she makes are so difficult. I think you are doing a wonderful job.' Such comments can often help a carer to feel that he or she does have someone who understands and has some interest in supporting him or her. So many times the focus is on the individual in need of care and the carer is ignored.

DID YOU KNOW?

There is a saying that 'The best way to keep on caring *about* someone is not to have to care *for* them'. There are many thousands of carers looking after relatives who would testify to the truth of that saying.

Some situations require much more than words of support, and giving practical, physical support to a carer or family may help to reduce the risk of abuse. The extra support provided by a professional carer can do this in two ways: firstly, it can provide the additional help which allows the carer to feel that he or she is not in a hopeless never-ending situation; and secondly, it can provide a regular opportunity to check an individual where abuse is suspected or considered to be a major risk.

There is now legislation protecting carers, and their situation is acknowledged as being very stressful and demanding. The Carers (Recognition and Services) Act 1995 means that carers have the right to ask for an assessment of their own needs. The national strategy for carers, 'Caring about Carers' (1999), identifies funding for support, information and consultation for carers. All of this can contribute to easing the burden on carers, and thus reducing the chances of abuse.

When resources are provided within the community rather than at home, this also offers a chance to observe someone who is thought to be at risk. Day centres, training centres, schools, after-school clubs and youth centres also provide an opportunity for people to talk to staff and to feel that they are in a supportive environment where they can talk about any abuse they have suffered and they will be believed and helped.

REMEMBER

- Preventing abuse is better than dealing with it.
- Support may make all the difference to a carer under stress.
- Only intervene directly if there is an immediate risk.
- Act assertively to stop any abusive behaviour.

TEST YOURSELF

1 If you had a situation where one service user was hitting another, would you:

    a physically pull them apart whilst shouting at them to stop?

    b go for help?

    c move as close as you safely could and repeat loudly 'stop now'?

2 Why is it important to recognise the work done by a carer?

3 If you consider an abusive incident to be minor and unimportant, what should you do?

The effects of abuse on all those concerned

Abuse devastates those who suffer it. It causes people to lose their self-esteem and their confidence. Many adults and children become withdrawn and difficult to communicate with. Anger is a common emotion amongst people who have been abused. It may be directed against the abuser, or at those people around them who failed to recognise the abuse and stop it happening.

One of the greatest tragedies is when people who have been abused turn their anger against themselves and blame themselves for everything which has happened to them. These are situations which require expert help, and this should be available to anyone who has been abused, regardless of the circumstances.

In an earlier section of this chapter you learned about the indications of abuse. Some of the behaviour changes which can be signs of abuse can be almost permanent, or certainly very long-lasting. There are very few survivors of abuse whose personality remains unchanged, and for those who do conquer the effects of abuse, it is a long, hard fight.

The abuser, often called the 'perpetrator', also requires expert help, and this should be available through various agencies depending on the type and seriousness of the abuse. People who abuse, whether their victims are children or vulnerable adults, receive very little sympathy or understanding from society. There is no public recognition that some abusers may have been under tremendous strain and pressure, and abusers may find that they have no support from friends or family. Many abusers will face the consequences of their actions alone.

> ## DID YOU KNOW?
> Prisoners who are serving sentences for child abuse, or for abuse of vulnerable adults, have to be kept in separate areas of the prison for their own safety. If they were allowed to mix with other prisoners, they could be seriously assaulted or even killed.

Care workers who have to deal with abusive situations react in different ways. There is no 'right way' to react. Everyone is different and will deal with things in his or her own way. If you have to deal with abuse, these are some of the ways you may feel, and some steps you can take which may help.

- You may feel quite traumatised by the abusive incident. It is quite normal to find that you cannot get the incident off your mind, that you have difficulty concentrating on other things, or that you keep having 'flashbacks' and re-enact the situation in your head. You may also feel that you need to keep talking about what happened.
- Talking can be very beneficial, but if you are discussing an incident outside your workplace, you must remember rules of confidentiality and *never* use names. You will find that you can talk about the circumstances just as well by referring to 'the boy' or 'the father' or 'the daughter'. This way of talking does become second nature, and is useful because it allows you to tell others about things which have happened at work whilst maintaining confidentiality.
- These feelings are likely to last for a fairly short time, and are a natural reaction to shock and trauma. If at any time you feel that you are having difficulty, you must talk to your manager or supervisor, who should be able to help.
- Alternatively, the situation may have made you feel very angry, and you may have an overwhelming urge to inflict some serious damage on the perpetrator of the abuse. Whilst this is understandable, it is not professional and you will have to find other ways of dealing with your anger. Again, your supervisor or manager should help you to work through your feelings.
- Everyone has different ways of dealing with anger, such as taking physical exercise, doing housework, punching a cushion, writing feelings down and then tearing the paper up, crying or telling your best friend. Whatever you do with your anger in ordinary situations, you should do the same in this situation (just remember to respect confidentiality if you need to tell your best friend – miss out the names). It is perfectly legitimate to be angry, but you cannot bring this anger into the professional relationship.
- The situation may have made you distressed, and you may want to go home and have a good cry, or give your own children or elderly relatives an extra hug. This is a perfectly normal reaction. No matter how many years you work, or how many times it happens, you may still feel the same way.
- Some workplaces will have arrangements in place where workers are able to share difficult situations and get support from each other. Others may not have any formal

meetings or groups arranged, but colleagues will offer each other support and advice in an informal way. You may find that work colleagues who have had similar experiences are the best people with whom to share this type of experience.

- There is, of course, the possibility that the situation may have brought back many painful memories for you of abuse you have suffered in your own past. This is often the most difficult situation to deal with, because you may feel as if you should be able to help because you know how it feels, but your own experience has left you without any room to deal with the feelings of others. There are many avenues of support now available to survivors of abuse. You can find out about the nearest support confidentially, if you do not want your workplace colleagues or supervisor to know.

- There is no doubt that dealing with abuse is one of the most stressful aspects of working in care. There is nothing odd or abnormal about feeling that you need to share what you have experienced and looking for support from others. This is a perfectly reasonable reaction and, in fact, most experienced managers would be far more concerned about a worker involved in dealing with abuse who appears quite unaffected by it, than about one who comes looking for guidance and reassurance.

REMEMBER

- Feeling upset is normal.

- Talk about the incident if that helps.

- Being angry is OK, but deal with it sensibly – take physical exercise, do the housework, cry.

- Do not be unprofessional with the abuser.

- If you are a survivor of abuse and you find it hard to deal with, ask for help.

TEST YOURSELF

1   What effects might abuse have on a child?

2   If you knew that an older person who had been abused was to be admitted to your care home, what sort of behaviour might you expect?

3   What reactions would you expect to see in a care worker who had dealt with an abusive situation?

4   What steps would you take to deal with your feelings following dealing with abuse?

Element Z1.3 | # Contribute to monitoring individuals who are at risk from abuse

What you need to learn

- How to share information
- Ways of assessing risk
- What to do if you suspect abuse in your own workplace

How to share information

Sharing information between different agencies and organisations can often be a vital way of ensuring that people at risk are protected.

There are often several care and other professionals involved with any child or adult considered to be at risk. One of the most important features of work with people at risk is co-operation between agencies.

Teamwork is vital, both with other involved professional care workers and within your own team. Information is always clearer and more comprehensive when it is shared, and you may find that different members of the team have observed slightly different aspects and so the picture will become more complete.

It may also be possible that people will have different views on any allegations or incidents which have taken place. It is important that all these views are taken into account. Some of the professionals involved may be working with the person alleged to be the abuser and they may have a different perspective to add to any discussions. Remember that there is always more than one story to be told, even though it may not always be easy to take account of the alleged abuser's perspective.

> **DID YOU KNOW?**
> Every report (called Fatal Case Inquiry) into child deaths from abuse in the past 30 years has highlighted the need for agencies to co-operate, work together and share information.

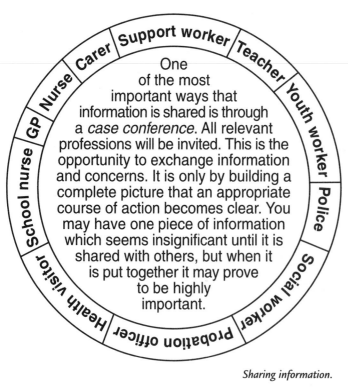

One of the most important ways that information is shared is through a *case conference*. All relevant professions will be invited. This is the opportunity to exchange information and concerns. It is only by building a complete picture that an appropriate course of action becomes clear. You may have one piece of information which seems insignificant until it is shared with others, but when it is put together it may prove to be highly important.

Sharing information.

Each local area has an Area Child Protection Committee (ACPC), which includes representatives of all relevant professionals: social workers, health professionals, teachers, police, and so on. The ACPC meets to lay down procedures which must be followed where child abuse is suspected or confirmed. It also ensures that a register of children who have been abused, or are at risk of abuse, is maintained by the social services department.

The Child Protection Register is a record of all the children about whom there are concerns. The register is held and maintained by social services, but the information can be shared with other relevant professionals. There are four main categories in the register: physical abuse, sexual abuse, neglect and emotional abuse.

Although there is no legal requirement for such a register for vulnerable adults, local authorities could make this part of the policy guidelines they develop as a result of the 'No Secrets' guidelines.

DID YOU KNOW?

Anyone, including a child, who has been abused by someone who has been tried in court and found guilty, can receive Criminal Injuries compensation. It is also possible for cases to be brought even where there is no criminal trial. It is vital that anyone who has been abused in any way should have a solicitor to act in his or her interests.

Ways of assessing risk

Decisions about abuse of adults are different from those about children because, ultimately, it is the adult himself or herself who will make the decision about how to proceed. Clearly there are some situations where this is not possible, but such circumstances are provided for under the law. If an adult has been abused, but he or she decides to remain in the abusive situation, then there are generally no legal steps which can be taken to prevent that.

CASE STUDY

Mrs C is 75 years old. She is quite fit, although increasingly her arthritis is slowing her down and making her less steady on her feet. She has been a widow for fifteen years and lives with her only son, R, who is 51. When R was 29, he was involved in a motorcycle accident which caused brain damage, from which he has never fully recovered. His speech is slow and he sometimes has problems in communication. His co-ordination and fine motor skills have been affected, so he has problems with buttons, shoelaces and writing. R also suffers from major mood swings and can be aggressive. Mrs C is R's only carer. He has never worked since the accident, but he goes to a day centre three days each week. Mrs C takes the opportunity to go to a day centre herself on those three days because she enjoys the company, the outings and activities.

Recently, Mrs C has had an increasing number of injuries. In the past two months she has had a grazed forehead, a black eye, a split lip and last week she arrived at the day centre with a bruised and sprained wrist. She finally admitted to the centre staff that R had inflicted the injuries during his periods of bad temper. She said that these were becoming more frequent as he became more frustrated with her slowness.

Despite being very distressed, Mrs C would not agree to being separated from R. She was adamant that he didn't mean to hurt her. She would not consider making a complaint to the police. Finally, Mrs C agreed to increasing both her and R's attendance at their day centres, and to having some assistance with daily living.

1   What do you think Mrs C should have done?
2   Can she be left with R?
3   Why do you think Mrs C will not take any action against R?

TEST YOURSELF

You have been appointed as care assistant to Mrs C and R. The work involves daily visits to their house for one hour to help them with household tasks and to monitor their welfare. One day you arrive to find R screaming at Mrs C and hitting her.

1 What would your immediate actions be?

2 Write a report covering the incident, including your actions.

3 Who would you give your report to?

4 Who else would need to be informed of this incident?

If you are unsure of any of these points, discuss them with your supervisor.

This kind of situation may cause a great deal of concern and anxiety for the care workers, but there are limits on the legal powers to intervene and there is no justification for removing Mrs C's right to make her own decisions.

Care workers faced with an abusive situation which cannot be resolved must assess the risks and work out ways of minimising the likelihood of further abuse. A 'risk assessment' will be carried out. Your workplace will have procedures about the way in which a risk assessment is carried out and how decisions are made. Many workplaces will have a system where decisions about level of risk are taken by a case conference. In others, decisions may be made by a team manager, who would need to be in possession of all the available facts. At no time would any worker be expected to make such judgements and decisions alone, or to accept full responsibility for this type of assessment.

DID YOU KNOW?

This type of shared responsibility and decision-making has only developed over the past 30 years or so in the case of children, and far more recently in the case of adults. Prior to that, workers were often left to make decisions without any support, and took the full weight of blame if things went wrong.

A risk assessment will consider all the elements in a situation and try to reach a judgement about potential dangers and what can be done. Clearly, the options are far more limited in respect of adults, because there is no overall legislation offering protection. It is also very rarely possible to act against the will of an adult, even where it may be in his or her best interests.

What to do if you suspect abuse in your own workplace

Blowing the whistle

One of the most difficult situations to deal with is when you believe that abuse is happening in your workplace. It is often hard to accept that the people you work with would abuse, but if you have evidence or good grounds for concern, then you will have to take action.

- The first step is to report the abuse to your manager.
- If you suspect that your manager is involved, or will not take action, you must refer it to the most senior manager who is likely to be impartial.
- If you do not believe that it is possible to report the abuse to anyone within your workplace, you should contact social services (or the NSPCC, if you prefer, for children).
- If you work for the NSPCC, social services or the health service and you are concerned about abuse, you should still follow the same steps, although you may need to contact a senior manager who is not directly involved with your workplace.

If you do not believe that there is anyone within your workplace or organisation who would take action on any concerns, or if you have reported concerns and nothing has been done, you should contact the National Care Standards Commission, which is responsible for registering and inspecting all health and care services. The Commission will investigate your concerns.

REMEMBER

- Consider all possibilities when there are any suspicions about the care of a vulnerable person.
- Abuse may be the last thing you would expect in a particular situation.
- Think the unthinkable – *listen* and *believe*.
- That does not just mean listening to what you are told: *listen* to what you see and *believe* what you feel.

Keys to good practice

✓ Always listen to and believe those who tell you they have been abused.
✓ Be prepared to accept the possibility of abuse where you don't expect it.
✓ Know the procedures and follow them strictly.
✓ Never underestimate the importance of sharing information.
✓ Protecting the vulnerable is your first priority.
✓ Never allow abusive behaviour to go unchallenged.
✓ Remember that people who disclose abuse want it to stop.
✓ You could make the difference – always be aware of the possibility of abuse.
✓ Do not try to deal with abuse alone.
✓ Use the support available for those who work with abusive situations.

The last word

Much of this chapter may sound as though the field of dealing with abuse is full of rules and procedures. It is – and for very good reasons. Abuse is very serious – it is potentially life-threatening. Systems and rules have been developed by learning from the tragedies that have happened in the past. Many of these tragedies occurred because procedures were either not in place, or were not followed. You must make sure that you know what the procedure is in your workplace and follow it to the letter.

Z1 UNIT TEST

1   Name three factors which may make you think that someone was being abused.

2   What are the different types of abuse which can occur?

3   What should you do if you suspect abuse in your workplace?

4   Are there different factors to consider when dealing with abuse of adults or children? If so, what are they?

5   Which is the only service user group with a legal right to protection from abuse?

6   Why is it important to record any evidence about abuse?

7   Who can take decisions in respect of adults who have been abused?

8   Which professional care workers would you expect to see at a case conference about:

   a   a child?
   b   a 25-year-old person with a disability?
   c   a 58-year-old woman with mental health problems?
   d   a 79-year-old man from a residential home?

9   What are the two key things to do when someone discloses that he or she has been abused?

Promote communication with individuals where there are communication differences

Unit CL2

Communicating in straightforward circumstances is dealt with in Chapter 2 (Unit CL1). This unit deals with communication where there are differences between the worker and an individual which can cause problems. It is likely that this chapter will provide useful knowledge for Unit CL5 from Option Group B.

It is important that you, as a health or care worker, understand how to communicate with people even though the differences may make that quite difficult. Communication is not just about talking to people when it is easy, it is also about managing to make contact with those people for whom it is much harder.

There are many ways in which you can help to make communication more effective, not just by talking, but by the actions that you take in making the environment better for communication or by making sure that communication is handled appropriately for the particular individual and that proper records are kept on the best way of communicating with each individual for whom you provide care.

It is important that you understand how to communicate with the people in your care.

Element CL2.1 Determine the nature and scope of communication differences

What you need to learn

- What communication differences are and their effects
- How to find out about likely communication problems
- How to record information

What communication differences are and their effects

Communication differences

Communication differences include:

- people speaking different languages
- either the worker or the individual having a sensory impairment
- distress, where somebody is so upset that he or she is unable to communicate
- a physical illness or disability, such as a stroke or confusion
- cultural differences.

Language

Where an individual speaks a different language from those who are providing care, it can be an isolating and frustrating experience. The individual may become distressed and frightened as it is very difficult to establish exactly what is happening and he or she is not in a position to ask or to have any questions answered. The person will feel excluded from anything happening in the care setting and will find making relationships with carers extremely difficult. There is the possibility that confusion and misunderstanding will occur.

Hearing loss

A loss or reduction of ability to hear clearly can cause major differences in the ability to communicate.

Communication is a two-way process, and it is very difficult for somebody who does not hear sounds at all or hears them in a blurred and indistinct way to be able to respond and to join in. The result can be that people become withdrawn and feel very isolated and excluded from others around them. This can lead to frustration and anger. People may present some quite challenging behaviour.

Profound deafness is not as common as partial hearing loss. People are most likely to suffer from loss of hearing of certain sounds at certain volumes or at certain pitches, such as high sounds or low sounds. It is also very common for people to find it difficult to hear if there is background noise – many sounds may jumble together, making it very hard to pick out the voice of one person. Hearing loss can also have an effect on speech, particularly for those who are profoundly deaf and are unable to hear their own voices as they speak. This can make communication doubly difficult.

Visual impairment

Visual impairment causes many communication difficulties. Not only is an individual unable to pick up the visual signals which are being given out by someone who is speaking, but, because he or she is unaware of these signals, the person may also fail to give appropriate signals in communication. This lack of non-verbal communication and lack of ability to receive and interpret non-verbal communication can lead to misunderstandings about somebody's attitudes and behaviour. It means that a person's communications can easily be misinterpreted, or it could be thought that he or she is behaving in a way that is not appropriate.

Physical disability

Depending on the disability, this can have various effects. People who have suffered strokes, for example, will often have communication difficulties, not only in forming words and speaking, but they often also suffer from aphasia (or dysphasia), which is the inability to understand and to express meaning through words. They lose the ability to find the right words for something they want to say, or to understand the meanings of words said to them. This condition is very distressing for the individual and for those who are trying to communicate. Often this is coupled with a loss of movement and a difficulty in using facial muscles to form words.

In some cases, the communication difficulty is a symptom of a disability. For example, many people with cerebral palsy and motor neurone disease have difficulty in controlling the muscles that affect voice production, and so speaking in a way which can be readily understood becomes very difficult. Other disabilities may have no effect at all upon voice production or the thought processes that produce spoken words, but the lack of other body movements may mean that non-verbal communication may be difficult or not what you would expect.

Learning disabilities

These may, dependent upon their severity, cause differences in communication in terms of the level of understanding of the individual and his or her ability to respond appropriately to any form of communication. This will vary depending on the degree of learning disability of the individual, but broadly the effect of learning disabilities is to limit the ability of an individual to understand and process information given to him or her. It is also likely that individuals will have a short attention span, so this may mean that communications have to be repeated several times in an appropriate form.

Dementia/confusion

This difficult and distressing condition is most prevalent in older people and people who suffer from Alzheimer's disease. The confusion can result ultimately in the loss of the ability to communicate, but in the early stages it involves short-term memory loss to the extent of being unable to remember the essential parts of a conversation or a recent exchange. It can necessitate the constant repetition of any form of communication.

Cultural differences

People's communication differences can result from differences in culture and background. Culture is about more than language – it is about the way that people live, think and relate to each other. In some cultures, for example, children are not allowed to speak in the presence of certain adults. Other cultures do not allow women to speak to men they do not know.

Some people may have been brought up in a background or in a period of time when challenging authority by asking questions was not acceptable. Such people may find it very hard to ask questions of doctors or other health professionals and are unlikely to feel able to raise any queries about how their care or treatment should be carried out.

Check it out

Try renting a video in a language other than your own, or watch a subtitled film on TV, covering the lower half of the TV screen where the subtitles are. Try to make sense of what is shown in the film. Note how difficult it is to understand what is happening and how frustrating it is. Notice how quickly you lose interest and decide that you will not bother to watch any more. Imagine how that feels if you are ill or in need of care, and everyone around you is speaking in a language you do not understand.

General effects of communication differences

The most common effect of communication differences is for the person receiving care to feel frustrated and isolated. It is an important part of your job to do everything in your power to reduce the effect of communication differences and to try to lessen the feelings of isolation and frustration that people experience.

CASE STUDY

Mrs C is 75 years old. She is Chinese and lives with her son and daughter-in-law in England. She has lived in England for over 30 years, but speaks no English and very rarely goes out apart from shopping within the local Chinese community. Mrs C has now developed a potentially life-threatening, but operable, bowel cancer. She is to have a series of tests which will be followed by surgery, a likely colostomy and radiotherapy. Her son is able to translate during the visits to the hospital, but he will not be able to remain with her during the entire time of her hospital stay.

1   How do you think Mrs C will be feeling?
2   If you were looking after her in hospital, what would be your first step to communicating with her?
3   What are the issues for her in having her son translate in these circumstances?
4   How could her condition be affected by poor communication?

How to find out about likely communication problems

You can discover likely communication problems by simply observing an individual. You can find out a great deal about how a person communicates and what the differences are between his or her way of communicating and your own.

Observation should be able to establish:

● which language is being used
● if the service user experiences any hearing difficulties or visual impairment

- if there is any physical illness or disability
- if there is a learning disability.

Any of these factors could have a bearing on how well a person will be able to communicate with you, and what steps you may need to take to make things easier. Observation will give you some very good clues to start with, but there are other useful sources of information for establishing exactly what a particular individual needs to assist communication. You may consider:

- asking the individual where this is possible – he or she is likely to be your best source of information
- discussing with colleagues who have worked with the individual before and who are likely to have some background information and advice
- consulting other professionals who have worked with the individual and may have knowledge of means of communication which have been effective for them
- reading previous case notes or case histories
- finding out as much as you can about an individual's particular illness or disability, where you have been able to establish this – the most useful sources of information are likely to be the specialist agencies for the particular condition
- talking to family or friends. They are likely to have a great deal of information about what the differences in communication are for the individual. They will have developed ways of dealing with communication, possibly over a long period of time, and are likely to be a very useful source of advice and help.

How to record information

There would be little point in finding out about effective means of communication with someone and then not making an accurate record so that other people can also communicate with that person.

You should find out your employer's policy on where such information is to be recorded – it is likely to be in the service user's case notes.

Be sure that you record:

- the nature of the communication differences
- how they show themselves
- ways which you have found to be effective in overcoming the differences.

Information recorded in notes may look like this:

Mr P has communication difficulties following his stroke. He is aphasic, with left side haemaplaegia. Speech is slurred but possible to understand with care. Most effective approaches are:

a) allow maximum time for communication responses
b) modify delivery if necessary in order to allow understanding
c) speak slowly, with short sentences
d) give only one piece of information at a time
e) physical reassurance (holding and stroking hand) seems to help while waiting for a response
f) can use flashcards on bad days (ensure they are placed on the right-hand side)
g) check Mr P has understood the conversation.

Keys to good practice

✓ Check what the differences in communication are.
✓ Remember they can be cultural as well as physical.
✓ Examine the effects of the communication differences for a particular individual.
✓ Use all possible sources to obtain information.

TEST YOURSELF

1   What would you expect to be the effects of partial hearing loss on someone's style of communication?

2   What sort of steps could you take to improve communication with someone following a stroke? List three.

3   What would you expect to be the cultural differences between an 80-year-old woman brought up in an industrial town and the 25-year-old son of an Indian consultant cardiac surgeon, who is working as a care assistant in the care home she lives in?

4   What is one of the most important ways of communicating with someone who speaks a different language?

5   An inability to communicate will not affect the rate of recovery or standard of physical care. True or false?

Element CL2.2 | # Contribute to effective communication where there are communication differences

What you need to learn

● How to communicate appropriately
● How to respond to communication and check understanding

How to communicate appropriately

Overcoming language differences in communication

Where you are in the position of providing care for someone who speaks a different language from you, it is clear that you will need the services of an interpreter for any serious discussions or communication.

● Your work setting is likely to have a contact list of interpreters.
● Social services departments and the police have lists of interpreters.
● The embassy or consulate for the appropriate country will also have a list of qualified interpreters.

You should always use professional interpreters wherever possible. It may be very tempting to use other members of the family – very often children have excellent language skills – but it is inappropriate in most care settings. This is because:

- their English and their ability to interpret may not be at the same standard as a professional interpreter and misunderstandings can easily occur
- you may wish to discuss matters which are not be appropriate to be discussed with children, or the individual may not want members of his or her family involved in very personal discussions about health or care issues.

It is unlikely that you would be able to have a full-time interpreter available throughout somebody's period of care, so it is necessary to consider alternatives for encouraging everyday communication.

Be prepared to learn words in the individual's language which will help communication. You could try to give the person some words in your language if he or she is willing and able to learn them.

There are other simple techniques that you may wish to try which can help basic levels of communication. For example, you could use flashcards and signals, similar to those which you would use for a person who has suffered a stroke. This gives the person the opportunity to show a flashcard to indicate his or her needs. You can also use them to find out what kind of assistance may be needed.

Some of the flashcards you may use.

The suggestions shown above are not exhaustive and you will come up with many which are appropriate for the individual and for your particular care setting. They are a helpful way of assisting with simple communication and allowing people to express their immediate physical needs.

The most effective way of communication with a person who speaks a different language is through non-verbal communication. A smile and a friendly face are understood in all languages, as are a concerned facial expression and a warm and welcoming body position.

However, be careful about the use of gestures – gestures which are acceptable in one culture may not be acceptable in all. For example, an extended thumb in this culture would mean 'great, that's fine, OK', but in many cultures it is an extremely offensive gesture. If you are unsure which gestures are acceptable in another culture, make sure that you check before using any which may be misinterpreted.

Overcoming hearing difficulties in communication

- Ensure that any means of improving hearing which an individual uses, for example a hearing aid, is working properly and is fitted correctly, that the batteries are fresh and working, that it is clean and that it is doing its job properly in terms of improving the individual's hearing.
- Ensure that you are sitting in a good light, not too far away and that you speak clearly, but do not shout. Shouting simply distorts your face and makes it more difficult for a person with hearing loss to be able to read what you are saying.

Some people will lip read, while others will use a form of sign language for understanding. This may be BSL (British Sign Language) or MAKATON, which uses signs and symbols. They may rely on a combination of lip reading and gestures.

> **REMEMBER**
> If you are able to learn even simple signing or the basic rules of straightforward spoken communication with people who have hearing loss, you will significantly improve the way in which they are able to relate to their care environment.

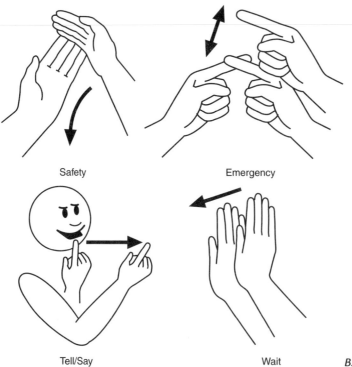

Safety   Emergency

Tell/Say   Wait   *BSL signs*

Other services which are extremely helpful to people who have hearing difficulties are telecommunication services, such as using a minicom or typetalk service. These allow a spoken conversation to be translated in written form using a form of typewriter, and the responses can be passed in the same way by an operator who will relay them to the hearing person. These services have provided a major advance in enabling people who are hard of hearing or profoundly deaf to use telephone equipment. For people who are less severely affected by hearing impairment there are facilities such as raising the volume on telephone receivers to allow them to hear conversations more clearly.

Overcoming visual difficulties in communication

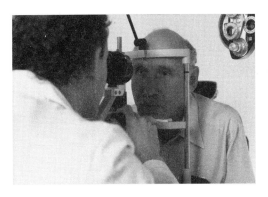

People should have their eyes tested every two years and their prescription should be regularly updated.

One of the commonest ways of assisting people who have visual impairment is to provide them with glasses or contact lenses. You need to be sure that these are clean and that they are the correct prescription. You must make sure that people have their eyes tested every two years and that their prescription is regularly updated. A person whose eyesight and requirements for glasses have changed will obviously have difficulty in picking up many of the non-verbal signals which you will be giving out when you are communicating with him or her.

For people with more serious loss or impairment, you will need to take other steps to ensure that you minimise the differences that will exist in your styles of communication.

Keys to good practice

When communicating with people who have visual impairment:

✓ Do not suddenly begin to speak to someone without first of all letting him or her know that you are there by touching and saying hello.

✓ Make sure that you introduce yourself when you come in to a room. It is easy to forget that someone cannot see. A simple 'hello John, it's Sue' is all that is needed so that you don't 'arrive' unexpectedly.

✓ You may need to use touch more than you would in speaking to a sighted person, because the concerns that you will be expressing through your face and your general body movements will not be seen. So, if you are expressing concern or sympathy, it may be appropriate to touch someone's hand or arm, at the same time that you are saying you are concerned and sympathetic.

✓ Ask the individual what system of communication he or she requires – do not impose your idea of appropriate systems on the person. Most people who are visually impaired know very well what they can and cannot do, and if you ask they will tell you exactly what they need you to do.

✓ Do not decide that you know the best way to help. Never take the arm of somebody who is visually impaired to help him or her to move around. Allow the person to take your arm or shoulder, to ask for guidance and tell you where he or she wishes to go.

Overcoming physical disabilities in communication

Physical disability or illness has to be dealt with according to the nature of the disability or the illness. For example, if you were communicating with somebody who had a stroke you would have to work out ways of coping with his or her dysphasia. This is best dealt with by:

- using very simple, short sentences, speaking slowly and being prepared to wait while the individual processes what you have said and composes a reply
- using gestures – they are helpful in terms of making it easier for people to understand the idea that you are trying to get across
- using very simple, closed questions which only need a 'yes' or 'no' answer. Avoid long, complicated sentences with interrelated ideas. For example, do not say 'It's getting near tea time now, isn't it? How about some tea? Have you thought about what you would like?' Instead say, 'Are you hungry? Would you like fish? Would you like chicken?' and so on, until you have established what sort of meal the individual would prefer
- try drawing or writing or using flash cards to help understanding.

Other illnesses, such as motor neurone disease or cerebral palsy, can also lead to difficulties in speech, although not in comprehension.

- The individual will understand perfectly what you are saying to him or her but the difficulty will be in communicating with you.
- There is no need for you to speak slowly, although you will have to be prepared to allow time for a response owing to the difficulties that the individual will have in producing words.
- You will have to become familiar with the sound of the individual's voice and the way in which he or she communicates. It can be hard to understand people who have illnesses which affect their facial, throat or larynx muscles.

Overcoming learning disabilities in communication

Where people have a learning disability, you will need to adjust your methods of communicating to take account of the level of disability that they experience. You should have gathered sufficient information about the individual to know the level of understanding that he or she has – and how simply and how often you need to explain things and the sorts of communication which are likely to be the most effective.

Many people with a learning disability are able to communicate on a physical level more easily than on a verbal level.

Many people with a learning disability respond well to physical contact and are able to relate and communicate on a physical level more easily than on a verbal level. This will vary between individuals and you should be prepared to use a great deal of physical contact and hugs when communicating with people who have a learning disability.

Overcoming cultural differences in communication

Communication is about much more than words being exchanged between two people – it is influenced by a great many factors. The way in which people have been brought up and the society and culture that they live in has a great effect on the way in which they communicate.

For example, some cultures use gestures or touch much more than others. In some cultures it is acceptable to stand very close to someone, whereas in others people feel extremely uncomfortable if others stand too close. You need to find out about the person's background when you are thinking about how you can make communication work for him or her. To find out the information you need, you could:

● look in the person's records
● speak to a member of the family or a friend, if this is possible
● ask someone else from the same culture, either a colleague or through the country's cultural representatives (contacting their embassy or consulate and asking for the information) – alternatively you could try a local multicultural organisation
● use reference books, if necessary.

It is also important that you communicate with people at the correct intellectual level. Make sure that you communicate with them at a language level which they are likely to understand, but not find patronising. For example, older people and people who have disabilities have every right to be spoken to as adults and not patronised or talked down to. One of the commonest complaints from people with physical disabilities is that people will talk to their carers about them rather than talk to them directly – this is known as the 'does he take sugar' approach.

Hello Jane. How is he today? Is his cold better?

Check it out

Find out the policy in your workplace for checking on people's cultural preferences. Ask who establishes the information about the cultural background of people who use your service, and what the policies are to ensure their needs are met.

How to respond to communication and check understanding

Although it is unacceptable to talk down to people, it is pointless trying to communicate with them by using so much jargon and medical terminology that they don't understand anything you have said. You must be sure that your communication is being understood. The most straightforward way to do this is to ask someone to recap on what you have discussed.

You could say something like: 'Can we just go over this so that we are both sure about what is happening – you tell me what is happening tomorrow', or you can rephrase what you have just said and check with the individual that he or she has understood. For example:

'The bus is coming earlier than usual tomorrow because of the trip. It will be here at eight o'clock instead of nine – is that OK?'

'Yes.'

'So, you're sure that you can be up and ready by eight o'clock to go on the trip?'

Communication through actions

For many people, it is easier to communicate by actions than by words. You will need to make sure that you respond in an appropriate way by recognising the significance of a touch or a sudden movement from somebody who is ill and bedridden, or a gesture from somebody who speaks a different language. A gesture can indicate what his or her needs are and what sort of response the person is looking for from you. You may be faced with a young person with challenging behaviour who throws something at you – this is a means of communication. It may not be a very pleasant one, but nonetheless, it expresses much of the person's hurt, anger and distress. It is important that you recognise this for what it is and respond in the same way you would if that person had been able to express his or her feelings in words.

REMEMBER

If you are planning communication with somebody who has a sensory impairment or who has a learning disability, you will need to take account of this and adjust your communication so that it is at a level he or she is are able to understand and make sense of. The single most important factor in communicating is that you are understood.

Encouraging communication

The best way to ensure that somebody is able to communicate to the best of his or her ability is to make the person feel as comfortable and as relaxed as possible. There are several factors to consider when thinking about how to make people feel confident enough to communicate. They are summarised in the table below.

Ways of encouraging communication

Communication difference	Encouraging actions
Different language	<ul><li>Smile</li><li>Friendly facial expression</li><li>Gestures</li><li>Use pictures</li><li>Warmth and encouragement – repeat their words with a smile to check understanding</li></ul>
Hearing impairment	<ul><li>Speak clearly, listen carefully, respond to what is said to you</li><li>Remove any distractions and other noises</li><li>Make sure any aids to hearing are working</li><li>Use written communication where appropriate</li><li>Use signing where appropriate and understood</li><li>Use properly trained interpreter if high level of skill is required</li></ul>
Visual impairment	<ul><li>Use touch to communicate concern, sympathy and interest</li><li>Use tone of voice rather than facial expressions to communicate mood and response</li><li>Do not rely on non-verbal communication, e.g. facial expression or nodding head</li><li>Ensure that all visual communication is transferred into something which can be heard, either a tape or somebody reading</li></ul>
Confusion or dementia	<ul><li>Repeat information as often as necessary</li><li>Keep re-orientating the conversation if you need to</li><li>Remain patient</li><li>Be very clear and keep conversation short and simple</li><li>Use simple written communication or pictures where they seem to help</li></ul>

Communication difference	Encouraging actions
Physical disability	● Ensure that surroundings are appropriate and accessible ● Allow for difficulties with voice production if necessary ● Do not patronise ● Remember that some body language may not be appropriate
Learning disability	● Judge appropriate level of understanding ● Make sure that you respond at the right level ● Repeat things as often as necessary ● Remain patient and be prepared to keep covering the same ground ● Be prepared to wait and listen carefully to responses

Use signing where it is appropriate and understood.

Check it out

Take some of the ideas from the table on pages 145–6 and discuss them with your supervisor. Ask him or her to give you other ideas and methods which have been found to be effective in your workplace.

Keys to good practice

The single most important thing that you need to remember is that you must tailor your response to the individual, not the condition.

CL2 UNIT TEST

1   What factors would you take into account when judging the best way to communicate with somebody from a different country?

2   What common mistake is made in talking to older people?

3   What do you need to do to encourage somebody with visual impairment to feel confident about communicating?

4   What is the most important purpose of communication?

5   Collect information about different cultures and the gestures which are used in communication.

6   Imagine you have to devise methods of communicating with:

   ● a blind French teenage girl
   ● an older man from Pakistan who is hard of hearing.

   a   What would be the problems you would expect to face?
   b   What are the likely differences in their communication needs?

Giving and receiving accurate information is vitally important for any care setting. The information could be about an individual who is being cared for in your workplace, a relative or friend, or it could be to do with the organisation itself, about or for somebody who works there, or for administrative purposes. The information could come to you in a range of ways:

- verbally, for example, in a conversation either face-to-face or on the telephone
- on paper, for example in a letter, a service user's health record or instructions from a health professional
- electronically, by fax or on a computer.

Whatever the purpose of the information, it is important that you record it accurately. It is also important that you pass on any information correctly, in the right form and to the right person. Recording information is essential in health and care services, because the services that are provided are about *people* rather than objects, so it is vital that information is accurate, accessible and readable. The information that is held in health and care records can seriously affect people's lives. The methods of storage and access to records are also important for the smooth and efficient running of the organisation that carries out the caring. Loss of files or records can cause serious delays in providing a service, can cause people to spend hours of time searching or could, in fact, have very serious consequences if services are provided or procedures carried out without proper records being available.

Element CU5.1 Receive and transmit information

What you need to learn
- Why the accuracy of information is important
- Ways of receiving and passing on information
- Restrictions on information giving
- Choosing the best way to pass on information

Why the accuracy of information is important

All kinds of different information will come into the place where you work. It could be messages for somebody who works there, information about appointments, information for somebody's records, dates of meetings, notices about outcomes of meetings or messages for a resident. The information could be minor or it could be very serious and important. However, it is not always possible to judge the importance of information unless you know all of the circumstances. You may consider a piece of information to be fairly trivial, but unless you know the reason why it is needed you are not in a position to make that decision, so you should pass on information as quickly as you can and make sure it is absolutely accurate. Look at these two examples:

- A message is received from the office supplies wholesaler saying that the computer printer cartridges will not be in until Friday. Failure to pass this on immediately could mean that a vital report for a case conference is written but cannot be printed, so verbal information will have to given at the conference. Lack of information means that a full picture is not available to everyone present, and particularly to those unable to attend. A wrong decision could be made.
- The meat supplier calls to say that the mince ordered for Thursday cannot be delivered until Friday afternoon. Failure to pass this message on could mean the planned menu for Thursday is not changed, so alternative meals have to be provided at very short notice. This could cause great difficulty in providing for some of the special diets and religious requirements, resulting in very disgruntled catering staff and service users!

Check it out

Find out what kinds of information come into your workplace. Make a list of the different types of information under different headings, for example information about service users, information about the organisation, information about supplies, etc.

Keys to good practice

Don't try to judge whether a message is important. Treat all messages as important and pass them on accurately and immediately to the right person.

Ways of receiving and passing on information

Today within health and care there are many ways in which information is circulated between agencies, colleagues, other team members, individuals receiving care, carers, volunteers and so on. The growth of electronic communication has meant a considerable change in the way that people receive and send information, in comparison to only a few years ago where information sharing was limited to either face-to-face meetings, telephone calls or posted letters.

Telephone

One of the commonest means of communication is the telephone. It has advantages because it is instant, straightforward and is a relatively safe and accurate way of communicating and passing on information. However, there are some disadvantages to the telephone in that it can often be difficult to ensure that you have clearly understood what has been said, partly because there can be problems with telephone lines which cause crackling and technical difficulties. It is also possible to misinterpret somebody's meaning when you cannot pick up other signals from them, such as facial expression and body language. If you regularly take or place messages on the telephone, there are some very simple steps that you can take to ensure that you cut down the risk of getting a message wrong.

- Make sure that you check the name of the person who is calling. If necessary, ask the person to spell his or her name and be sure that you have it right. Repeat it to make sure. It is easy to mix up Thomas and Thompson, Williams and Wilkins, and so on. You may also need to take the person's address, and again it is worthwhile asking him or her to spell the details to ensure that you have written them correctly.

- Always ask for a return telephone number so that the person who receives the message can phone back if necessary. There is nothing more infuriating than receiving a message on which you have some queries and no means of contacting the person who has left it for you. You should read back the message itself to the person who is leaving it just to check that you have the correct information and that you have understood his or her meaning.

Incoming post

If it is part of your role to open and check any incoming post, you must make sure that you:

- open it as soon as it arrives
- follow your own workplace procedures for dealing with incoming mail – this is likely to involve stamping it with the date it is received
- pass it on to the appropriate person for it to be dealt with or filed. Check the next section for advice on how to deal with confidential information.

Faxed information

The steps for dealing with an incoming fax message are as follows.

- Take the fax from the machine.
- Read the cover sheet – this will tell you who the fax is for, who it is from (it should include a telephone and fax numbers) and how many pages there should be.
- Check how many pages there should be and make sure that they have all been received. If a fax has misprinted or has pages missing then you should contact the telephone number identified on the cover sheet and ask for the information to be sent again. If there is no telephone number, then send a fax immediately to the sending fax number asking them to resend the fax.

- Follow your organisation's procedure for dealing with incoming faxes. Make sure the fax is handed to the appropriate person as soon as possible.

Check page 153 for information about dealing with confidential information which comes in by fax.

E-mail

E-mail is a very frequently used means of communication within and between workplaces. It is fast, convenient and easy to use for many people. Large reports and complex information which would be cumbersome to post or fax can be transmitted as an attachment to an e-mail in seconds. However, not everyone in all workplaces has access to e-mail and not all electronic transmission is secure. Be aware of this if you are sending highly sensitive and confidential material. If you do send and receive information by e-mail you should:

- follow the guidelines in your workplace for using e-mail and the transmission of confidential material
- open all your e-mails and respond to them promptly
- save any confidential messages or attachments in an appropriate, password-protected file or folder, and delete them from your inbox unless that is also protected
- return promptly any e-mails you have received in error
- not give your password to anyone.

Outgoing mail

If you have to write information to send to another organisation, whether it is by letter or by fax or e-mail, you should be sure that the contents of your letter are clear, cannot be misunderstood and are to the point. Do not write a rambling, long letter which obliges recipients to hunt for the information they need.

It is likely that, within many organisations, you will need to show any faxes or letters to your supervisor or manager before they leave the premises. This safeguard is in place in many workplaces for the good reason that information being sent on behalf of your employer must be accurate and appropriate. As your employer is the person ultimately responsible for any information sent out, he or she will want to have procedures in place to check this.

Restrictions on information giving

Computer-based information

The Data Protection Act 1998 provides the basic principles which govern access to all data held about anyone. This covers many types of records, not just those held on computer. The principles are that data must be:

- fairly and lawfully processed
- processed for limited purposes
- adequate, relevant and not excessive
- accurate
- not kept longer than necessary

- processed in accordance with the data subject's rights
- kept secure
- not transferred to countries without adequate protection.

Individuals are allowed to see their own records, whether they are medical, care records, credit records or any other personal information. The Act, however, restricts the release of any personal information to others without the consent of the individual. You must be very sure that you do not reveal information which your organisation holds about individuals.

REMEMBER

- Access to information held about service users is restricted.
- The person the information is about has a right to see it, but no one else has that right.
- It can only be used for the purpose for which it was obtained, for example to provide care.

See the section 'How to refuse to give information' on page 154.

Keys to good practice

The basic rule when you are asked for information is:

Do not give any information without seeking the consent of the individual concerned, unless you know that the caller has a right to have that information and a need to know it.

Written records

The confidentiality of written records is also extremely important. You will need to make sure that, when you receive information in a written form (perhaps intended for somebody's file or a letter concerning somebody you are caring for), the information is not left where it could be easily read by others.

Do not leave confidential letters or notes lying in a reception area, or on a desk where visitors or other staff members might see it. You should ensure that the information is filed, or handed to the person it is intended for, or that you follow your agency procedure for handling confidential information as it comes in to the organisation.

You may need to stamp information which is confidential with a 'Confidential' stamp so that people handle it correctly.

Do not leave confidential material lying around in public areas.

Telephone

It may be that you will have a telephone request for information, or that you are involved in taking messages over the telephone which concern confidential matters.

- You must be very sure that you do not hand out confidential information over the telephone without first checking the identity of the caller.
- If necessary, ask for a telephone number and agree to ring the caller back. Just because somebody says that he or she is a social worker, or from a doctor's surgery, or from another care organisation, does not necessarily mean that is the case.
- You have a duty to check a person's identity and his or her rights to any information before you hand it out.
- A great deal of information about individuals which ought to be confidential is inadvertently handed out over the telephone to unauthorised people simply because they have claimed to work in a particular setting or claimed to have a right to the information.
- If you are unsure as to how much you should tell someone, take the telephone number and offer to call back, then check with your supervisor.

Faxes

Fax machines have presented a new type of problem in terms of confidentiality of information coming into any work setting. Many agencies and organisations will have a fax machine in a central point. This can often mean that incoming faxes are received in a very public area and can be left lying in the fax tray or can be read by anybody who happens to be standing in the office.

Check it out

Your organisation should have a policy for dealing with incoming faxes. It is important that you check what this policy is and discuss it with your supervisor. Ensure that you follow whatever guidelines are in place for maintaining confidentiality of faxed information.

Organisational information

Obviously, there is some information which callers may ask for which is generally available to the public, such as visiting times, directions to your place of work, and so on.

In most places of work this sort of information is readily available and given to anyone who asks. However, if you worked in a women's refuge, for example, then certainly the address or telephone number would not be given out to anyone who asked for it. So there are always considerations to take into account before passing on information, and you should always check if you are unsure.

Keys to good practice

✓ Always check before giving out any information concerning an individual.
✓ Never leave confidential information in a place where it can be seen.
✓ Make sure that confidential information is marked as such.

The dos and don'ts of dealing with information

Type of information	Do	Don't
Telephone calls incoming	Check the identity of the caller	Give out any information unless you are sure who the caller is
Telephone calls outgoing	Make sure that you are passing on information which the caller is entitled to	Give out details that the individual has not agreed to
Written information	Check that it goes immediately to the person it is intended for	Leave written information lying around where it can be read by anyone
Receiving faxed material	Check your organisation's procedure for dealing with faxed material. Collect it as soon as possible from any central fax point	Leave it in a fax tray where it could be read by unauthorised people
Sending faxed material	Ensure that is clearly marked 'Confidential' and has the name on it of the person to whom it should be given	Fax confidential material without clearly stating that it is confidential and it is only to be given to a named person. If in doubt, do not use a fax to send confidential information
Receiving e-mailed information	Save any confidential attachments or messages promptly into a password-protected file. Acknowledge safe receipt of confidential information	Leave an e-mail open on your screen
Sending e-mailed information	Ensure that you have the right e-mail address for the person who is receiving the information. Clearly mark the e-mail 'Confidential' if it contains personal information. Ask for the recipient to acknowledge receipt	Leave an e-mail open on your screen. Send confidential information to an address without a named mailbox e.g. info@ ...

How to refuse to give information

It can be quite hard to refuse to give information to someone, especially if he or she is insistent. It is also hard if the person is known to you, perhaps as a relative or friend of a service user. If you are placed in this position, try to remember some simple facts:

● The law is on your side.
● You must act in your service user's interests, no matter how much you sympathise with the person asking for information.
● Be polite, but firm – never allow yourself to be bullied.

- If someone becomes rude or aggressive, do not argue – offer to arrange for him or her to speak to a more senior member of staff.
- Try saying something like 'I'm sorry, I'm afraid I can't give you that information. Only [name of service user] can give permission for that information to be passed on.'

Choosing the best way to pass on information

Sometimes the method of communication is dictated by the circumstances. If the situation requires an immediate response, or you need to find essential information urgently, then you are unlikely to sit and write a long letter, walk down to the post office, put it in the post and wait until next week to get a reply! You are far more likely to pick up the telephone and see if you can contact the person that you need to speak to, or send a quick e-mail. Or you may choose to fax your request, or fax information in response to a telephone request from someone else. These methods are fast, almost instant, and relatively reliable for getting information accurately from one place to another.

There may be other occasions when, on the grounds of confidentiality, something is sent through the post marked 'Strictly confidential' and only to be opened by the person whose name is on the envelope. This method may be entirely appropriate for information which is too confidential to be sent by fax and would be inappropriate in a telephone conversation or to be sent by e-mail.

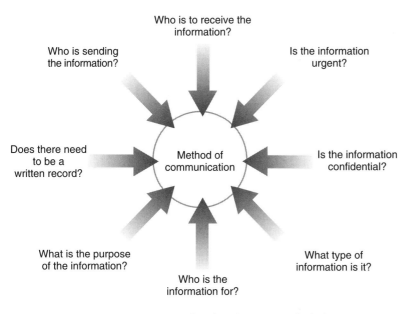

Factors to consider when choosing a method of communication.

You will have to take a number of factors into account when deciding which method to use, as the diagram above shows.

Types of information

The types of information you wish to convey can vary from the simplest day-to-day information to the most complicated and detailed information on somebody's history, background, diagnosis and prognosis.

Simple information

You may simply wish to communicate to a colleague that an individual you are caring for is probably not well enough to go out for a walk today. However, you have agreed with the colleague that you will go in with a cup of tea and see how she is feeling. You do not wish to shout the information in public, thus making the individual the object of general interest, and you have agreed with your colleague that you will check the situation and give her a nod or a shake of the head to let her know. This is a very simple example of the way that information can be sent from one person to another by physical signals, without the need for words.

Two-way exchange

The information that you have to share may be of a kind that requires a conversation with a colleague or relative or the individual himself or herself. The advantage of a verbal exchange of information is that it can be two-way, and you can receive information at the same time as you are sharing what you know.

Written information

Other information is of a nature that requires it to be written down. This could include detailed records on someone, or information that may need to be shared with more than one person and may be for inclusion in a person's health or care records. In this case you would probably choose to write the information and send it by fax, by post or by e-mail.

Making a decision between these three means of communicating written information may be based on:

- availability of fax or e-mail
- the nature and level of confidentiality of the information.

The person receiving the information

One of the factors you must consider when choosing the best method of passing on information is the person who is going to receive it.

- Make sure that the method is appropriate for the person who will receive it.
- Do not send a letter to a person who is visually impaired unless you know he or she has a method of having it read.
- Do not attempt to pass on information by telephone to someone with hearing loss unless you are using an adapted telephone system.
- Use language which is at the right level for the person receiving it.

CASE STUDY

Mr S had been receiving support in his own home for the past two years. His health and mobility had been deteriorating and he had found it increasingly hard to manage even with support. A review had been held at his home where Mr S, his key worker, the occupational therapist and the community nurse had all decided that his needs would best be met by a move into residential accommodation. His home carer had not been able to attend the review, neither had his niece who was a regular visitor. Following the review, Mr S's key worker passed on the following information:

Telephone call to Mr S's niece:

'Hello, Mrs Patel, this is Maria, your uncle's key worker. I promised your uncle I would call to let you know how the review went. Your uncle decided, and we all agreed, that he would be better to move into residential accommodation. He would quite like to go to Maidstone House, but if you and he decide you want to look at any others, I'll be happy to arrange it if you like. Of course, we will send you a copy of the review notes, but I wanted to let you know as soon as possible.'

Telephone call to home carer:

'Hi Sue – Maria. Mr S went for residential, as you hoped. He wants Maidstone House – I'll have to check vacancies, it's always really popular. I think he'd like you to carry on working with him until he goes in – he's very fond of you. I'll keep you up to date with progress.'

E-mail to Maidstone House:

```
Hi Jo

How are you - not caught up since that last training day -
hope things are going well. What's your vacancy position? Can
you let me know ASAP, I've got quite an urgent male admission
if there's any hope??

Speak soon

Maria
```

Letter to GP:

Dear Dr Sida

Re: Mr W. S   27 Miranda Street

Please find attached a copy of the review notes for records of the above gentleman who is a patient of yours. The plan is to arrange his admission to residential care as a matter of urgency. I will advise you of the date for admission.

Please do not hesitate to contact me if I can provide any further information.

Yours sincerely

Maria Perez

Social worker

1 Which different styles of information giving can you identify?
2 Why were the different styles appropriate?
3 Did Maria take the Data Protection Act into account?
4 Would any of these styles have worked if they had been used with a different recipient?

Check it out

Keep a record for a week of the types of information that come into and go out of your workplace. Note the methods used for different types of information. Ask people why they have chosen to pass on information in a particular way.

TEST YOURSELF

1 Describe three different methods of sending and receiving information.

2 What would be an appropriate way of passing on the records of a case conference or case meeting?

3 What are the safeguards that need to be taken about faxed material?

4 What are the steps that you can take to maintain accuracy with telephone information?

5 In what sorts of situation would the verbal exchange of information be appropriate?

Element CU 5.2 Store and retrieve records

What you need to learn
- The purpose of keeping records
- How to record information
- Methods of storing and retrieving records

The purpose of keeping records

In any organisation records are kept for a variety of different purposes. The type of record that you keep is likely to be dictated by the purpose for which it is required. It could be:

- information that is needed for making decisions
- information to provide background knowledge and understanding for another worker
- information about family and contacts of people who are important to an individual
- information to be passed to another professional who is also involved in providing a caring service
- information to be passed from yourself to a colleague over a short space of time to ensure that the care that you provide offers an element of continuity
- information to help in planning and developing services.

The kind of information that you may record to pass on within your own organisation may well be different from the types of record that you would keep if you were going to send that information to another agency or if it was going into somebody else's filing system.

Sally

Mary Johnson

Please could you make sure that you check on Mrs Johnson several times during the next shift. Nothing I can put my finger on, nothing that could go on the handover record, but she just doesn't seem herself. Please keep an eye on her.

See you tomorrow.

Sue

An informal note like the one above is often used to pass on information which is not appropriate for a formal file or record sheet, but it is nevertheless important for a colleague to take note of. This is different from information which has to go outside the organisation – it would need to be formally written, and word processed using a more structured format.

Medical records

One of the very common means of transmitting information and keeping records in health and care is an observation chart recording temperature and blood pressure, like the one on page 160.

This is done in a very simple form on a graph so it is easy to see at a glance if there are any problems. The purpose of this record is simply to monitor a person's physical condition so that everybody who is caring for him or her is able to check on the person's well-being.

If you were to put a written record into someone's case notes or to write a report for another agency or another professional, it is unlikely that you would include the actual charts. It is far more likely that you would include a comment or an interpretation of the information on the charts similar to the one below.

Mrs J has shown no significant abnormalities in terms of raised temperature or blood pressure for the past week. It would seem to indicate her infection has now cleared up and her temperature has returned to normal after the very high levels of ten days ago.

Other types of record

Information which is likely to be used in making decisions about someone is very important. It may concern a child or older person who has been the subject of a protection conference, or a young person who has been in trouble with the law and is the

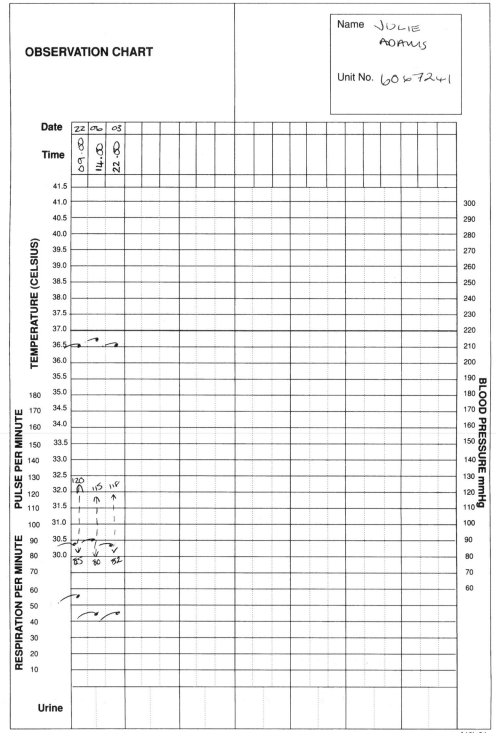

An observation chart.

A10b 94

subject of a report for the courts, or someone with mental health problems where a background report is being provided to assist in decisions about how to best treat him or her.

Where such records are being kept for the purpose of assisting with decision-making, it is important that reports are not written in such a way that people have to read through vast amounts of material before finding the key important points. It may be necessary to include a significant amount of information in order to make sure that all of the background is there, but a summary at the beginning or the end that covers the main points is always useful for a reader in a hurry.

Check it out

Find out how many different types of record are kept in your workplace. There may be reports, charts, notes, index cards... these are just a start. Check how many there are and note what each is used for.

How to record information

If you think about the purpose for which the information is to be used, this should help you to decide on the best way to record it. There would be little point in going to the trouble of typing out a piece of information that you were simply going to pass over to a colleague on the next shift. Alternatively, if you were writing something which was to go into somebody's case notes or case file and be permanently recorded, then you would need to make sure that the information is likely to be of use to colleagues, or others who may need to have access to the file.

Check it out

Find out if your organisation has a policy about record-keeping and about where different types of information should be recorded and kept. Check whether there are clear guidelines on what should be handwritten and information that needs to be word processed.

You must make sure that you follow the guidelines and provide information in the format that your organisation needs. If you are unsure about how you should produce particular kinds of records, ask your supervisor or manager.

Keys to good practice

There are certain golden rules which are likely to be included in any organisation's policy about keeping records and recording information:
- ✓ All information needs to be clear.
- ✓ It needs to be legible (particularly if you are handwriting it) – there is nothing more useless than a piece of information in a record file which cannot be read because somebody's handwriting is poor.
- ✓ It should be to the point, not ramble or contain far more words than necessary.
- ✓ Any record should cover the important points clearly and logically.

There is a great deal more information about how to record things effectively in Chapter 2 (CL1.2).

Methods of storing and retrieving records

Imagine going into a record shop which has thousands of CDs stored in racks but in no recognisable order; they are not filed by the name of the artist, nor by the title of the album. Imagine how much time it would take to trace the particular album that you are looking for. Anything from REM to the Rolling Stones to Mantovani would be all jumbled together! This is exactly what it is like with a filing system – unless there is a system that is easily recognisable and allows people to trace files quickly and accurately, then it is impossible to use.

Records are stored in filing systems. These may be manual or computerised. All organisations will have a filing system, and one of the first jobs you must undertake is to learn how to use it.

> ## ! REMEMBER
> Someone who uses an organisation's filing system incorrectly can soon cause chaos!

Some organisations have people who deal specifically with filing, and they do not allow untrained people to access the files. This is likely to be the case if you work for a large organisation, such as an NHS trust. Smaller agencies are likely to have a general filing system which everybody in the organisation has access to and uses directly. This is exactly the kind of situation where files and records are likely to go missing and to be misplaced.

If you learn to appreciate the importance of records and the different systems that can be used for their storage, then you can assist rather than hinder the process of keeping records up-to-date, in the right place and readily accessible when people need them.

Manual systems

In a manual filing system the types of file used can vary. The most usual type of life is a brown manila folder with a series of documents fastened inside. Other types include ring binders, lever arch files and bound copies of computer printouts.

All of the files have to be organised (indexed) and stored in a way which makes them easily accessible whenever they are required.

Alphabetical system

An alphabetical card index.

If there are not too many files, they can be kept in an alphabetical system in a simple filing cabinet or cupboard. In this sort of system, files are simply placed according to the surname of the person they are about. They are put in the same order as you would see names in a telephone directory, starting with A and working through to the end of the alphabet, with names beginning *Mc* being filed like *Mac* and *St* being filed as *Saint*.

GPs' patient records are usually kept using an alphabetical system.

Numerical systems

Where there are large numbers of files an alphabetical system would not work. Imagine the numbers of M. Johnsons or P. Williams who would appear as patients in a large hospital! In that situation an alphabetical filing system would become impossible to manage, so large organisations give their files numbers, and they are stored in number order. Clearly, a numerical system needs to have an index system so that a person's name can be attached to the appropriate number.

A hospital is likely to give a patient a number which will appear on all relevant documentation so that it is always possible to trace his or her medical notes. However, there still needs to be an overall record to attach that person's name and address to that particular set of case notes, and these days this is normally kept on a central computer.

Other indexing systems

It could be that, instead of files being organised alphabetically, they may be organised according to the different services an agency offers. For example, they could be kept under 'Mental health services', 'Care in the community services', 'Services for children' and so on. Within these categories files would be kept in alphabetical order. In a similar way, files may be organised under geographical areas.

Computerised systems

If your organisation uses a computerised system, there will be very clear procedures which must be followed by everybody who accesses the system. The procedures will vary depending on the system used, but usually involve accessing files through a special programme, which may well have been written either especially for your organisation, or is one which is specifically about record-keeping in health and care.

You are unlikely to be able to delete or alter any information which is in someone's file on a computer. It is possible that you will only be able to add information in very specific places, or it could be that files are 'read only' and you cannot add any information to them. This process, because it will not allow people to change or alter files, does have the advantage that information is likely to remain in a clear format. It is less likely to become lost or damaged in the way that manual files are. After all, it is really not possible to leave a computer system on a bus!

A computerised system enables organisations to keep a great deal more information in much less space. Although they can be expensive initially to install and to set up, the advantages outweigh the disadvantages in the long run. It also means that everybody in the organisation has to learn how to operate the system and how to use the computer – this is a new skill for a great many people! It is, however, a skill worth learning if it enables you to record and use information more accurately and effectively.

Check it out

Find out about the filing system used in your workplace. Check how much information is kept in files, and how much on computer. Find out if the system is alphabetical or numerical, and ask someone who understands it to show you how to use it.

Other types of records

Most organisations maintain electronic records for accounts, suppliers, personnel and all essential business records. There will be a back-up for any electronically held information; this may be a paper system or off-site electronic back-up.

Useful information about advice and support services in the area could be maintained in a resource area or filing system, so that helpful leaflets and information packs are not left in a heap on a shelf or a window sill! An electronic index of useful websites, with links, can be very valuable for service users and their families if they have computer access and are comfortable accessing information in this way.

REMEMBER

Filing systems can work extremely well if they are properly run. They work efficiently and effectively in most organisations as long as a few basic rules are followed by everyone who uses them (see the table below).

Some basic rules about filing

Do	Don't
Leave a note or card (or something similar) when you borrow a file from a manual filing system	Remove an index card from a system
Return files as soon as possible	Keep files lying around after you have finished with them
Enter information clearly and precisely	Alter or move around the contents of a file, or take out or replace documents which are part of somebody's file
Be sure that you access electronic files strictly within your permitted level of access	Make any changes to files unless permitted to do so
Make sure you log in and out correctly	Copy any part of an electronic record system
	Forget to log out

CU5 UNIT TEST

1   Name the two main ways of storing information.

2   What are the main disadvantages of a manual filing system?

3   Name two different ways of indexing files in a manual system.

4   Name two advantages of a computerised filing system.

5   If you were passing information to a colleague on the next shift, would you:

   a   type it?
   b   handwrite it?
   c   ask someone to pass on a message?

6   If you were providing some information for your supervisor who wanted to take it to a conference about one of your service users, would you:

   a   handwrite it?
   b   phone her and tell her about it?
   c   type a report?

7   You have to tell six people that there has been a change in time for a meeting next week – a colleague from a similar workplace to yours, the service user's social worker, the service user's GP, an officer-in-charge from another care home, the service user's mother who is very deaf and the service user's friend who has poor literacy skills.

   a   How you would contact each person?
   b   How would you record your contacts?
   c   Why would you record your contacts?

8   You receive a telephone call from someone who says she is your service user's niece. She asks for details about her aunt's condition and well-being. You have never heard your service user mention a niece, and to your knowledge she has never visited her aunt. How would you deal with this telephone call? Give reasons for your answer.

Unit NC12 Help clients to eat and drink

This unit is about helping service users to choose the food and drink that they want and also, if necessary, helping them to eat and drink it. The unit is only about food and drink consumed by mouth, and does not include learning about types of artificial feeding. You may be working as part of a care team that includes dieticians and occupational therapists, and you may need to know how to use special equipment and keep records of food intake. To achieve this unit you will also need to know about basic food hygiene preparations and the processes involved in handling food hygienically – it is likely that you will participate in a food hygiene course and obtain a basic certificate in food hygiene. You may well find that some of the knowledge that you will need for Unit NC13 will also be obtained by working on this unit.

Eating and drinking is vital to life for everyone, but it is also a social activity and one which provides enjoyment and pleasure. Above all, your aim must be to help people to be independent, to eat and drink with dignity and work to make eating and drinking an enjoyable experience.

Element NC12.1 Help clients to get ready for eating and drinking

What you need to learn

- The importance of food and drink
- Making it possible for people to have choice
- Dietary and hygiene requirements
- How to provide an enjoyable and relaxed environment

The importance of food and drink

Food and drink are basic essentials for human beings to survive. We can survive for far longer without food than it is possible to survive without drinking. Human beings become dehydrated very quickly if they don't take any fluid, whereas it is possible to survive – although not very well – for several weeks without food.

Food is an important part of social events in most cultures and there are often special customs associated with eating. Food is associated with enjoyment and social contact with others. It is usual when celebrating an event with family or friends that a meal or food of some kind is provided as part of the celebrations. Most significant events are marked by sharing a meal with the important people in someone's life. The form and the content of the meal varies from culture to culture, but the providing of food as part of any form of celebration or welcome is fairly universal across cultures.

Food also has an emotional significance. It is seen as part of the process by which babies and children are nurtured and provided with love and care from their parents. This again is common throughout most cultures.

Making it possible for people to have choice

It is important to give people in your care some choice in the food they eat. This will make meal times more enjoyable. Just imagine being unable to prepare food for yourself and having to sit down day after day to eat boring or unappetising or badly cooked food!

Choice should be offered both in the type of food, the way it is cooked and the quantity of food that is provided. It may also be useful, if possible, to vary the times at which food is provided, so that service users can choose the time at which they wish to eat rather than having to fit in with the arrangements of their care setting. You will also need to consider the religious requirements and personal preferences that people have in respect of food. The situations you may come across include the following.

- Vegetarians do not eat meat or meat-based products.
- Vegans are vegetarians who also do not eat dairy products, eggs or any animal-related foods.
- Muslims do not eat pork or meat from carnivorous animals and will only eat meat killed in a particular way (Halal). Alcohol is forbidden.
- Jewish people do not eat pork and do not eat meat and milk together. Meat must have been killed and prepared in a particular way (Kosher).
- Hindus do not eat beef, and many are vegetarian. Alcohol is forbidden.
- Until recently Roman Catholics did not eat meat on a Friday, traditionally eating fish on that day.
- Sikhs do not eat beef and do not drink alcohol.
- Rastafarians are mainly vegetarian, although those who do eat meat cannot eat pork.

Keys to good practice

✓ Ensure that people's religious preferences are discussed with them.
✓ Make sure these preferences are recorded in their plan of care and are observed by everybody who is providing care for them.
✓ The personal likes and dislikes of each individual should be discussed with him or her and recorded.
✓ It should be clear to any new member of the care team that there are particular types of food which a person does not eat or does not like.

It is likely that people's preferences will vary according to their life stage. For example, young children are likely to have quite different tastes from those of adults or older people. A meal of burger, chips and ice cream may be very attractive to a ten-year-old, and to a considerable number of adolescents, but may not be welcomed by an older person.

A typical entry on a care plan may read:

1 WARNING: MRS C HAS NUT ALLERGY – CHECK ALL FOOD FOR NUT TRACES

2 Mrs C is vegetarian. Please make sure that no meat, suet or animal fats are offered. She will eat any food which does not contain meat, and will eat fish. CHECK FOR NUT CONTENT – ALLERGY

3 Likes tea and coffee with hardly any milk

Problems

People may be reluctant, or may even refuse, to eat certain types of food which have been noted in their plan of care as a requirement for their condition – such as a diabetic diet, a weight-reduction diet or a gluten-free diet. This can cause difficulties in terms of being able to offer freedom of choice. You may feel that this places you, and other care staff, in a very difficult position.

If someone is determined to ignore medical advice and to follow a different diet, this should be reported and discussed amongst the care team and the medical staff responsible for the person's care. Ultimately you have little control over a diabetic who buys and eats Mars bars and sweets. However, you do have a responsibility to provide full information and explanations, and to repeat the explanations regularly to the person and to make every effort to persuade him or her to comply with the dietary requirements. If a person chooses, in the full knowledge of the consequences, to ignore medical advice, then that is his or her choice.

REMEMBER
Your responsibility is to inform, explain and advise. You cannot normally force anyone to follow medical advice about diet.

The situation is different, however, for children, people who are compulsorily detained under the Mental Health Act or subject to guardianship, and older people who are very confused or severely demented. All of those situations require a high degree of tact, skill and understanding. It is important that you report immediately any difficulties involving a person's consumption of food and drink.

How food is served

The way in which food is served can often reflect the kind of care setting and can show a great deal about the way in which that setting is run and the way in which the individuals who use the care facility are thought about. The factors which are significant are:

- the presentation of food
- the variety of food which is offered
- the choice of how people sit – at large tables, in small groups or individually, or with a tray on their knee in front of the television
- whether meal times are flexible.

The way in which food is served can reflect the quality of the care setting.

All these are indications of how much choice and individuality are available for service users in a particular setting. Obviously, for people who are living in their own homes these issues are not so relevant, although those who are dependent on others to prepare and serve their meals may share some of the same considerations.

Keys to good practice

✓ Be as flexible as you can be in giving people choice.
✓ Choice is about more than the menu – consider how food is served and the general atmosphere.
✓ Always discuss an individual's wishes and meet them as far as possible.

Check it out

Find out how your workplace copes with special diets and food preferences. Are the procedures the same with diets followed for medical reasons as with those followed for religious or cultural reasons? Is someone who is a vegetarian by choice given the same treatment as someone who is a diabetic? If there appear to be differences ask your supervisor about the reasons.

Dietary and hygiene requirements

All human beings require essential nutrients in order to survive. They are classified into five major groups: proteins, carbohydrates, fats, vitamins and minerals. Human beings also need to consume about 2 litres of liquid each day. The liquid can be water, fruit juice, tea, coffee, soda or any kind of non-alcoholic liquid.

It is important that a healthy diet balances the amounts of different nutrients which are taken each day. Clearly the amounts needed will vary depending on the individual. Some older people will require less food, for example, than an active teenager. Lifestyle and the amount of exercise that is taken must be taken into account when deciding on the overall amounts of food that people will consume, but it is important to get the balance of nutrients right regardless of quantity.

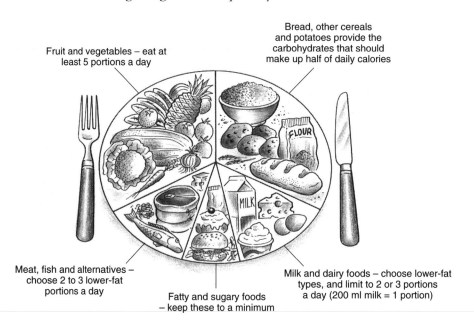

A balanced diet.

Carbohydrates should make up more than 50 per cent of the calories in food eaten each day. Carbohydrates are found in fruits, vegetables, cereals, bread, peas and beans. The remaining 50 per cent should be made up of about 20 per cent of protein, which comes from lean meat, poultry, fish, beans, nuts and dairy products, and the total fat intake should be no higher than 30 per cent of daily calories. A variety of foods is the most likely way to ensure a balanced diet and a good intake of vitamins and minerals.

Proteins, carbohydrates and fats

Nutrient	Where found	Purpose
Proteins	Found in meat, fish, eggs, milk, cheese, nuts, cereals, tofu and beans	Proteins promote growth and are essential for the replacement and renewal of body cells. They are essential for everyone and they must be eaten each day as the body is not able to store protein

Nutrient	Where found	Purpose
Carbohydrates	Found in potatoes and some root vegetables e.g. yams, sweet potato, and in bread, flour, rice, cereals, pasta. Also all products which are sugar-related	Carbohydrates, also known as starches, are used to provide energy and heat by the body. They are essential to provide an energy source for the body, but if they are eaten to excess they will be stored as fat
Fats	Found in butter, margarine, cooking oil, dripping, meat fat, cream, milk, cheese, egg yolks	Fats are a very concentrated source of heat and energy. If they are eaten to excess they will be stored by the body in the adipose layer just beneath the skin

Vitamins and minerals

Nutrient	Where found	Purpose
Vitamin A	Found in liver and fish oils, milk, butter, eggs and cheese and can be made by the body from carotene which is found in carrots, tomatoes and green vegetables	Protects from infection and contributes to growth. A lack of vitamin A can cause eye problems
Vitamin B group (there are several)	Found in cereals, liver, yeast and nuts	This is a large group of complex vitamins, all of which are essential for maintaining a good skin. It may be that a lack of vitamin B is responsible for some diseases of the nervous system
Vitamin C	Found in citrus fruits, strawberries, potatoes and some green vegetables	Vitamin C cannot be stored so it must be taken each day. A lack of vitamin C can cause scurvy, a disease which affects the gums and causes bleeding – an extremely serious condition. People who have a lack of vitamin C are also more likely to be affected by viral infections and coughs and colds
Vitamin D	Found in eggs and fish oils, and made by the body when the skin is exposed to sunlight	Vitamin D enables calcium to be absorbed to strengthen and develop bones and teeth. A severe shortage of vitamin D will lead to rickets, a deforming disease seen in children where bones do not develop adequately
Vitamin E	Found in wheat germ, cereals, egg yolks, liver and milk	This helps prevent cell damage and degeneration
Minerals, e.g. iron, calcium, sodium	A wide range of minerals, essential for health, are found in eggs, cocoa, liver, baked beans, cheese and milk	Iron is important for the formation of red blood cells, and a lack of iron can lead to anaemia. Calcium is used for developing firm bones. Sodium is important for maintaining the fluid balance of the body and an excess of sodium can be a contributory cause of oedema (fluid retention)

Vitamins are essential for maintaining good health and maintaining the human body in good condition. Some vitamins are in certain foods in very small quantities, but they are nonetheless essential, as are minerals which similarly may be found in small quantities. All vitamins and minerals have very specific purposes within the body, as the table on the previous page shows.

TEST YOURSELF

1   Name the three main food groups.

2   What is each food group important for?

3   If you were told that someone had eye problems as a result of a lack of vitamins, which vitamin would he or she be short of?

4   The lack of which vitamin and mineral can cause problems with bones?

5   Why is iron important?

6   Which group of people is often given iron supplements?

DID YOU KNOW?

A calorie is defined as the heat energy needed to raise the temperature of 1 gram of water by 1°C.

Hygiene requirements

If you are preparing areas or equipment for people who are about to eat or drink, it is important that you follow basic hygiene procedures. This will also involve you in knowing how to store and prepare food safely in order that people are able to eat it safely. Ensuring that food is not contaminated by bacteria is a matter which raises many questions, for instance:

Q   What personal precautions do I need to make to ensure that I am hygienic?

A   You must make sure that if you have long hair, it is tied back or covered. You should ensure that your nails are short and clean and that you are not wearing any jewellery in which food could become trapped, such as rings with stones, etc. You must ensure that you wash your hands thoroughly at each stage of food preparation and between handling raw food and cooked food, or raw meat and food which will not be cooked. You must always wash your hands after going to the toilet. Do not touch your nose during food handling or preparation.

Q   What should I do if I have a cut or sore on my hands?

A   You must wear a special blue adhesive plaster dressing. This is because no food is blue, and if the plaster should come off during food preparation it will be easy to locate.

Q   How does food become contaminated?

A   Food is contaminated by bacteria which infect food directly, i.e. food which is not heated or chilled properly, or by cross-contamination, which is where bacteria are spread by somebody preparing food with unclean hands or equipment.

Q   What are the main bacteria that cause contamination of food?

A   Salmonella, campylobacter and e-coli are types of bacteria that can cause serious food poisoning in people who are old, ill or in young children.

Q   How can infection and cross-contamination be avoided?

A   Raw meat is a source of bacteria and you should be sure to use separate utensils and chopping boards or areas for raw food and for cooked food. For example, do not chop the raw chicken breasts and then chop the lettuce for the accompanying salad on the same chopping board or with the same knife. This is sure to give everybody who eats your salad a nasty dose of salmonella. You should keep separate chopping boards for meat and vegetables, and ensure that you use different knives. Remember to change knives and wash your hands between preparing different types of food.

Q   Does it matter whether food is to be cooked or not?

A   It is possible to kill bacteria by cooking food. But be careful with foods which are not cooked, such as salads or mayonnaise, that you are not using contaminated utensils to prepare them.

Q   How hot does food have to be to kill bacteria?

A   A core temperature of 75°C will kill bacteria. Hot food should be heated or re-heated to at least this temperature.

Q   How cold does food have to be to kill bacteria?

A   By law, food should be stored at below 8°C. However, good practice dictates that food is stored below 5°C to be free from any risk of contamination with bacteria. A fridge with the door left open rapidly warms up to above 5°C or 8°C, and food can deteriorate quite quickly and become dangerous. Food in a fridge where the door has been left open or where the power has been cut off should be discarded.

Q   What other safety steps should I take with the fridge?

A   When you arrange food in a fridge, you should be sure that you put any raw meat on the bottom shelf to stop any moisture or blood dripping from the meat onto any of the foods stored below – moisture or blood from uncooked meat could be infected with bacteria. Fridges should be kept scrupulously clean and should be regularly washed out with an anti-bacterial solution. Do not allow particles of food to build up on the inside of the fridge. It is also important that the fridge does not become 'iced up' as this will make the motor work harder in order to keep it cold and could result in a warming of the fridge.

Q   What about 'best before' dates?

A   These are provided by the manufacturers to ensure that food is not kept by retailers beyond a date when it is safe to eat. Many manufacturers now include instructions about how soon the food should be consumed after purchase. These should be followed carefully. As a general rule, unless the manufacturer indicates otherwise, you should consume food by its 'best before' date in order to ensure that it has not begun to deteriorate.

CASE STUDY

Two of the residents, A and P, of an independent living unit for people with a learning disability were about to prepare their evening meal when the support worker arrived for her evening visit.

The two women were about to prepare a ham salad – they took the salad and ham from the bottom of the fridge and noticed that the chicken which they had taken out of the freezer that morning had dripped onto the ham and onto the lettuce.

'We'll need to wash this lettuce and dry off the ham – look, it's all soggy,' said A.

'Absolutely not – you should not eat the ham or the lettuce,' said the support worker.

'Why not?' P asked.

1 Why did the support worker not want the women to eat the food?
2 What mistakes had they made with storing the food?
3 What illness do they risk contracting?
4 What should the support worker do now?

Check it out

What are the rules of hygiene in your workplace? Are they clearly displayed? Do you have the chance to go on a food hygiene course? Look at your own fridge – how hygienic is it? Be honest!

How to provide an enjoyable and relaxed environment

As well as storing and preparing food and making sure that people are being given a balanced and healthy diet, you also need to ensure that the environment is safe and hygienic for service users to eat food. The place where food is consumed in your work setting should be clean and pleasant. Whether your workplace has an arrangement of people sitting together in small groups or around a large table, it is important that that environment is kept scrupulously clean and that it can be used by everyone with or without assistance.

If you are dealing with people who are bedridden, you will need to prop them up into a comfortable position. Special arrangements will have to be made to feed service users who are lying flat. If a person needs to be moved in order to eat his or her meal, you should offer any assistance necessary, but otherwise encourage the person to get to the eating area by himself or herself.

People who need to have protective napkins should be provided with them before the start of the meal. You must take care that you do not patronise service users or treat older people as if they were children by tucking bibs around their necks. Sometimes it is necessary to protect clothing and for comfort and cleanliness to protect a persons' neck and chest if he or she does have some difficulties in eating. It is far better to offer some kind of protection and allow people the dignity and independence of eating by themselves than to feed them simply because they make a mess.

You will need to make sure that people are given the opportunity to wash their hands and go to the toilet before a meal and also to complete any religious ceremonies which may be important to them.

Keys to good practice

✓ Ensure hygiene procedures are observed when preparing food.
✓ Follow safe procedures for storing food.
✓ Make sure that areas for serving food are clean and safe.
✓ Make mealtimes enjoyable.
✓ Treat people with dignity.
✓ Encourage independence as far as possible.

The consuming of food and drink should be an enjoyable and sociable occasion as well as a necessity for life. You can contribute to this by ensuring that you take note of all of your service users' needs and wishes, and offer them pleasant, well-cooked and well-prepared food in an enjoyable and stimulating environment.

TEST YOURSELF

1   Name some ways in which food can be contaminated.

2   What are the basic nutrients that everyone requires?

3   Why are mealtimes an important occasion?

4   How should you arrange a fridge?

5   How would you arrange a dining room in a residential home? Why would you choose this arrangement?

ement NC12.2 Help clients to consume food and drink

What you need to learn
● How to identify when assistance is needed
● How to assist service users to eat and drink

How to identify when assistance is needed

Some service users will experience difficulties in eating and drinking because of their condition, their level of confusion or their level of understanding. There could also be difficulties in someone eating and drinking properly because of environmental or emotional factors, if he or she is unhappy or dislikes the care setting. The vast majority of people that you deal with will be able to feed themselves perfectly well, but some may need a level of assistance which can be provided through special adapted utensils and others may need considerable assistance to make sure they maintain a healthy intake of food and drink.

You may notice that some individuals are apparently experiencing difficulty in eating by themselves. Their problems could cover a wide range:

- They may be unable to raise their arms and hands to their mouths.
- They may be unable to grip a knife and fork.
- They may be unable to cut up their food.
- A visually impaired person may be unable to see the food and to know what he or she is eating.
- There could be problems where somebody is confused and forgets that he or she is in the process of eating and needs to take another mouthful or another drink.
- The problems could be as simple as badly fitting dentures or other dental problems which could be relatively easily resolved.
- Alternatively, the problems could be caused by medication which can mean that people lose their appetite and may need some assistance and encouragement to make sure they eat an adequate and appropriate diet.
- Sometimes people may have problems with swallowing. This can be due to illness or to their condition, and you will need to make special arrangements to ensure that they are able to eat.
- There could be an emotional cause, for example if someone is worried or unhappy and does not feel like eating.
- There could be more serious eating disorders where a service user is having problems in dealing with food.

How to assist service users to eat and drink

The most important thing you need to do is to establish with the individual whether he or she requires your assistance. You should never impose help on a person – it is far better to encourage independence, if necessary through the use of specially adapted utensils, rather than to offer to feed him or her yourself.

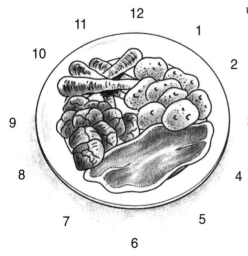

Some people would be perfectly capable of eating by themselves if they were given a minimal amount of assistance, perhaps in the form of specially designed eating and drinking aids such as those shown on page 177.

All of the aids shown opposite are designed to allow people to maintain independence with only minimal assistance from others.

There are also special ways of helping people who have particular needs, for example, a visually-impaired person is often able to feed himself or herself if you can help to prepare the plate of food in advance. If you

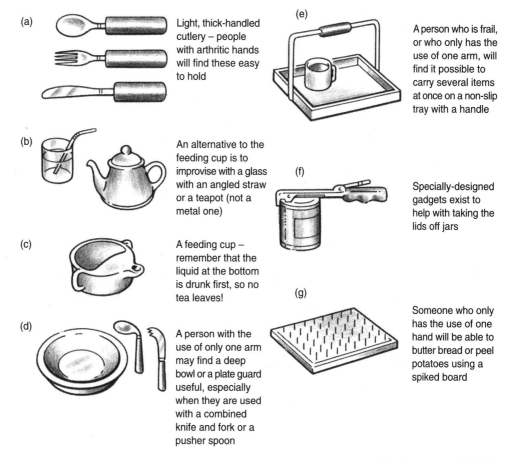

(a) Light, thick-handled cutlery – people with arthritic hands will find these easy to hold

(b) An alternative to the feeding cup is to improvise with a glass with an angled straw or a teapot (not a metal one)

(c) A feeding cup – remember that the liquid at the bottom is drunk first, so no tea leaves!

(d) A person with the use of only one arm may find a deep bowl or a plate guard useful, especially when they are used with a combined knife and fork or a pusher spoon

(e) A person who is frail, or who only has the use of one arm, will find it possible to carry several items at once on a non-slip tray with a handle

(f) Specially-designed gadgets exist to help with taking the lids off jars

(g) Someone who only has the use of one hand will be able to butter bread or peel potatoes using a spiked board

Aids for eating and drinking.

arrange the food in separate portions around the plate and then tell the person, using a clockface as a comparison, that potatoes are at 2 o'clock, meat at 6 o'clock, sprouts at 8 o'clock, and so on, then this is often enough to allow the person to work out what he or she is eating and to enjoy the meal.

If you do need, because of additional requirements, to feed a person who has visual impairment then you should try to avoid expressions like 'open', which could be patronising, to indicate that you are ready with the next mouthful of food. Perhaps a signal like a tap on the hand or 'OK' would be appropriate. You can agree with the person in advance what signal he or she would like you to use.

Dentures

One of the commonest causes of eating problems, particularly for older people, is badly fitting dentures. This can often be a source of difficulty for people eating, partly because it is physically difficult to eat and also because they could be embarrassed by the fact that their dentures do not fit properly and can fall out or become clogged with food. This is a problem that can be resolved very simply by making arrangements for the dentures to be properly fitted, perhaps by the use of denture adhesive.

If people have dental problems, a sore mouth or difficulty swallowing, you may need to provide food which has been liquidised or puréed to make it easier to eat.

If someone is reluctant to eat or drink, you will need to talk with him or her and try to find out the reason for the problem. You will need to establish if it is one of the physical reasons mentioned above or if it is emotional and to do with being unhappy, frightened or worried. If so, you should use your communication and listening skills to try to find out the nature of the concerns and to establish if there is anything you can do to assist. It may be that with some reassurance or some greater involvement in settling in to a new care setting, or with some sympathy and understanding, it may be possible gradually to improve the individual's interest and appetite.

Keys to good practice

When assisting people who cannot eat by themselves, remember the following.
- ✓ Wash your hands.
- ✓ Check that you have everything you will need: the meal, salt and pepper, feeding utensils, etc.
- ✓ If the person is completely unable to eat by himself or herself, you should position him or her comfortably, either propped up or sitting in a chair. The upright position is the easiest to assist digestion of food and so people should be in this position where possible.
- ✓ Ensure that the person is comfortable before you begin the meal. Help him or her to use the toilet or commode if necessary and to wash his or her hands.
- ✓ Offer the chance to see the meal before you begin and ask what he or she would like to start with. For example, he or she might want the potatoes first or the meat, or may not have a particular preference.
- ✓ Establish whether he or she likes to eat food piping hot or whether it should be allowed to cool down.
- ✓ Sit down beside the person, slightly to one side and in front of him or her.
- ✓ Regardless of whether you feed with a fork or a spoon, you should make sure that you leave enough time for each mouthful to be properly chewed and swallowed.
- ✓ Bear in mind that if somebody is ill, he or she may take a considerable amount of time to eat. Make sure that you do not rush and find yourself hovering with the next spoonful before he or she has finished the last one.
- ✓ Make sure that the person takes regular drinks before, during or after the meal.
- ✓ Chat and keep up an interesting conversation throughout the meal, even if the person is unable to respond to you. But beware of the dentist's trick of asking a question that requires an answer just after you have put a spoonful of food into the person's mouth!
- ✓ Help the individual to wash, if necessary, at the end of the meal, or he or she may be happy with just a wipe of the mouth and to rinse the hands.
- ✓ Remember that some people may have religious requirements for particular types of washing and cleaning after food.

This unit does not deal with feeding an unconscious service user. It is vital that you never attempt to give anyone who is unconscious or semi-conscious a drink or anything to eat as the swallowing reflex is lost when a person lapses into unconsciousness. In this situation, feeding will be through a tube, usually passed through the mouth and into the stomach.

Check it out

You will need to do this with a friend or colleague. Sit down and practise being fed. Then swap places and practise feeding. Make a note of how it felt and the things which were difficult. Note the speed at which you were fed. Were you ready for the next mouthful? Was the food the right temperature? Were the right sorts of food put into your mouth together?

Make sure the person you are helping to eat or drink is comfortable.

Check for a bad reaction

Occasionally, you may find that a service user has an allergic reaction to a particular food.

The commonest signs you may see are:

- flushed or swollen face, neck or mouth
- coughing or choking
- vomiting
- sweating and muscle cramps
- rash or other skin reaction.

There may be other, less immediate allergic reactions to food. Clearly, all of these must be reported immediately to your supervisor and medical help must be summoned at once. Be sure that you:

- tell the doctor or paramedic exactly what food has been eaten and how much
- keep any food left over in case it is needed for analysis
- record clearly in the person's notes or case file that they are allergic to the particular food.

TEST YOURSELF

1 What type of drinking utensil could you use for somebody who is unable to drink without assistance? How is it used?

2 What factors would you take into account when judging how much help to offer a service user?

3 List at least five factors you need to consider when you are assisting a service user to eat.

4 What types of special help may people need?

Creating a pleasurable environment

The vast majority of people that you deal with will be able to feed themselves. The best way that you can assist in that is to ensure that both the food and the setting in which it is served are as attractive as possible. Such touches as nice table cloths and attractive crockery, some flowers or pretty napkins, all help to make eating a pleasurable occasion. Also the role of the care worker in prompting good conversation and encouraging people to talk to each other during meal times is invaluable.

The role of the care worker in prompting good conversation at mealtimes is invaluable.

As a care worker you are the person who is in the best position to assess how well someone is eating and drinking. You will notice if he or she is refusing to eat certain types of food or having any difficulties with foods listed in the care plan as essential. You are in a good position to liaise with other members of the care team who are designing menus and producing meals, so that they are aware of the needs of individuals and can try to accommodate those needs within their general planning. If at any point you are working with someone who refuses to follow a particular diet, you must report it immediately.

There is no reason why people receiving care should not have exactly the same consideration about the presentation, the flavour, content and attractiveness of their food as is given to diners in top restaurants where great trouble is taken with presentation. It is amazing what some careful presentation can achieve with the simplest meal in terms of making it more appetising, more attractive and more likely to be eaten and enjoyed.

Check it out

Make a list of suggestions for making the eating environment in your workplace more attractive. Remember that your ideas can include people as well as physical resources.

NC12 UNIT TEST

1   Give three reasons why it is important that people are offered choice in the food they eat.

2   Which groups of people are unlikely to eat pork?

3   Which foods contain vitamin C? Why is it important to take some every day?

4   For food safety, at what temperature should a fridge be kept?

5   Apart from physical problems, which other factors could cause a service user to have difficulty with eating?

6   Describe some ways in which you could help a visually impaired person enjoy a meal.

7   Name four possible signs of an allergic reaction to food. What action would you take if you saw any of these signs?

8   Describe what you would do if a person in your care regularly refused to follow a diet recommended in his or her care plan.

Contribute to the ongoing support of clients and others significant to them

This chapter will look at how you can support people you are caring for, and help them to keep on being the person they have always been. You will learn about how people grow through the various life stages, and about the importance of relationships with others. The unit is also concerned with your role in supporting the families and friends of the service users you work with. You will have the opportunity to find out about the importance of interests and how they help to meet individual needs, and you will be able to examine the basis of human needs and how they can be met.

It is likely that this chapter will provide useful knowledge for Unit W8 from the Option Group B, particularly W8.1.

Element W2.1 Enable clients to maintain their interests, identity and emotional well-being whilst receiving a care service

What you need to learn

● Human needs ● Self-esteem ● Maintaining interests

Human needs

All human beings have needs which must be met in order for them to achieve comfort and the feeling of well-being.

There are different ways of looking at human needs, and we will consider two of them:

● PIES
● Maslow's Hierarchy of Needs.

PIES

This is one of simplest ways to think about needs and to remember what they are, as the diagram opposite shows.

Physical needs

These are things like food, warmth, shelter, sleep and drink.

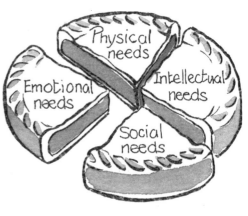

Human needs – PIES.

Physical needs are usually very basic, and it is impossible to survive without them. Of course, the needs will vary with the age of the individual and the stage of life he or she is at. But, generally, human beings have a greater range of physical needs at the start of their lives and in old age. These tend to be the times when physical needs are greater than just food, warmth and shelter. At the beginning of life an individual is likely to require assistance with moving, feeding and cleaning of body waste. Some or all of these needs may recur in the later stages of life.

Intellectual needs

This is not about being clever! Intellectual needs are about mental stimulation and having varied interests. Everyone needs to keep his or her brain active – this is not to suggest that everyone should try to be Einstein, but simply that all humans need to have something which holds their interest or makes them think. Like physical needs, intellectual needs change to fit the life stage: a baby will be stimulated by colours and simple shapes or by new sounds. But, as many of you will know, an older child or adolescent requires considerably more to prevent boredom! An adult will benefit from having interests and outlets which offer a challenge and a change. Later adulthood is a vital time to ensure that intellectual needs are met, as maintaining interests and having access to mental stimulation become increasingly important if physical abilities decline.

Emotional needs

Most people like to be liked; most people like to love and be loved. At the various stages of our lives, the needs will be different, but basically everyone needs to feel secure, nurtured and loved. A new-born child needs to feel safe and secure, or he or she will become distressed and unhappy. As children grow, they benefit from receiving love and caring, as well as having boundaries, limits and routines which provide security. As adolescents progress into adulthood, emotional fulfilment is likely to come from developing a close emotional bond with another person. Throughout the life of most human beings the need to be emotionally contented is of great importance.

DID YOU KNOW?
Children who are deprived of love and affection become silent and withdrawn. They fail to thrive and have difficulty in developing normally.

Social needs

Social needs are about relationships with other people. No one lives in a vacuum, and most human beings like to relate to other human beings! As a species, we have never lived a solitary existence. Humans have always sought to meet their social needs by living in groups alongside others. All cultures have a history of people grouping together in villages and towns or simply in tribes or families.

Maslow's Hierarchy of Needs

This approach, one of the most useful, was suggested by the psychologist Abraham Maslow.

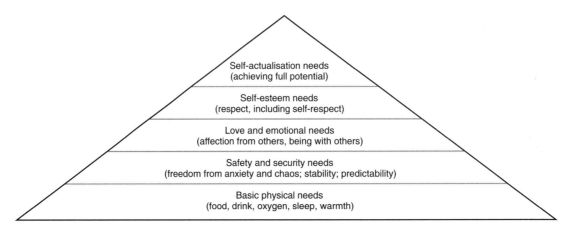

Maslow's Hierarchy of Needs: people need to satisfy the needs at the bottom of the triangle before going higher.

Basic physical needs

People will do whatever is necessary to meet their basic physical needs. These needs rank as the most important when people are placed under threat. Most people are fortunate enough to be able to take the basic physical needs for granted, but all human beings, if they are deprived of them, will go to great lengths to satisfy those needs. For example, if a person is starving it becomes his or her overriding priority to find food. All of the other higher-level needs fade into insignificance when compared to needs like food, warmth and shelter.

Safety and security needs

These are the needs which people will try to satisfy once they have met their basic needs. When they have sufficient food, some heat and a shelter, then they will look to feel safe and secure. Safety and security means different things to different people, but safety from physical danger is what most people will look for. Freedom from fear is something which is important to everyone, and individuals will try to achieve that and will see it as a higher priority than establishing relationships. Stability and security also include the need to live in a stable and unchaotic society. Humans also need to be free from anxiety as well as from fear, and will take steps to try to regulate the environment in which they live to achieve this.

Love and emotional needs

Human beings need to reach out and form relationships with other human beings. They need to love and to be loved in return, to express affection and caring for others, and to feel cared for and nurtured in return. It is about more than having a close relationship which we would define as love. It is also about contacts with others – friends, colleagues, neighbours – and the opportunity to co-operate and work alongside others. Most individuals dislike feeling like outsiders or not being accepted by a group, and a failure to make relationships with others is likely to make people feel very badly about themselves. The need to form relationships with other human beings only becomes important after basic needs and safety and security needs have been achieved.

Self-esteem needs

Self-esteem is about the way people feel about themselves. It is important that people feel that they have a valuable contribution to make, whether it is to society as a whole or within a smaller area such as their local community, workplace or their own family.

Feeling good about yourself also has a great deal to do with your own experiences throughout your life and the kind of confidence that you were given as you grew up. All human beings need to feel that they have a valuable place and a valuable contribution to make within society.

Self-esteem is discussed in detail on page 186.

Self-actualisation needs

This is about every human being's need to reach his or her maximum potential. This might be through setting out to achieve new goals or meeting new challenges, or through developing existing talents. Abraham Maslow suggests that if our other needs have not been met (from the most basic needs up to self-esteem needs), then this need will never be met, because people will continue to try to achieve the needs lower down the hierarchy, and will never attempt self-fulfilment and will never reach their full potential.

REMEMBER

Maslow may be right in his hierarchy of needs. Think about the number of times that you have seen people who are confused, depressed, dirty and malnourished who, within a few days of having their basic needs of warmth and food met, have started to make relationships and to try to meet some of their higher needs.

CASE STUDY

Miss J had lived alone in a very large, cold house since her mother died about 15 years ago. She was always viewed as a bit odd by the local neighbours. She appeared quite grubby and unkempt and never spoke to or smiled at anyone. She was very thin, and seemed to be just skin and bone. The milkman and paper girl, who were the only people who ever went to the house, said that it looked very messy and dirty inside and there was never any evidence of heating, even in the depths of winter.

She was admitted to hospital one day after the milkman looked through the window and saw her on the floor when she didn't answer his knock. She had fallen and fractured her femur.

At first, Miss J didn't speak to anyone apart from asking to be left alone. She agreed to a bed bath and having her hair washed, and ate the meals which were brought to her. The nurses and health care assistants noticed that after about a week, she began to respond to their conversation and seemed to look forward to having a shower and eating her meals. Gradually, she began to talk to other patients on the ward and it became clear that she was a well-informed and intelligent woman with a keen sense of humour.

When she was ready for discharge, she decided to go on to convalescence and to sell her house and buy a flat in a retirement community, where she would meet other people and yet retain her independence.

1   Which of Miss J's needs were met by coming into hospital?
2   What effect did that have on her behaviour?
3   What next level needs is Miss J going to meet?
4   What may have happened if she had not had the fall?

Self-esteem

Self-esteem is about how people value themselves and how they see themselves (their self-image). People have different levels of self-confidence, and it is very common to hear that somebody is not very confident or does not have a very high opinion of himself or herself.

The reasons why people have different levels of self-esteem are complex. The way people feel about themselves is often laid down during childhood. A child who is encouraged and regularly told how good he or she is and given a lot of positive feelings is the sort of person who is likely to feel that he or she has something to offer and can make a useful contribution to any situation. But a child who is constantly shouted at, blamed or belittled is likely to grow into an adult who lacks belief in himself or herself, or finds it difficult to go into new situations and to accept new challenges.

Not all the reasons for levels of self-confidence and self-image come from childhood. There are many experiences in adult life that can affect self-confidence and how people feel about themselves, for example:

● being made redundant
● getting divorced
● the death of somebody close
● the loss of independence, possibly having to go into residential care or into hospital
● the shock of being burgled
● having a bad fall, which results in a feeling of helplessness and a lack of self-worth.

All of these experiences can have devastating effects. Very often, people will become withdrawn and depressed as a result, and a great deal of support and concentrated effort is needed to help them through these very difficult situations.

Look at the tree diagram above. It shows people at a great many stages and in a great many different situations. Study them all carefully.

1   Where do you think you fit? Are you the person at the top of the tree smiling, or the person near the top of the tree but not very happy? Are you falling, or being pushed? Are you hanging on by a thread or having great fun? Are you climbing up, or sliding down?

2   Which figures look the happiest?

3   Which figure would you most like to be?

4   Which figure would you least like to be? Why?

> ## REMEMBER
> The people you provide care for all see themselves at different stages on the tree, and have probably seen themselves at different stages at various points in their life. Nobody stays at the same point on the tree forever. As circumstances change, so do people's views of themselves and how they fit in.

Maintaining interests

One of the most important factors in maintaining the well-being of a person who is receiving care is that person's involvement in some kind of interest or activity. This may be within the person's own home, in a residential setting or in hospital. The activities and interests may well be restricted by physical limitations, but their importance cannot be over-estimated. Interests and activities serve three purposes. They encourage:

- mental well-being
- physical well-being
- emotional well-being.

Mental well-being

When people are ill, disabled, becoming elderly and in need of support and care services, one of the problems is that the loss of physical abilities is often accompanied by a loss of interest in other activities. You will probably have seen a formerly intelligent, bright, active and cheerful elderly person become withdrawn, sitting for hours dozing or watching TV, following an illness, a fall or some kind of deterioration in his or her physical abilities. Maintaining interests is vital, therefore, for providing mental stimulation.

Whether you are working in a residential or a community setting, it is important that you give thought to the kinds of activity that you can arrange and the sorts of interest that you are able to encourage, for which you can offer support.

Activities which maintain mental stimulation include:

- reading
- doing crossword puzzles
- writing
- taking part in conversations
- joining discussion and debating groups
- going on visits and outings
- seeing visitors
- chess or similar games.

You must be sure that you are responding to indications from an individual about his or her interests. You should not impose your ideas about activities that you consider would be appropriate.

Keys to good practice

✓ Make sure that it is what the individual wants – not what you think might be good for him or her!
✓ Agree the programme with the care team and include it in the plan of care
✓ Make sure that books and reading materials are accessible – in large enough print, appropriate language, etc.
✓ Consider ways to help people to write – specially shaped writing materials can help, or how about a word processor? It's never too late to learn!

✓ Think about a link with a local school – information can go two ways. There is always something of interest which people can offer. It may be knowledge of local history, or a particular skill or craft. The school may be interested in sharing a project to develop a new service.

✓ Organise a discussion or debating group. If you work in the community, you could try to arrange visits or visitors who will stimulate conversation. You could find articles or news items about areas of your service user's interest and be prepared to talk – and learn – about them.

✓ Arrange outings and visits to places of interest which have been identified by your service users.

People who are confused

If you work with people who are very confused or disorientated, you may be involved in specific activities which are designed to provide mental stimulation. These are things like recall therapy, which involves a care worker beginning a discussion about things which have happened in the past, what the local area used to be like in the past, the sort of food people used to eat, the clothes they wore, the experiences that people went through together, perhaps the war, perhaps extreme poverty or hardship. Gradually it is often possible to see even the most confused people beginning to join in and to pick up words and concepts which are familiar to them from a time that is often easier to recall than more recent events.

Another practice that may be familiar in your workplace is reality orientation. In its simplest form, this might be a wall chart showing the day, the date, the weather, where people are, and other very basic details which will assist people to orientate themselves in time and place.

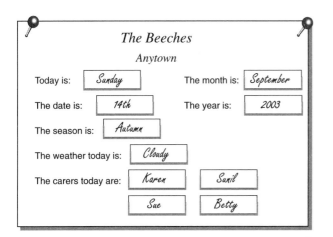

A reality orientation chart assists people to orientate themselves in time and place.

Check it out

1 Why would a chart like the one above be helpful to someone who is confused?

2 Why is it important?

3 Have you seen a chart like this used in a workplace? If so, was it effective?

REMEMBER

Mental stimulation is not only important for people who are confused, it is essential for general well-being. Many people will know the relief of having adult company after spending the entire day with a small child or baby who does not yet talk. If you know how that feels, imagine how much worse it must be for somebody who is isolated, unable to take part in much physical activity and very rarely has any company at all. Unless a person is able to maintain mental stimulation through interests and contacts, he or she is likely to become depressed and unhappy, and suffer as a consequence.

Physical well-being

Physical exercise and activity, within limits, is tremendously important for everyone regardless of physical ability. Most people are able to maintain some level of physical activity, even if that is severely limited by their physical condition.

Physical activities might include:

- mountain climbing
- hang gliding
- gardening
- aerobics
- walking
- playing ball
- dancing
- simple hand jiving.

There may be some activities in that list which you are unlikely to be asked to arrange for the individuals you care for – but you never know! You should never assume that just because a person falls into a particular 'category' he or she will not be interested in a particular type of activity. Do not assume that everybody, once they have turned 65, wants to play bingo or go on coach trips – although a great many of them do!

Never assume that just because a person falls into a particular 'category' he or she will not be interested in a particular type of activity.

Appropriate levels of activity

Physical activity should be relative to an individual's capabilities. For example, a person in a wheelchair may only be able to carry out physical activity with his or her arms, but that can include wheelchair marathons, basketball, archery and all kinds of other sporting activities. It could also include playing musical instruments and participating in wheelchair dancing or acting.

For someone who has just undergone surgery, the maximum level of physical activity he or she is able to manage may be a short walk along the ward, but that will represent a vast increase on the previous day when all he or she could do was sit in a chair.

It is important to maintain physical activity at a level that is appropriate for a particular individual.

The human body is not designed to be inactive. Muscles need to be kept moving or they develop problems, internal body systems work better if they get some exercise, and the skeleton is not designed to be immobile. It is important that you encourage, support and help people towards whatever kind of physical activity they are able to manage in order to keep them as healthy as possible.

You could help to arrange:

- walks around local places of interest
- exercise or dance classes
- gardening
- bowls
- team or individual sports such as golf
- helping with housework
- for service users who are bedridden or unable to move from a chair, hand and arm exercises to music.

Keys to good practice

✓ Make sure that any type of physical exercise programme is agreed with the appropriate professional – usually the physiotherapist.
✓ Make sure that it is agreed with the care team and is part of the plan of care.
✓ Encourage, but do not force, people to participate.
✓ Little and often is the key to enjoyable and effective exercise.
✓ Don't make assumptions about what people will want to do.

DID YOU KNOW?

In a recent survey, almost 60 per cent of people aged between 70 and 75 had done some gardening in the previous month. Over a third of people over 60 had been for a walk of between 2 and 5 miles in the previous month.

Emotional well-being

The social side to maintaining interests and hobbies is very important. Many hobbies which people follow will lead them to meet with others:

- People who are gardening may well belong to a gardening club which provides the kind of contact that is always welcome.
- People who enjoy dancing, or chess, or even a luncheon club or a ramblers association have the opportunity to meet with others whilst continuing to follow their hobby or interest.

It is difficult to identify the factor that provides the greater sense of well-being – is it the hobby itself, or is it the contact that it brings with others?

Encouraging people to maintain interests and activities is a valuable contribution to their emotional well-being, because it also allows them a sense of achievement and personal fulfilment and this contributes to their emotional health.

REMEMBER

- Offering support to individuals to participate in particular interests or activities is a vital and constructive part of your work in providing care. However, it is important to remember that the activities must be ones in which the individuals have expressed interest, and not activities which you, or someone else, thinks will be good for them to participate in.

- One of the most useful roles which you can play is to encourage an individual to express his or her interests, and to give the kind of support he or she may need to revive or maintain an interest.

CASE STUDY

Mr Z is 73 years old. He came to this country as an asylum seeker from Eastern Europe several years ago. Although he was living with his son, he found it difficult to cope in their very small house as his mobility was very poor following a stroke. Reluctantly, Mr Z agreed to residential care. His English is poor, but he understands quite a lot. Following his admission he was withdrawn and not willing to communicate or to join in any activities. One day one of the care assistants noticed he was drawing on a paper napkin, and his drawing was very good. She began to ask him about drawing and painting, and discovered that he had a real talent and love of art. Mr Z was encouraged to attend the art group held each week in the home. He seemed to enjoy the group and talked to other residents in the group about the paintings. The art therapist taking the group felt that Mr Z's work was too good just for their little group, so encouraged him to meet the art group from the local gallery.

This led to Mr Z going to regular meetings and classes, visiting other galleries with the group, and even putting an exhibition of his work in the local library. His English improved and although his mobility was still limited, he was motivated to get out and about using support and walking aids.

1 What may have happened if the staff member had not noticed Mr Z's drawing?
2 Why do you think the changes in Mr Z were so noticeable?
3 What factors made Mr Z's situation worse?
4 What other ways could Mr Z have been helped?

TEST YOURSELF

1 What are human needs?
2 Why is it important to have needs met?
3 List at least three ways of meeting emotional needs.
4 Why are interests important?
5 Give two examples of activities you could carry out in your workplace to encourage mental well-being.
6 What factors do you need to take into account when you are promoting physical well-being?

Enable clients to maintain contact with those who are significant to them

What you need to learn

- What are relationships?
- Why relationships are important
- How you can help to maintain contact

What are relationships?

No one lives in a vacuum. Most people have other people in their lives who are important to them and who make a difference to how they feel and to their overall well-being. Not everyone has relatives, but most people have somebody in their lives who is significant to them. This may be a friend or a neighbour, even a pet.

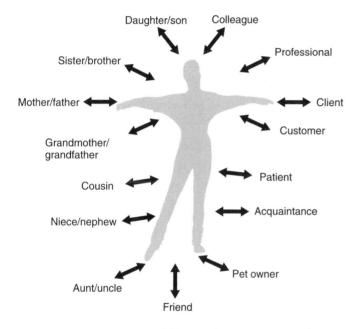

Everybody has a complex system of relationships.

Relationships are very varied and everybody has a very complex system of relationships. If you think about the number of different people that you have different relationships with, you will begin to see how complex a picture it is.

You can see from the diagram opposite that your relationships with large numbers of people are all different. You are only a daughter or a son to one or two people, whereas you can be friend to many and a colleague or an acquaintance to a great many more. Each of those relationships has with it different expectations, and you will find yourself with a different role in each of those relationships.

Check it out

Think about the number of different relationships that you have. Make a list of them. Then, next to each one say why it is important and why it is different from the one next to it in the list.

Why relationships are important

It is good for the well-being of all individuals that they are able to relate well to others. Particularly when people are in need of care, and possibly in a physical state which has deteriorated, it is important that they are able to make links to other people who are important to them and not to lose touch with them.

Check it out

Relationships meet many different needs. The table below gives some ideas about the way different needs are met by different kinds of relationship. Think about the people in your workplace, both service users and colleagues, and complete a chart for three of them, showing which relationships meet which needs.

How relationships may meet human needs

Type of relationship	Needs which may be met

Close relationship:
  husband/wife/partner
  close relative
	Emotional

Close friend, confidant	Emotional and social
Acquaintances, people who share interests	Social and intellectual
Colleagues	Intellectual, social, self-esteem

It is very easy for relationships and contacts to disappear slowly, as people become less able to get out and about and visit, or perhaps move into residential care or into hospital. In these situations, the opportunities to maintain relationships with friends or even family can often be affected.

It is very important in your role of providing care that you establish with each individual:

● Who are the people who matter to you?
● Do you have any family that you see regularly and with whom you have a good relationship?
● Is it friends or neighbours who are the people who are most significant in your life?

Once you have established who the important people are, you need to ensure that the individual is encouraged to maintain those contacts.

However, you must be sure that the contacts that you are encouraging are contacts that the individual wishes to maintain. You may believe that it would be very good for somebody to maintain contact with his or her daughter. However, it is matter of choice whether that is something he or she wishes to do, and you must make sure that you respect the choice the individual has made.

Sometimes it may appear that an individual refuses to see somebody or to allow the person to be contacted for no good reason. This is always a difficult situation to handle, particularly if the person he or she is refusing to see has no idea why and is distressed by the refusal. The only action that you can take in these circumstances is to try to explain to the relative or friend that the individual has refused and that this is his or her choice. You need to be assertive and direct, and to respect the choice of the individual about the people he or she wishes to contact. There is more in Chapter 3 (Unit CU1) about how to deal with this difficult situation.

CASE STUDY

K lived in a small children's home. She was 15 years old and had lived in the home for just over a year. Her mother had a long history of mental health problems and had committed suicide after suffering with depression for many years. K had no family who were able to look after her – she and her mother had never had any contact with her father, and her grandmother had a history of mental health problems herself and could not cope with K.

K did have a friend with whom she had grown up in the town where she used to live until she was 10. The two girls had written, but had gradually lost touch. K found it difficult to make friends and did not relate well to the other four residents. Her school described her as a loner who had seemed to relate only to her mother and not to have any friends.

K was very keen to get back in touch with her old friend and asked one of the staff at the home to help her.

Together, they checked the last address that K had. The family was still there and had a phone number. The staff member telephoned, with K's agreement, and spoke to the friend's mother to explain the situation. K's old friend was happy to speak to her and the girls wanted to meet up.

Although the town was only 25 miles away, transport was quite difficult to arrange as no one had a car. Using the Internet, K and the staff member checked the times of the buses and agreed that K's friend, along with her mother, would visit the home the following weekend. After this, the visits were alternated and occurred about once a month. The girls got on as well as ever. Re-starting this relationship seemed to give K the confidence to make other contacts and she began to make friends with others in the home. Soon she started getting invitations to go out with other girls from her school.

1 Why was it important to help K in making the first contact?
2 What could have happened if she had had no help?
3 How do you think K felt after finding her friend again?
4 How do you think she had been feeling before that?

Keys to good practice

✓ Never forget the importance of relationships.
✓ Do a 'relationships chart' for each of your service users.
✓ Encourage relationships, both old and new.
✓ Make sure that you are following the service user's wishes.

How you can help to maintain contact

There are several ways that you can assist people to maintain their contacts, by:

- written communication
- telephone
- visits.

Written communication

Often letters are a useful way to keep in touch with family and friends, particularly for older people. Most people enjoy receiving letters, although fewer enjoy writing them! It can be useful for an older person to receive a letter, because it can be referred to as often as necessary if some of its contents have slipped his or her memory. Letters can also be a very useful means of communication for people with hearing difficulties, where telephone calls may be extremely difficult without the use of aids.

There may be occasions where you can offer help to write a letter. If somebody has difficulty in holding a pen or managing to write clearly then an offer of assistance would probably be welcome. It should go without saying that you are very much bound by the rules of confidentiality when you are assisting somebody by writing a letter, or by reading out a letter for somebody who has impaired sight. If you are writing a letter for somebody, you must make sure that you write exactly what he or she says and that you are not tempted to alter the content of the letter to resemble something that you may consider to be a little more appropriate.

Look at the example below.

Dear Joan,

How are you? As you can see, I am now living in a new place. This is so much nicer than the hospital. It is a small home where we all have our own room and there is a lovely lounge and gardens. The staff are very kind and the other residents seem very nice, although it's not the same as the old neighbours.

Do you see much of the people who bought my house? It upsets me sometimes to think of them living there after all those years, but it was too much for me. Is the road still the same? I expect Sue has had the baby by now. If you tell me what they had I'll send a card.

It would be lovely if you could manage a visit, but I know it's a long way on the bus. Please write soon, it would be lovely to hear from you.

From your old friend and neighbour

Ada Johnson

Dictated by A Johnson to K Morris (Care Assistant)

E-mail

If friends or relatives of service users have e-mail, it may be a useful means of keeping in touch. Electronic methods are very convenient for people who find it difficult to get out to post a letter, or who are hard of hearing and find the telephone difficult to use. You may need to support people to use e-mail if:

- it is new to them
- they have difficulty using the keyboard
- they simply need encouragement.

If you write e-mails on behalf of people, the process is the same as writing a letter. You must be sure to write and send exactly what they tell you – even if it not what you consider to be appropriate.

Telephone contact

Telephones are an everyday means of communication, and are used without a second thought by most people. However, some older people are not comfortable using a telephone, or have not had much experience in making or receiving telephone calls. They may require assistance, or it may be more appropriate to find other means of encouraging them to maintain contacts.

If people are happy to use a telephone, you may still need to provide assistance. You may need to:

- take them to a telephone
- bring a telephone to them
- look up or dial a telephone number
- set the receiver at a higher volume
- arrange for a call to be taken in a private and quiet place.

An individual may ask you to make a telephone call on his or her behalf in order to arrange a visit with relatives or friends. If you are asked to do this, you should do it promptly and clearly, and make sure that you report back to the individual the outcome of the conversation.

If there is an incoming telephone call for someone you are caring for, you should try to make sure that he or she is able to take it somewhere private and quiet, where the conversation will be uninterrupted, rather than being overheard by other residents in a lounge or disturbed in a busy hallway or a bustling ward.

Check it out

1 Find out where all the phones are in your workplace.

2 Find out which ones you can move.

3 Check which phones, if any, have adjustable volume controls.

4 Identify quiet and private places in your workplace for telephone conversations.

5 Make a note of this information for the next time you need it.

REMEMBER

When you are communicating for someone, whether it is by letter, a phone call, fax or e-mail, that person is simply talking through you. It is as if you are an interpreter – you must only communicate exactly what the person has told you.

How to deal with visits

Visits are usually very important to individuals who are receiving care. It is essential, however, that you make sure the individual concerned is happy to see the particular visitors. This basic rule applies regardless of the setting in which you work, although there are different factors to take into account depending on where you work.

Visits in hospital

If you work in a hospital environment, it is usually not possible to control visiting as there are set visiting times and restrictions on who may visit. For example, children may not be able to visit at all times and pets are rarely allowed.

You should notice, however, if people do not have visitors and if there are particular individuals who always seem to be alone at visiting times. You will need to make the time to talk to such individuals about people whom they could contact in order to arrange visits. If they indicate to you that they would be glad of some company and welcome visits, then it may be appropriate for you to refer this to an agency which organises hospital visitors, such as the hospital's League of Friends or the hospital chaplain. Make sure that this is agreed with the care team and is included in the care plan.

Alternatively there may be a person who always seems to be surrounded by a large group of noisy relatives, and may often appear exhausted at the end of visiting time. Try to find out if the person would like you to limit the number of visitors who come to see him or her at any one time. Often people do not feel able to ask visitors to leave or to visit in smaller numbers, and are grateful for the request to come from hospital staff. This enables them to say 'I'm sorry – they won't let me...'

Visits at home

Clearly, when people are receiving visitors in their own home, they will have their own ways of doing things. They may be glad of some assistance, and an offer to prepare refreshments or to be there to let the visitors in may be welcome.

Giving information to visitors

You may be asked by visitors for information about an individual. It is not correct to assume that just because somebody has appeared to be glad to see a friend or relative that he or she is willing to have information about him/her given out. You must, at all times, discuss with the individual concerned how much information he or she is willing for you to share with any family or friends who visit. You must never assume that just because someone is a close relative that information can be given without seeking permission from the individual.

Keys to good practice

Try to keep a mental checklist about visiting, like the one below. If you always mentally run through the items on your checklist before somebody has visitors, you are less likely to make any mistakes in how you handle the situation.

Visitors checklist

1.	Well enough for visitors?	✓
2.	Are these visitors welcome?	✓
3.	Have I seen them before?	✓
4.	Do they need refreshments?	✓
5.	Do they tire him/her out?	✗
6.	Can they have information?	✓

TEST YOURSELF

1 Name three ways of helping service users to maintain contact.

2 What would you do if your service user's daughter visited and your service user did not want to see her?

3 What are the key things to remember about telephone calls?

4 a Can information about service users be given to their friends? Yes/No
  b Can information be given to their relatives? Yes/No

5 Name three ways in which you have an important role in respect of visitors.

Support those who are significant to the client during visits

What you need to learn

● How to deal with visitors
● Involving family and friends
● Supporting family and friends

How to deal with visitors

In the last element you looked at why visitors are important to the individuals you care for, and how you can help them to maintain contact. This element concerns the visitors themselves and the people who are important to those that you care for. As the person who greets visitors and welcomes them, you have a very important role to play in creating the atmosphere of the setting in which you work. You have the ability to make people feel welcome and a valuable part of the care that their friend or relative is receiving – or you could make them feel that they are an unwelcome nuisance and an interference in the routine of the establishment!

> **REMEMBER**
>
> In many cases, the care setting has become the individual's home. The individual is no longer able to receive his or her own visitors at home as in the past, so you have to do this on his or her behalf. Try to remember this and greet visitors as you know the individual would want them to be greeted and offer the kind of courtesy and consideration that they would have received from the individual.

Being welcoming is about more than just providing the basic courtesies. It is about offering information which allows people to feel that they have a part to play in the overall care which their friend of relative is receiving.

An individual may feel more at ease if it is possible to receive his or her visitors in private – in his or her room, for example, rather than in a communal lounge with other people around. This is something you will need to find out from the individual, and it may depend on who the visitors are or the reason for the visit. Be guided by the wishes of the individual, not the visitors, and make sure that the individual knows that privacy is possible, if needed.

How you provide privacy will depend on the care setting. In a hospital, it may be sufficient to draw curtains around a bed, or a separate room may be available. In a residential setting, it should be possible for individuals to receive visitors in their rooms (if they do not share a room), in a separate room that isn't in use, or in a quiet corner of a communal room.

Occasionally visits do not go well. Visitors may appear to upset or distress an individual, there may be arguments or disagreements or you may even feel that the individual is under threat from a particular visitor or group of visitors.

Steps to take if there are problems with visitors

- Report this at once to your manager.
- Be very clear about why you are concerned.
- Explain the effect that the visitors appear to have on the individual.

It may not be as clear cut as an argument or open disagreement, but there will be times when you will notice that an individual always appears quiet or withdrawn after visits from a particular relative or friend. If this is the case, you should certainly report what you have noticed and discuss with your manager whether it would be appropriate to try to talk further in order to establish what the problem might be, and to use some of your communication skills to try to get the individual to talk about what the problem is, and whether or not he/she would like you to stop those particular visits.

Involving family and friends

It is often useful to involve regular visitors in the care planning for the individual. If activities, outings or exercising are planned, it may be that these can be arranged to coincide with visits and that relatives and friends can be encouraged to arrange outings or to participate. Providing that you always gain agreement first, this can be a very useful way of encouraging an individual to become more active and outgoing. The fact that some familiar people are taking part in his or her care can often be very beneficial.

CASE STUDY

M is a 27-year-old man with cerebral palsy. He was admitted to residential care about six months ago because of his mother's deteriorating health. She had cared for him alone since her husband had left shortly after M was born. M requires total care, he needs feeding, washing and dressing, he is doubly incontinent and has no independent mobility. His mother had done all the lifting and handling and moving him between bed and wheelchair. M's speech is poor, but his mother can understand him. His understanding of both spoken and written communication is excellent.

M's mother had a heart attack and he was admitted to residential care as an emergency. On admission he was found to have several pressure sores and was very dirty – his skin was in poor condition, and his buttocks and genitals were very sore. Clearly, as his mother's deteriorated she had been able to do less and less for him and the level of care required was simply too much for her.

When his mother began to visit, she would only stay for a few minutes, make an excuse and leave. If the staff asked her opinion about M, she would say 'I don't really know, dear. I'm sure you all know best.' M would become very distressed when his mother left and would shout and rock and be very difficult to work with for long periods of time.

M's key worker has gradually involved his mother in M's care plan. She arranged for his mother to be part of the exercise programme designed by the physiotherapist. She asked his mother if she would continue to cut his hair as she had always done. As she has become more involved in M's care, his mother has stayed for longer and seems more relaxed and less keen to rush away. M is happier now that his mum is there for a part of each day, and the arrangements seem to suit everyone.

1 Why do you think M's mum only stayed for a short time?
2 What do you think her feelings may have been?
3 Do you think the key worker handled the situation well?
4 What could have happened if M's mother had not been involved in his care?
5 Do you think anything could have been done to stop this situation arising?

Check it out

Think about the care plan for one particular person you are caring for. List the items in the care plan and think about where relatives or friends could be involved. There are obviously some areas of personal care where their involvement may be inappropriate and unacceptable to the individual, but in other areas of more social or physical aspects then the individual may be happy to have his or her family involved.

The activities on your list may include outings or card games, recall therapy (which involves talking about events in the past), simple physiotherapy exercises, or other activities which contribute to somebody's well-being, such as hair washing or choosing new clothes.

Supporting family and friends

Very often relatives or friends may ask for information about where they can obtain support. You will need to make sure that you have plenty of up-to-date and accurate information available about the sorts of organisation that may be able to offer help to relatives. These may include organisations which specialise in offering help and advice for specific conditions, such as Scope, MENCAP, Alzheimers Society, Schizophrenia Fellowship, MIND, and so on.

In addition you must make sure that relatives are aware of the facilities that are provided locally by the social services department. They may also be interested in private sector provision, such as nursing homes, home-care services or night-sitting services.

More than just a visit

It may often be the case that visitors have a great many worries, concerns and feelings of their own that they would be glad to discuss with someone. The admission into care of a relative or friend can be very traumatic and can leave people with all sorts of feelings:

● They may feel anxious or concerned about what is going to happen to their loved one.
● They may feel guilty, that they should have been able to prevent this from happening, or that they should be able to provide care themselves.
● They may feel angry and perhaps let down by the system or even angry towards the individual who is receiving care.
● The range of emotions and feelings is likely to be complex and you should try to use your communication skills in order to offer them the opportunity to ask questions and express their own feelings and concerns.

How visitors may feel.

Make sure that you feel confident about dealing with any of the feelings that may be expressed. As soon as you feel that you are out of your depth or that something is beyond the level that you have been trained to cope with, then you must consult your manager. You may also find, from time to time, that relatives and friends want to discuss areas of an individual's care for which you have no responsibility and no specialised knowledge. You must be very careful in this situation.

For example, if you work in a hospital you are very likely to be approached by relatives asking about the medical treatment that someone is receiving. It is not your role to make any comment whatsoever in respect of medical treatment. You must refer them to someone with medical expertise. Similarly, in a residential setting if you have somebody who is querying the financial assessment which has been made in respect of a relative, this is not something that you can deal with and you must refer the person to the appropriate member of staff.

Keys to good practice

✓ Do not give information you are not qualified to give.
✓ Refer the relatives to somebody who can give specialist information.

Possible problems

Relatives and friends may not always find it easy to offer unconditional support to someone who is receiving care. For all the reasons we discussed in the last section they may find it difficult to be involved, or to be involved in a supportive way. Where you notice that there are such difficulties, it is very important that you make sure that these are referred on through your manager. People may also experience very simple practical difficulties, such as transport difficulties or the cost of fares involved in visiting their relative in hospital or residential care. If this is the case, make sure that you pass on this information and that you do tell the relatives that you have done so and that help is available.

TEST YOURSELF

1 What should you notice about the effect which visitors have?

2 What steps would you take if you noticed that someone did not have any visitors?

3 Note at least three different emotions which relatives may feel about someone being in care.

4 In what circumstances should you refer visitors to another member of staff?

5 What would you do to offer support to a relative?

What you need to learn
- How to offer support to carers
- What carers need to know
- How to give advice
- Caring for carers

How to offer support to carers

Caring for people is a lonely job. The very nature of looking after somebody who is ill or disabled in their own home means that it is a very isolated task to undertake. It is also an unending task, and carers who are family or friends do not have limits to their hours of work, nor the salaries of professional carers. You should never assume that the people who care voluntarily for friends or family are in the same position as those who care for others as a profession.

The key thing about offering support to anyone is to make sure that it is the right support and that it is the kind of support that the person is looking for. There is no point in offering a carer a friendly chat and a sympathetic ear when what she is actually looking for is somebody to come in for three hours so she can visit a friend or go shopping.

When supporting a carer, you must be careful to remember that your main role is still to support the individual who needs care. The two roles should not conflict, but occasionally they may, and you may find that you need to ask for assistance to provide support to the carer while you continue providing support to the individual needing care.

Ideally, both the carer and the individual should be able to ask for help from the care team as and when they need it.

> **DID YOU KNOW?**
> A project is currently in progress researching 'Virtual Community Care'. This means looking at how the Internet can be of help to people who are isolated as carers in the community.

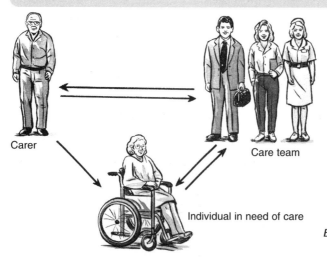

Carer

Care team

Individual in need of care

Both the carer and the individual should be able to ask for help from the care team.

There may come a time when an individual can longer be cared for in his or her own home. A move to another care setting may be long-term, in a residential home, or short-term for treatment in hospital, or for respite care if the individual's carer needs a break or is ill. You will need to support both the individual and the carer during this process of change, by giving them as much information as possible to help them make decisions, answering their questions honestly, giving them constant reassurance, and allowing them time to get used to the change. Chapter 9 (Unit W3), particularly Element W3.1, deals with supporting individuals experiencing change. The advice it gives for supporting individuals also applies to supporting their carers.

What carers need to know

Many carers will not have any of the basic skills which are necessary to provide physical care for someone. Things which may seem very commonplace to you, and a part of your everyday routine in your work, may be things which they have never before had to do. Such skills include:

- how to bath somebody
- how to get someone on and off a commode
- how to get someone in and out of a chair.
- how to give a bed bath
- how to move someone safely

All of the basic safety requirements are skills which a new carer may need to be taught, and even experienced carers may need regular support. Particularly in areas like lifting and handling, carers often need advice to ensure that they do not hurt themselves or the person that they are caring for.

Carers will also need to know what actions they should take in an emergency. This can be one of the most frightening aspects of caring for somebody and clear knowledge of the steps which they need to take can often be very reassuring. Make sure, when you give advice about aspects of practical care, that you are only advising in areas that you really know about. If you think that more expert advice is needed, you should refer the matter to your manager. For example, you may not feel you have enough knowledge about lifting and handling to be able to advise a carer on the safe methods that he or she can use, or you may not know about all of the aids and adaptations which would be appropriate in that situation. A referral to an occupational therapist may well be the best course of action.

Carers also need to know about facilities that can be provided to give them a break. These can range from local volunteers who are able to come and sit with an individual for an afternoon or an evening, through to full-scale residential respite care, either on an occasional or a regular basis. One of the commonest things carers say is that they may not have made use of all of the facilities that were available, but often just knowing that they were there if they needed them made it possible for them to cope.

REMEMBER

Caring for someone is one of the hardest jobs in the world – there is no pay, few perks and often little thanks. People who care may never make use of any support you offer, but they need to know that they can – don't stop offering the help.

How to give advice

One of the most important things about giving advice is never to make people feel that they are somehow inadequate because they need the advice. Caring for somebody full-time is one of the most difficult jobs, and people need the maximum amount of encouragement and support to carry out this task. When you offer information and support, it is important that you do it in a way which makes them feel that they are being helped rather than being criticised.

Many carers are very unsure that they are doing a good job, and they can easily feel undermined by you, as a professional, if you appear to know all the answers. Make sure that you are not making somebody feel inadequate when what you should be doing is giving encouragement.

CASE STUDY

Scenario 1

Carer: I'm glad to see you, I really need to talk to someone.

Professional: Yes, what can I do for you?

Carer: I don't know really – I'm just finding it so hard to cope with Peter, he's so difficult sometimes. I know he can't help it and he's angry, but then I get short with him, and I know I shouldn't.

Professional: No – you really shouldn't get short-tempered with him – his behaviour is as a result of his accident. He did have a massive brain injury you know. He's done really well to have progressed as much as he has. Things could have been much worse.

Carer: Yes, I know you're right. Everyone has been so wonderful in what they've done for him – I feel as though I'm letting everyone down by finding it all so hard.

Professional: Well, it certainly sounds as if you're not coping. Perhaps it would be better for Peter if he came back into the unit, then he can have his outbursts handled properly – I'll arrange it if you like.

Carer: Well – I suppose you'd better – I'm obviously not managing here and he should be with people who can look after him better. I really did want him home, though.

Scenario 2

Carer: I'm glad to see you, I really need to talk to someone.

Professional: It's nice that someone's glad to see me! – how can I help?

Carer: I don't know really – I'm just finding it so hard to cope with Peter, he's so difficult sometimes. I know he can't help it and he's angry, but then I get short with him, and I know I shouldn't.

Professional: I'm not surprised you get short – he really can be very difficult. We certainly had some very difficult days with him at the unit. Even though you know it's not his fault and it's because of the accident, there are still moments . . . At least we get to go home

▶

at the end of the shift, but you never get a break – I think you're amazing.

Carer: Do you really think so? Everyone's done such a lot for him, I feel as though I'm 'the weakest link'.

Professional: Of course you're not, you're doing such a good job here. In fact everyone at the unit was only saying that the other day. It sounds as if there are times when you could scream, though – how about joining in the carer's support group?

Carer: I couldn't – there's no one to look after Peter.

Professional: No problem – its only one afternoon a week – I can arrange for a support worker to come in to give you a break.

Carer: Yes please, that sounds great. I feel so much better now.

1. What are the main differences between the two approaches?
2. What is there about the first approach that may undermine a carer?
3. Why is the second approach likely to make a carer feel more encouraged?

Caring for carers

The government has developed a National Strategy for Carers, called 'Caring for Carers'. This has come about because of the recognition of the huge numbers of people who are caring for others; there are almost 6 million carers in the UK, and currently three-fifths of them receive no support at all. Many are young carers, under the age of 18 – there are thought to be about 50,000 young carers. The strategy's main action points are the following.

- Carers must be consulted and included in any plans made for care of the person they look after.
- Carers can ask for their own assessment by the local authority, even if the person they care for has refused one.
- Carers should be able to take a break from caring and the strategy has provided resources to local authorities to enable this to happen.
- Carers who are working can now have unpaid leave for family emergencies. This means that many carers are able to carry on working rather than having to give up.
- There is a recognition of the importance of carers' own health, with an NHS Direct helpline for carer information.
- Carers must be consulted by local authorities on the provision of services.

DID YOU KNOW?

Research carried out by the carers' national association showed that 51 per cent of carers had suffered injuries such as a strained back since they began caring, and 52 per cent had been treated for a stress-related illness since becoming carers.

Informal carers are an essential part of the community care strategy. The whole concept of ensuring that people can remain in their own homes for as long as possible, rather than being looked after in residential care, is built on the idea that a vast number of informal carers will be involved, and that these carers will be supported to greater or lesser degrees depending on need and the availability of resources. The support for carers often varies from area to area. In some parts of the country support, such as respite care, domiciliary support, aids, adaptations, hospices or carers' groups, is readily available, and in others there is a long waiting list or support is simply not available.

Caring can be extremely stressful. If you are involved in working with carers, either supporting them on a day-to-day basis or supporting them by being part of a respite care package for a relative or friend they are caring for, it is important that you recognise the signs that a carer is experiencing problems. If difficult situations can be picked up early, they can be dealt with before there is a breakdown in care.

The table below lists a range of symptoms and signs of stress. You may notice some or all of them. All individuals are different and will show stress in different ways. As you get to know a carer, it will be easier to notice when all is not well and he or she is showing signs of difficulty in coping.

Signs of stress

Physical signs	Emotional signs
Rapid breathing	Crying easily
Sweating	Expressing feelings of guilt
Trembling	Feeling anxious
Shaking hands	Showing aggression
Difficulty sleeping	Irritability
Poor appetite	Tension
Increase in smoking or drinking	Having difficulty making decisions
Restlessness	Poor concentration
Nervous or inappropriate laughter	Over-sensitivity to criticism
	Being poorly organised

Stress may be evident not only in the carer but also in the family. You will need to be aware of this and think about the pressures on other family members, if an individual is being cared for within a family home. Of course, the ultimate concern, where a carer or family are under considerable stress and pressure, is that an abusive situation might develop. Stress is one of the warning signs for potential abuse, so be very careful in a situation where you know carers are experiencing difficulties and be on the alert for signs of abuse. The signs of abuse are covered in Chapter 4 (Unit Z1). Make sure that you know what they are and that you watch for them.

Keys to good practice

✓ Never undermine a carer.
✓ Keep offering support, even if it is not taken up.
✓ Be ready to recognise when things are getting too much.
✓ Offer practical help that people can use.
✓ Don't offer advice on anything you are not sure about.

W2 UNIT TEST

1 Why is it important for people to maintain outside interests when they are in care?

2 Name three different types of activity and their purposes.

3 Name two ways in which you could keep somebody in contact with important friends and relations.

4 What are the important things to remember about giving information to friends or relatives?

5 Name three possible signs of stress in carers.

6 What are the practical ways in which help can be offered to carers?

Unit W3

Support individuals experiencing a change in their care requirements and provision

This unit is about learning what you can do to support people who are having to undergo a change. Changes can be exciting, interesting and a challenge, but they can also be frightening, worrying and cause a great deal of anxiety and distress. Your job is to make people feel better able to cope with the changes that they will experience. You then need to be able to help them adapt to the changes after they have taken place. Once someone has actually moved into a new care setting, you have a vital job in helping him or her to settle in and to readjust to the new surroundings. This unit will cover the basic skills that you need to learn to ensure that the settling-in process is as constructive and useful as possible.

The changes you might have to deal with include an older person coming into care in an emergency, somebody with mental health problems moving out of supported accommodation and into his or her own accommodation in the community, a child or young person moving from residential into foster care, a change in the level of domiciliary care provided for an individual, or a change in the person carrying out that domiciliary care. These sorts of situations can raise concerns for the individuals involved.

Element W3.1 Enable individuals to prepare for, and transfer to, different care requirements

What you need to learn
● How people cope with change
● How to explain change to service users
● How to assist a transfer

How people cope with change

Most people who receive care will experience a change at some point, regardless of what that change is – whether it is something as apparently small as a new home carer or something as great as a residential home closing down and a move to somewhere new, it is still going to be worrying for the individual concerned.

There are two types of change that affect most people's lives. One is caused by predictable events and one by unpredictable events. Predictable events are things like:

● starting school
● getting married

● leaving school
● moving house.

Unpredictable events are things like:

- a sudden death
- accident
- redundancy
- winning the lottery.

People tend to cope in different ways with the two different types of event. Generally, it is easier to cope with a predictable event because people have had time to plan, to organise and to get used to the idea that it is going to happen. Unpredictable events can be much more difficult to cope with. Even nice changes like winning the lottery can be quite traumatic, although it is probably a way that most of us would like to be traumatised!

Check it out

Think of major events that have happened in your life. Make two lists with three or four items on each: one of unpredictable events and one of predictable events. Next write down what you can remember of your feelings about each of these events. Some of your memories may be a bit vague if they happened some time ago, but try to remember what you can. It is feelings which are important. Try to write down as many as you can.

You have probably found that many of your feelings, even about the planned and predictable changes in your life, were to do with anxiety and worry about how things would turn out. A new job can be something that you welcome, look forward to and are excited about, but that is still mixed with feelings of worry and anxiety, and questions like: Will it be alright? Will they be nice people? Will I be able to do the job? Imagine how much greater those feelings must be when people are moving from one care setting to another. Even a planned move can still bring with it a great many concerns and worries.

Unpredictable or unplanned events can obviously be even more difficult for people to cope with. Having to move into residential care, perhaps as the result of the death of a partner, the illness of a carer at home, because of a fall or because of illness, can make it very difficult for people to adjust to the new setting they find themselves in. This is hardly surprising – they have had no chance to think, to adjust, to plan or to ask questions and get any answers.

DID YOU KNOW?

The expression 'ringing the changes' is not about change at all! It comes from an old, complicated sequence in bellringing called 'change ringing'.

Helping people to cope with change

The best way for people to cope with change is generally to have the maximum possible amount of information. One of the key roles you will have in supporting people who are going through change is ensuring that their questions are answered and that they have information on which to base decisions and make plans. There have been many studies carried out into how people cope with major changes caused by loss – the death of a close relative or the loss of a limb, or major physical changes following an accident or an illness. Although a transfer from one type of care setting to another may not seem as drastic as any of these changes, it certainly can have similar effects for some people.

One of the most common findings in all of the research is that there are a number of stages in people's reactions to major and traumatic change. In general they follow a pattern of:

- *Stage 1: Shock and disbelief*
- *Stage 2: Denial*, where people tend to pretend that the change is not happening or that it is not as large a change as it may appear to be
- *Stage 3: Frustration*, a stage where the change is still not accepted and there is a great deal of frustration and anger about the fact that nothing can be done to change the situation
- *Stage 4: Depression and apathy*. This is the stage at which people say 'What is the point? How can I carry on?'
- *Stage 5: Experimental stage*, where people begin to accept that the change has happened, and start to experiment with the new situation
- *Stage 6: Decision*, where people start to decide how they are going to move forward from this point in their lives. They are accepting the change and coming to terms with it
- *Stage 7: Integration*, where change is now fully integrated into a person's life, he or she has completely come to terms with it and it is now a part of the way he or she lives.

All of this takes time, and the length of time varies depending on the nature of the change. The accepted time to work through these stages, for example in the case of bereavement, is about two years. Clearly other situations may take less or more time. Adjusting to a change to a new care setting is unlikely to take as long as adjusting to something as drastic as a bereavement, but nonetheless acceptance may not be immediate. So do not be surprised if a new resident, who has been admitted as an emergency, does not seem very friendly or chatty or want to take part in the activities of the care setting.

Give people as much information as possible, and offer reassurance and support.

The best way to support people through the stages of coping is to ensure that they are constantly reassured and constantly given information so that they can reach their own conclusions about the new situation. Always offer information and always make sure that you take the time to answer questions. Try to ensure that you include anybody new in any activity which is going on in your care setting. There is nothing worse than arriving somewhere new, perhaps where you do not want to be, feeling strange and also feeling left out and not knowing how to begin to join in.

CASE STUDY

T has been a resident in a small children's home for the past two years. She is 13 years old and attends the local school. Her mother died following an overdose and during most of T's life had had an intermittent drink and drugs problem. T maintains occasional contact with her grandmother, who is not able to care for her. Her father has had no contact with her throughout her life. T has generally adjusted well to life in care. She has made good relationships with the other young people and the staff, and apart from the occasional outburst and tantrum, has never presented any major difficulties with behaviour. A decision has been taken by the social services department that, in line with its policy of extending its community provision for young people, T's children's home is to close along with three others. The young people are to be relocated, either in one of the remaining children's homes in the city or in foster care.

Individual reviews have been held with all of the young people from the home and plans have been made. T has decided that she wants to go to a foster home and the care team are happy to agree to this. T has been asked if she has any preferences about the kind of family she wants to live with. She has decided that she would like other children to be in the family, but that she does not mind if there are one or two parents. T wants to live in town rather than the country, does not mind if she has to change school and wants a family who have a dog. A suitable foster home has been found for her, she has been told about it and shown photographs. T decided that she would like to meet the family. So introductory visits have been made, after which both T and the family have decided that they want to go ahead. Finally, the date arrives for T to move on a permanent basis.

1   What do you think T's feelings will be?
2   What issues should have been considered before the move was planned?
3   From the information given, do you think they were all considered? Was anything missed?
4   What sort of behaviour could you expect from T?
5   What help do you think that T may need in the immediate future?

In the case study of T it is clear that she was given a lot of information. She was able to meet her new foster carers and visit them, the reasons for the home closing were obviously explained to her and she had time to plan. However, this is not always the case, as the following case study shows.

CASE STUDY

Mr P has terminal cancer. He is 65 years old. He is cared for by his wife, with the support of Macmillan nurses. He has always remained at home for most of his treatment and both he and his wife have been adamant that they do not want to consider any form of hospital or hospice care. Mr P is now at a stage where he is taking a fairly substantial number of painkillers and his mobility has decreased. Although he gets up each day, he only moves into the lounge, where he sits by the window overlooking the garden. On mild days he is able to walk out onto the patio, but this is the furthest he can manage.

On the way back from the local shops one day, his wife was involved in a serious car accident. She was admitted to hospital and is likely to be there for several weeks. Mr P was taken to the local hospice by his Macmillan nurse. He had never been to the hospice before, but he has been told about his wife's condition and knows that he may have to remain there for some time.

1 What is Mr P likely to be feeling?
2 What immediate help does he need?
3 What would have been the ideal way of his coming into the hospice?
4 What would you say to Mr P now? Tomorrow? Next week?

Change without information is a time of anxiety and confusion.

Change is easier to manage with information.

The two case studies show two very different situations – one where there was plenty of opportunity to plan and for T to have all the information she needed, and the other where Mr P had virtually no information at all. The two individuals concerned are likely to have responded very differently to their two experiences and your role in each situation would be different, but still concerned with achieving the same result – an acceptance of the change that they have experienced.

How to explain change to service users

In many ways, explaining change to people and thus giving them the opportunity to ask questions and to understand is the key to achieving a happy transition and an acceptance of the new circumstances. You must be sure that the individual understands completely the reason why the change or transfer is necessary and has every opportunity to reinforce that information. Even if you feel you are repeating the same thing over and over again, it is still very important to keep on giving information.

The type of information you provide, and the way you provide it, should be suitable for an individual's level of understanding, for example, whether you are dealing with an adult or a child. Sometimes there may be barriers to communication and understanding, such as individuals who are confused, who do not understand English very well, or who have a hearing or visual impairment. In such cases, you may need to call upon others to help you explain the change – your colleagues, the individual's family or friends, a signer or an interpreter. You may find that you need to speak more slowly, repeat information several times and simplify the information (without missing out anything important!). Verbal information may need to be supplemented with written information, pictures, plans or with visits, to ensure that the individual gains as much understanding of the change as possible.

One of the hardest situations to deal with is change or transfer because a facility is closing down and it is something which has been forced on the individual. It is also quite likely that the decision to close is unwelcome to the staff and one that you have difficulty in supporting. This makes it doubly difficult to achieve a positive outlook for everyone who is to make the transfer.

Keys to good practice

Steps towards explaining change

✓ Ensure that the individual has the opportunity to express how he or she feels about the change.

✓ Make sure the individual has all possible information about why the change is taking place.

✓ Make sure the individual has all the information about what the changes will mean – this could include making visits, looking at plans and photographs, and anything at all which will help to give a clear picture.

✓ Make sure the individual has all the information about any possible legal or financial implications of the move.

✓ Make sure the individual is thoroughly prepared and that you offer whatever assistance he or she may need with the transfer.

It can be very hard to support and explain a change that you do not agree with. However, it has to be done in the interests of the individual concerned, in the hope that he or she can be helped to make as easy a transfer to a new situation as possible. The realities have to be explained – it is unfair and unkind to give people a false reassurance that things 'may be alright' or may not have to change. If you are absolutely clear about a change being permanent – for instance, if you know that a facility is about to close, or if the individual has already been told that he or she is unable to return home, or if a child or young person knows that following a review a decision has been made about a move – you must reinforce that decision and explain to the individual the reasons for it and the fact that it is inevitable and try to help him or her to prepare to deal with it in a constructive way.

If you disagree with a change, it is perfectly reasonable for you to join with residents in protesting about the closure of a home or a day centre, because you are fighting on their behalf and acting as an advocate for them. However, at the stage where it becomes clear that it is no longer feasible to change such a decision then you do have to accept the inevitable and begin to prepare the individuals in your care to accept the change in a positive way.

Make sure individuals have every opportunity to express their feelings about the transfer.

Keys to good practice

✓ Give plenty of information about the new facility.
✓ Provide written information, plans, photographs.
✓ Arrange a visit to the new facility.
✓ Arrange a visit from staff who work there and others who use the facility.
✓ Make sure you answer all questions and concerns.
✓ Inform any friends and relatives, as requested by individuals.

How to assist a transfer

Your role in assisting a smooth transfer from one facility to another is crucial, whether it be:

● from hospital to residential care
● from home into hospital
● from residential care to foster home
● from residential care to supported living, or
● from supported living to independence.

The key thing that you must do is to establish the level of assistance an individual actually wants. It is very easy for people to lose the feeling that they have any kind of control over the transfer, if you simply take over and arrange everything for them. Discuss with the individual the level of assistance that he or she is going to need.

● If the transfer is going to require transport, find out if you need to arrange it.
● If it is going to involve moving personal property and belongings, ask the individual what he or she wants to move and what you can move for him/her.
● Find out from the individual:
  – who needs to be told of the move
  – who he or she will tell
  – who you can tell on his or her behalf.

Never assume that somebody wants you to do something without checking with him or her first. If people are able to do things for themselves they are far more likely to feel a part of what is happening and to feel more committed to it. If a person just feels like a spectator, he or she is going to find the change much more difficult to come to terms with.

A change may not mean an individual moving from one care setting to another. It may simply be a change of carer or a change of service. For example, the agency providing a person's care may change, the home care assistant may change, or perhaps the individual may begin to receive care at night as well as during the day. In this sort of situation, it is just as important that you help the individual to prepare for the change he or she is going to experience. There may be fewer physical changes and arrangements to make, but it is just as important that the individual should receive the maximum amount of information and have the opportunity to ask questions.

Making links

It may be that you can offer a useful role in giving somebody a link between the place that they are in now and the new place they are moving to, by physically going with the person and helping him or her to settle in. Alternatively, you may be able to arrange for a care worker from the new establishment to accompany the individual (and perhaps you) to the new care setting and to help to settle the person in. Make sure that, where the transfer does involve a physical move, carers in the new setting are aware of all of a service user's personal preferences: likes and dislikes, views, beliefs and all the personal details that are very important to ensure that a person's needs are met and that he or she settles more quickly.

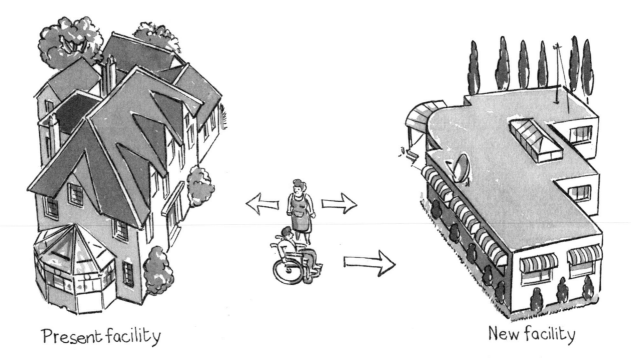

Present facility   New facility

The care worker acts as a 'bridge' between the old and the new care setting.

It is helpful, for example, if the new carers know how an individual likes his or her room to be set out. Perhaps he or she prefers the bed to face the window or to be near to the door. Some people may like particular plants or flowers in their rooms. If there are touches which you know would mean a lot to an individual, in addition to his or her personal belongings, then that is invaluable information to be passed on, so the person can feel that his or her own personality and wishes are being taken into account.

Some of this personal information (including diet, religion, next of kin, doctor and medication) will be included in the individual's records, which will need to be transferred to the new setting. It is important to check that any records you complete are clear, accurate and up-to-date before the transfer takes place. On the day of the move, the records should be handed over to the appropriate member of staff at the new setting.

Check it out

Think about what you miss about home when you go away on holiday. Make a list. It is unlikely to be only people you miss – perhaps your immediate family or a close friend – but often things like your own bed, a decent cup of tea, your favourite biscuits, a comfy chair, your garden, your dog or cat. When you have finished your list, think about how much worse it must be for someone going somewhere new, and missing all those things – but without the knowledge that they will be going home after a week or two.

TEST YOURSELF

1 Why is it important to give people information about changes?

2 What practical help may you need to provide?

3 What emotional support may you need to offer?

4 What is the most important factor to check with the service user?

5 What are the main stages in adapting to change?

Element W3.2 Enable individuals to become familiar with new care requirements

What you need to learn
- How to prepare a new environment
- How to give information about a new setting
- How to assist the settling-in process

How to prepare a new environment

The information which should have come to you from an individual's previous care setting will help you to make sure that the new setting is as ready for him or her as possible. If the information is not volunteered by the previous establishment, you should make sure that you ask for the information you are going to need to help the individual adjust to the new surroundings. You will need to know about a person's:

- likes and dislikes
- preferences regarding his or her room if you are in a residential setting
- food preferences and/or dietary requirements or restrictions
- personal beliefs and values.

You will also need to know about any special arrangements that need to be made regarding access and visits.

All of this information is just as important whether you are dealing with an older person, someone with a disability, a child, someone with mental health problems or someone who is confused.

Their needs will be different, but the basic information that you need to know will be the same for all of them. Keep a checklist that you always follow whenever somebody new comes to your care setting or whenever you take over a caring function for a new individual. The list that you need could look like the one below.

Checklist for new residents

1. How much will the individual decide for himself or herself? ✓
2. Family and friends – who's special/significant? ✓
3. Special arrangements for room? ✓
4. Food – likes/dislikes? ✓
5. Religion/values/beliefs? ✓
6. Activities – likes/dislikes? ✓
7. Particular requirements? ✓

The more information you have in advance of someone's arrival, the better the chance that he or she will feel welcomed and settled in the new place or with new people. Provided the individual is able to communicate, you should ensure that he or she is the first person that you speak to when finding out information. Ask the individual to tell you what he or she needs and any arrangements that he or she would like to be made. It is only in situations where a person is unable to give you some or all of the information you need that you should go elsewhere for personal information.

How to give information about a new setting

As always, information is the key to whether or not people are able to settle. There are some situations in which the giving of information is very difficult. For example, if a person is very confused and disorientated, it may be hard. He or she may appear not to be able to take in the information that you are giving. However, this does not mean that you should not attempt to give as much information as you can and to try to familiarise the person with the new environment.

A move to a new setting can be very disruptive, particularly for older people. It can cause confusion and disorientation. A person who was not previously confused may become very muddled when he or she moves to somewhere new. If this happens, it is important that you report it – it could be an indication of a problem and some intervention may be needed. On the other hand, it could be a reaction to being in unfamiliar surroundings. Be careful about attributing every problem to the new surroundings – there may an illness developing which needs medical help.

Steps to giving information

- You will need first to consider the person you are giving information to and what his or her needs may be.
- If you are talking to a child or young person, the sort of information that he or she will want about the new surroundings will be quite different from that given to an older, confused person, or perhaps to somebody with a learning disability. See the table below.
- It is important that the information you give is at a level that the person receiving it can understand. Everyone's needs are different and the amount of information that each can absorb will be different.
- You will need to think about any special arrangements that you need to make for giving information, such as particular language difficulties, interpreters or signers who may be needed, and the person's general level of understanding.
- You may find that you have to repeat the same information several times. This may reflect the individual's level of understanding, or may be because of his or her level of anxiety about the changes.
- Consider whether you should provide some written or taped information that the individual can refer to when needed.

The different sorts of information people may want

Individual	Type of information
Teenager	How late can I stay out? How loud can I play my music? How do I get to school? How many mates can I have in my room at once? Can my mates stay the night? What time is tea? Can I go to the clubs in town? Do I have to share a room?
An adult with a disability	What kind of transport will there be? What arrangements are there for physio and other services? Will the finances be any different? Is there much social life? Is there access to any sports or other organised activities? Do we have to eat together, or can we help ourselves when we get in?
An adult with a learning disability	Are people nice here? Can my room be pink? Will there be a disco? Can my mum come and see me? Do I go on the same bus? Can I go to the same centre?
Older person	Why do I have to move? Will the food be very different? Will it cost any more money? Will my friends still be able to visit me? How will my niece get here? Will the staff be as nice? Will I still get a chiropodist? Does the hairdresser come?

Find out what information your workplace gives to new service users. Check the formats in which it is available. Is it available in large print? Can it be given out on tape? Is it for service users, or aimed at relatives? If there is no pack available, think about talking to your supervisor about putting one together.

How to assist the settling-in process

Showing people around a new care setting

You will need to show a new arrival around the care setting. In a residential setting, you will need to show the person first and foremost the area which is to be his or her own space.

Whether the setting is a residential home, supported living, hospital care or a nursing home, the single most important factor is the space that a person is able to call his or her own, whether that is a room or simply a bed with a curtain around it on a ward. Whatever that space consists of, it is the first thing that an individual should be introduced to, and to have a chance to get to know.

Next, the individual needs to be able to get his or her bearings and to find out how to get from his or her room to the communal facilities, such as the lounge or dining room, the bathrooms, or out into the garden, if there is one. You will need to be aware, as with other information, that the pace at which you introduce a person to a new environment must be at a level he or she can cope with. There is no value in giving an older person, who is muddled and distressed by a move, a full guided tour of a residential facility, all at once. However, a bright and interested individual who has a physical disability may well want to know every nook, cranny and cupboard and want lots of details about how the place operates.

REMEMBER

A curious ten-year-old may want to explore, but a confused 80-year-old may possibly just be able to cope with learning how to get from his or her bedroom to the lounge.

Introductions

Introductions are obviously about more than places – they are also about the people who are in them. If you have a new resident you must make sure that he or she is introduced to everyone else who lives there, again bearing in mind the person's ability to cope with vast amounts of new information. This needs to be carefully handled so that he or she is not overwhelmed. Some people, of course, may be keen to meet as many new people as possible and very excited by being in their new surroundings. Staff will need to be introduced, particularly the key workers and the team leader for each shift.

It is very important that a new individual is told the systems to use in emergencies and how to obtain help when needed. The system in the previous establishment may have been different and it is vital that he or she learns immediately how to get help.

Making plans

You may need to make individual plans for people who come to your establishment. Some may be shy or confused or not particularly sociable, and in this case you may decide that an introduction to one or two people would probably be better, rather than trying to meet everybody at once. It is often possible to 'match' people up where you know people share similar interests, or where you know somebody is particularly warm, friendly and welcoming. Everyone has met the situation where an existing 'clique' bands together to make a newcomer feel unwelcome and, in the process, attempt to make themselves feel more secure. This behaviour has to be gently discouraged and a way around it established, either by introducing an individual who shares an interest or by involving the new person in the activities of the clique.

You may find that you have to repeat introductions and directions several times. It is very easy to forget things you have been told when you are feeling nervous or flustered at the start of something new.

> **! REMEMBER**
>
> Think about a time when you have felt nervous or unsure of yourself – perhaps the first day of a new job, the first day at college, going to an event, or meeting somebody for the first time. Try to remember how you felt, and particularly remember the feeling that you were unable to take in everything that was said to you.

The atmosphere of a new place can have a tremendous influence on how easily people are able to settle.

The whole atmosphere of a new place can have a tremendous influence on how easily people are able to settle. Somewhere which feels warm, welcoming and friendly is always easier to adapt to and to learn about, than a place which seems to have a lot of rules and regulations and where it is easy to feel afraid that you will do the wrong thing or make a mistake.

Special requirements

There are some situations that you need to give special consideration to when thinking about helping people to settle in. Someone who has impaired sight or hearing will need special introductions, both in terms of people and orientation to the place in which he or she is. Remember, too, that particularly for people with impaired vision, you will need to re-run an introduction to their surroundings if those surroundings are ever changed in any way by moving furniture, changing the use of rooms, or having building works carried out.

For someone who has hearing difficulties, you must find out what he or she needs from you in order to be able to communicate. This could vary from a signer for somebody who is profoundly deaf, to merely ensuring that you speak clearly or on a particular side for someone who is hard of hearing. People who are confused and disorientated frequently find it extremely difficult to adapt to somewhere new. To try to learn the layout of a new building or to become familiar with new faces is a massive task and can only be tackled in small pieces. Simple techniques of reality orientation can be useful here in giving reminders about where they are, the day, the time, and which room they are in – whether it is the dining room, the lounge or the bedroom. Carers' name badges are also useful. Be sure, though, that you do not mix up temporary confusion and disorientation, brought on by a move to new surroundings, with a long-term, permanent dementia.

You may need to spend extra time with somebody new and make sure that you join with him or her in activities, meal times and other social events until he or she begins to make friends and contacts with others in the care setting. It is important that familiar visitors are encouraged to come and see the individual in his or her new setting, partly so that the individual is reassured that visitors will still come and that he or she will be able to maintain contacts with the people who are close, and partly because anything which is familiar and reassuring is very important at this stage.

All people are individuals and all their needs will be different, but the steps outlined in this chapter are a blueprint that will apply in general no matter who the individual is or what is the nature of his or her circumstances.

CASE STUDY

Mrs W is 83, physically frail but mentally alert. She has glaucoma and has been blind for the past eight years. The residential care home she has lived in for the past seven years is closing and all the residents have to move. She is very apprehensive about the move and, like all her fellow residents, does not want to go.

Recently, Mrs W made an introductory visit to the new care home. She was met by Karen, who was to be her key worker. Karen touched Mrs W on the arm and introduced herself. She took her to what was to be her room and described the corridor they were walking down. She took Mrs W into her room and described everything in there, including all the colours and the patterns on the curtains and quilt cover. Mrs W was able to touch everything and find her way around.

Karen repeated this throughout the home. Then she and Mrs W sat and had a cup of tea and a chat with some of the other residents before Karen took her on a walk around the garden, where Mrs W was delighted with the raised beds and large numbers of scented plants and flowers.

Before she left, Karen gave her a tape she had made which reminded Mrs W of all the things she had shown her. Mrs W said she felt much better about going and was even quite looking forward to it!

1   Was the introduction handled well?
2   What do you think Mrs W's feelings were before the visit?
3   What were her feelings after the visit?
4   Why was the tape important?
5   Why was it important that Karen described patterns and colours?

Keys to good practice

✓ First, show people their own 'space'.
✓ Go at the individual's pace.
✓ Give the person the information he or she needs and is able to handle.
✓ Make the person feel welcome.
✓ Introduce the individual to other people he or she will live with.
✓ Give the individual time, and be prepared to repeat information.
✓ Agree all your actions with the care team and include them in the plan of care.

W3 UNIT TEST

1 Name three different circumstances in which people may have to transfer to a different care setting.

2 Why is it important to allow the individual to say how he or she feels about a move?

3 What should you do if you disagree with the move?

4 Name at least three important pieces of information which you should pass on to a new care establishment.

5 State why each of these pieces of information is important.

6 If you were welcoming a new individual to your care setting, what is the first thing you would do?

7 Which individuals find it most difficult to transfer from one establishment to another?

8 Name at least two situations in which you would have to make special arrangements for introduction.

Unit Z6

Enable clients to maintain and improve their mobility through exercise and the use of mobility appliances

Exercise is extremely important for health and for giving a feeling of well-being. The benefits of exercise for any individual, regardless of level of disability or dependency, are both a physical and an emotional improvement of his or her condition. You will need to know about how to maintain people's mobility, despite their age or infirmity or the level of disability or difficulties they may experience. It is important that you are able to offer them encouragement and to help them to exercise to their maximum potential.

Mobility appliances help with walking and getting around, and can make a major difference to someone's life. Being able to be mobile allows people to maintain their independence and allows them to avoid relying on human assistance. There is a world of difference between being able to go where you want, when you want to, even if you go there very slowly, and having to wait while arrangements involving someone else are made.

It is likely that this chapter will provide useful knowledge for Unit Z5 from Option Group B.

Element Z6.1 Enable clients to exercise

What you need to learn

- What is exercise?
- Why exercise is important
- How to help individuals to follow an exercise programme

What is exercise?

Exercise can be a formal programme, assessed by a physiotherapist, or a specific form of exercise designed to increase mobility or to improve strength, stamina or suppleness. But more importantly, it includes the simple day-to-day activities which everyone carries out involving some form of physical movement.

At its simplest, exercise is the contraction and relaxation of muscles in order to produce movement. These muscle movements use energy and raise the heart rate and breathing rate. These increased heart and breathing rates strengthen the cardiovascular system, while the movement itself tones and strengthens the muscles.

The effects of exercise

Exercise → Increased heart and lung activity → Improved cardiovascular system

Exercise → Increased use of muscles → Improved muscle strength and tone

All of those outcomes can be achieved through a properly designed exercise programme. They are also encouraged by the day-to-day activities which most people carry out, such as getting up from a chair, walking across a room, washing, dressing, going up and down stairs. This is why it is important to encourage service users to be as mobile as possible within the limits of their physical condition.

Why exercise is important

Exercise matters because:

- it strengthens and tones muscles
- it improves the cardiovascular system which controls breathing and the circulation of blood
- it improves sleep
- it uses up calories and keeps weight balanced
- it promotes a feeling of well-being.

The diagrams on pages 228 and 229 show how the skeletal muscles and cardiovascular system are arranged within the body and how they are all interlinked.

The diagram of the muscular system illustrates how muscles are attached to the bony skeleton. Muscles work like hinges or levers – they pull and move particular joints. When a muscle contracts (gets shorter), it pulls a joint in the direction that it is designed to move. Muscles can become slack and make movement slower and more difficult, but when muscles are regularly used they are firm and easy to move.

The diagram of the cardiovascular system shows how the heart is basically a pump made up of muscle which pumps the blood around the body to keep organs and muscles alive. The vessels which carry the blood are called veins and arteries. Together with the heart they comprise the cardiovascular system. The oxygen which the body needs is provided through the lungs, and both the lungs and the heart are improved by being exercised regularly.

DID YOU KNOW?

During exercise, the heart can pump over 30 times more blood around the body than when at rest. The blood vessels expand to cope with the extra volume of blood.

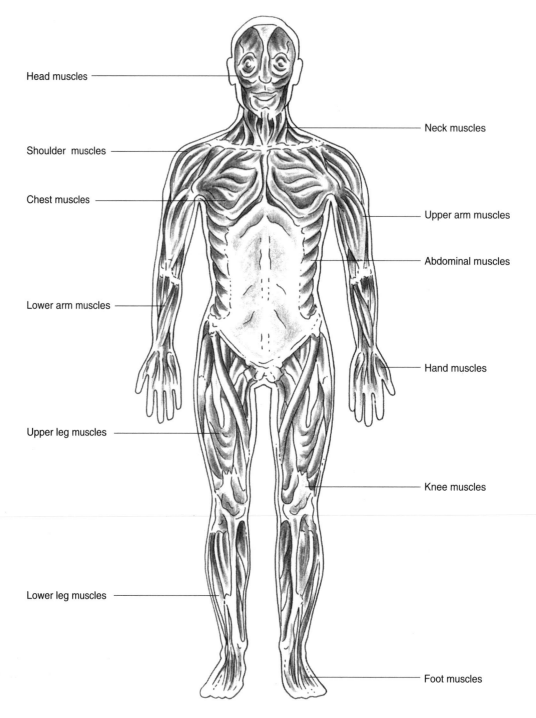

Head muscles

Neck muscles

Shoulder muscles

Chest muscles

Upper arm muscles

Abdominal muscles

Lower arm muscles

Hand muscles

Upper leg muscles

Knee muscles

Lower leg muscles

Foot muscles

The muscular system.

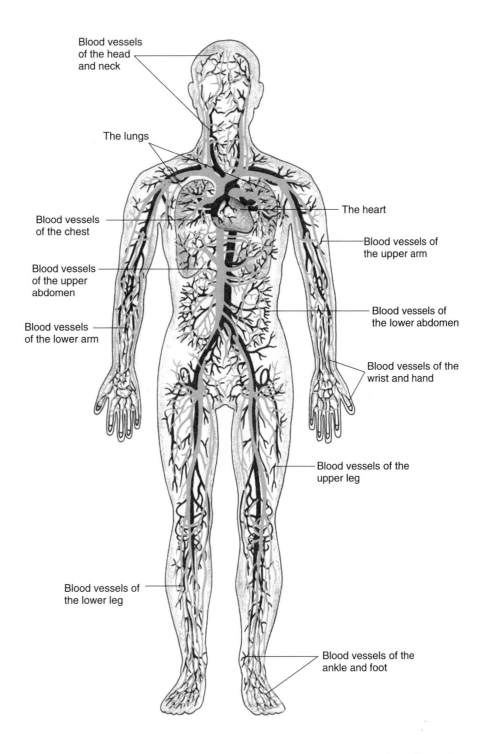

Blood vessels of the head and neck

The lungs

Blood vessels of the chest

Blood vessels of the upper abdomen

Blood vessels of the lower arm

Blood vessels of the lower leg

The heart

Blood vessels of the upper arm

Blood vessels of the lower abdomen

Blood vessels of the wrist and hand

Blood vessels of the upper leg

Blood vessels of the ankle and foot

The cardiovascular system.

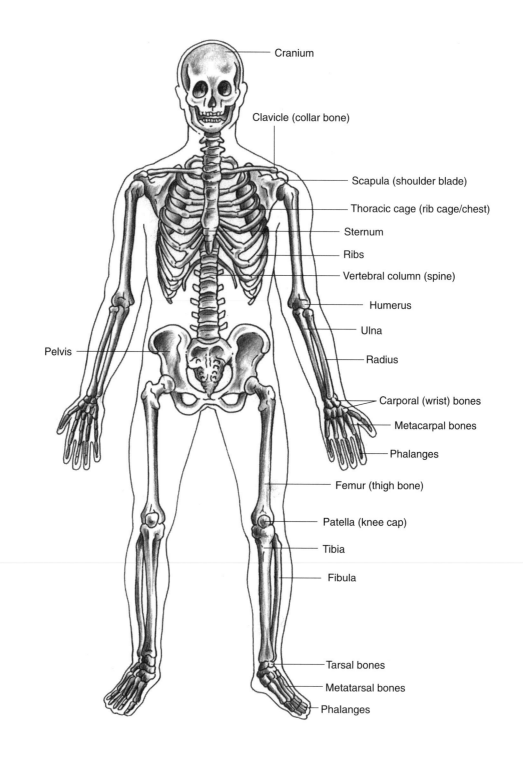

The skeleton.

(a) Types of joint

Hinge joint, e.g. the knee, which can straighten or bend in the same way a door hinge opens or closes

Pivot joint, e.g. the elbow, which allows the lower arm to rotate

Saddle joint, e.g. the thumb

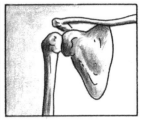

Ball and socket joint – the most flexible free-moving joint, e.g. the shoulder and the hip

(b) How the knee moves

The muscles responsible for moving the knee run from the upper to the lower leg. Those in the front of the upper leg (the **quadriceps**) pull on the tibia (lower leg bone) to straighten the leg. The muscles at the back of the upper leg make the knee joint bend.

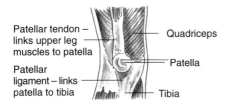

Patellar tendon – links upper leg muscles to patella

Quadriceps

Patella

Patellar ligament – links patella to tibia

Tibia

(c) How the upper arm moves

The large muscles in the upper arm work together to raise and bend the arm. The most powerful arm muscle is the **biceps brachii**. If you bend your arm up and down, you will feel your biceps working.

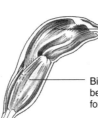

Deltoid muscle – raises the arm sideways, pulls it forward and backward and rotates it onward and outward

Biceps brachii – the bulging muscle which bends the arm at the elbow and rotates the forearm so the palm of the hand faces upward

How joints and muscles work together.

Exercise can be specifically defined to improve particular conditions. A physiotherapist would make an assessment and design a particular programme for an individual with this in mind. For example:

● Following a stroke, an exercise programme will be designed by a physiotherapist to work on strengthening the areas weakened by the stroke.
● Following surgery to replace a hip joint, the key to recovery and regaining full use of the joint will be the plan devised by the physiotherapist.
● Many people who use wheelchairs may have special exercise programmes to ensure that their muscles remain active as far as possible, and to promote their general fitness levels.
● Exercise programmes are vital for asthmatics and others with chest problems. Exercise strengthens and helps to expand airways to make breathing easier.

DID YOU KNOW?

The latest research has developed a device for asthmatics which actually strengthens the lung muscles. The theory is that this will reduce wheezing. Early trials are showing great success.

If you are working with older people you should never assume that it is 'just old age' when they begin to slow down or become less mobile. There may be a physical condition which is causing the loss of mobility and, if this is noticed at an early stage, it can often be treated or at least alleviated so that many of the mobility problems are reduced.

Mr K is 72. He is a former schoolteacher who lives with his wife. They are both fit and well and are very involved in the local historical society and interested in art, literature and the theatre. Both are also active members of the local dramatic society and involved in all their productions. Mr K's greatest joy in life is reading, and his lately discovered interest – the Internet.

Recently he noticed that his eyesight was getting worse. He had had his glasses renewed recently, so he put the deterioration down to increasing age. He had to stop reading unless he was sitting in bright sunshine, and could not see the computer screen properly. He stopped attending the dramatic society because he could not read the scripts and he was becoming depressed about his lack of ability to enjoy his interests.

Eventually, his wife persuaded him to see the doctor about his eyes, although he still insisted it was 'old age' and nothing could be done. However, the doctor immediately diagnosed cataracts and Mr K was referred for a simple surgical procedure first in one eye and then the second, which completely restored his sight and enabled him to carry on with a full and active life.

1   How common do you think it is for people to dismiss problems as 'old age'?
2   What could have happened if Mr K's wife had not persuaded him to see the doctor?
3   Which aspects of Mr K's needs would not be met if he stopped his activities?
4   What could be the effects?

Exercise is vital as people grow older. It can make the difference between an active old age and one spent sitting in a chair and shuffling around. It does not have to be a specially designed programme, but just remaining active. Walking around the house, preparing a meal and taking a walk are all valid forms of exercise which you must encourage.

There are many active older people who live busy and fulfilled lives.

How to help individuals to follow an exercise programme

If you are working with an individual who has been given an exercise programme, it is important to remember that the programme will have been devised by the physiotherapist, or other specialist, for a specific condition or to improve general fitness and mobility. It must, therefore, be carried out exactly as it has been planned.

You must ensure that:

- the exercise programme is detailed in the plan of care
- it is followed accurately
- the individual is given encouragement and support to follow the programme
- progress in carefully recorded, and achievement is recognised and applauded
- any problems are immediately reported to your manager and to the professional who designed the programme.

However, if you are simply trying to encourage someone to be more active, you need to be aware of all the simple activities that can be undertaken. This includes encouraging the person to go and get something for himself or herself, rather than you getting it because it is quicker. It may be much easier, when somebody says he or she has forgotten a cardigan, for you just to nip back to get it, but it may be better to encourage the person to do it himself or herself. You should encourage people to do something active rather than sit and watch TV. If it is possible, within their physical limitations, people should be assisted and encouraged to:

- walk where possible
- climb stairs if they are able
- go swimming or take part in an active game
- do stretching exercises.

Check it out

Find out what the exercise programme is for your workplace. Is it formal and organised? Is there a policy of encouraging activity? What is the attitude towards encouraging people to move around and do things for themselves, even if this takes a long time?

Keys to good practice

✓ Explain any exercise plan clearly to the individual before you begin and make sure that he or she is in agreement with it and willing to participate.
✓ Never attempt to impose any kind of exercise or activity regime on anybody unless he or she is willing, because the programme simply will not work unless a person is happy to join in.
✓ Encourage people to do as much as possible for themselves, because part of the benefit of exercise is an increase in independence.

You will need to make sure that an individual is able to exercise in a safe environment. This will include:

- checking that the floor surfaces are safe
- checking that there is nothing that can be tripped over or that could cause injury.

If the exercise is being carried out by a person sitting in a wheelchair:

- check that the wheelchair is absolutely stable and steady
- check that the brakes are firmly on.

If the exercise is being carried out by someone in bed:

- make sure that it is stable and steady
- ensure that the bed brakes are firmly on.

If a service user is using any kind of walking aid, you will need to ensure that it is being used properly and has been measured correctly to make sure it is the correct size.

Clothes

The clothes that an individual wears are a part of the exercise environment. You should make sure that they are appropriate for exercise. It is no coincidence that the tracksuits and trainers worn by athletes for many years have now been adopted as regular wear by people relaxing or taking part in leisure exercise, as they are so comfortable and easy to wear.

This type of clothing may be suitable for all kinds of people undertaking exercise. You

The correct clothing helps to maintain the person's dignity as well as safety.

will need to make sure that shoes are firm and comfortable and offer support, and that any exercise which involves standing or moving the feet is not carried out in loose or ill-fitting shoes or slippers, but in firm, well-fitting, well-supporting shoes with safe, non-slip soles. The correct clothing also helps to maintain people's dignity, as they need not fear that the exercise will involve them in exposing parts of themselves which they would rather keep covered!

If you are assisting a person to follow a programme designed by a physiotherapist, your role may be quite clearly defined. There may be times when you need to lend physical assistance or you may be required to assist in the case of exercise aids which are used as part of the programme. For example, someone who has had a stroke may be squeezing a rubber ball in his or her hand in order to strengthen the arm and hand muscles on one side of the body. Your job may be to count the number of repetitions of an exercise.

> ## REMEMBER
> If you are involved in a policy within your workplace to encourage a higher level of activity amongst the people whom you care for, your best contribution may be not to help! By not helping you can encourage people to be much more active and hence improve their own mobility.

How to encourage individuals and record progress

One of the most significant factors which affects how well people carry out exercise programmes is whether or not they feel confident – and support and encouragement can play a major part in this.

You will need to ensure that any exercise plan is being properly followed. It is important that you do not alter any aspect of an exercise plan. If someone is having problems following the exercises as they have been set, because they are too difficult, too strenuous or are causing discomfort, you must report this immediately to the physiotherapist or to your supervisor.

Do not ever advise anyone to do an exercise in a different way, even though it may seem to you that, if he or she simply moved a little to the left or to the right, or did it a little bit differently, it would be easier and less painful or difficult. You should never make such a suggestion, as you could cause serious injury or further discomfort or pain to the person. Any difficulties should be reported to the professional who prepared the programme.

Keys to good practice

✓ Follow the exercise plan as it has been designed.
✓ If a person is in pain or discomfort, stop, and report this to your manager.
✓ Do not attempt to adapt the exercise.

It may not be necessary for you to assist a person physically in order to give him or her support; it may be sufficient for you simply to be there offering verbal support and encouragement as he or she carries out the exercise programme. Your support and encouragement could range from going along to the local gym to support one of your residents who plays in a wheelchair basketball team, to giving words of encouragement to a paralysed stroke victim who is lying in bed trying to raise an arm by two or three inches.

Recording progress

Recording a person's progress on an exercise programme is important. The physiotherapist will want regularly to review the progress that is being made so that he or she can change and update the programme as necessary. You should take careful notes about how many times an exercise has been repeated and whether there is any evidence that flexibility, suppleness or strength is improving as a result. If the person's participation is aimed at becoming more active generally, you should regularly note in his or her records the differences that a more active approach is making to his or her general level of fitness, alertness and mobility.

CASE STUDY

Strawberry Mill is a hostel for people with mental health problems. The effects of medication and the previous lifestyles of several residents have contributed to the fact that most of the residents (and staff!) are unfit. At a house meeting, it was decided to start a fitness programme. The residents decided to call it 'Best Foot Forward'. It was decided to hold an exercise class every other evening, with a basic exercise video for everyone to follow. They also decided that everyone would walk to the shops instead of getting a lift or using the bus for just two stops, and that there would be a rota for taking the hostel dog for a walk, instead of leaving it to the officer in charge!

Some residents also decided they would try to stop smoking and stop eating so many sweets and chocolates.

They started by weighing everyone, and by asking people to record what they could do before getting out of breath. Most could not even get up the stairs without puffing. After four weeks everyone was weighed again and asked how they felt. Out of the eight who had started, six were still doing the programme. They had lost an average of four pounds each and they all said they felt much better and less lethargic. All the six people felt that they had more energy. One person had stopped smoking and three were eating sweets only on Saturday nights.

1 What do you think helped to make the programme work?
2 What would you have expected the results to be?
3 What other activities could the group have tried?
4 How can they keep motivated to carry on?
5 What other benefits may come from this programme?

Element Z6.2 Assist clients to use mobility appliances

What you need to learn

- What mobility appliances do
- How to use mobility appliances
- How to monitor and record progress

What mobility appliances do

At their simplest, mobility appliances assist a person to become or to continue to be mobile, either by providing support or, like a wheelchair, by providing the actual mobility.

Mobility appliances such as walking sticks, crutches, quadrupeds and walking frames work by providing support for people who have become unsteady or whose joints or muscles are weak or painful. They also provide additional security where someone has had a fall or is recovering from illness. Often, the loss of confidence after an incident such as a fall is as damaging to mobility as any injury sustained.

How to use mobility appliances

Mobility appliances will be recommended by an appropriate professional, either a physiotherapist or occupational therapist. This professional will have explained to the individual how the appliances are to be used, and there will have been an opportunity to try them under supervision. However, you will need to reinforce the advice and continue to support service users until they are confident and are using appliances correctly.

There are particular ways of using the various mobility appliances in order to get the maximum benefit from them. It is important that you ensure that individuals are using them in the correct way, because otherwise they are likely to cause injury or discomfort.

It is also important to explain to individuals how different floor surfaces and floor coverings affect the use and safety of appliances.

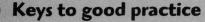

Check it out

One of the most useful things you can do before beginning to teach or encourage anyone in the use of walking aids is to try them out yourself, using the correct methods (see pages 239–243), so that you know how it feels to use the walking aid and the difficulties that you might encounter. Ask your supervisor if you can try the appliances available in your workplace.

Think about how different floor surfaces may affect the use of the appliance you are trying – consider slopes, steps, gravel paths, tiled floors, carpeted floors, etc. Some surfaces, such as steps, may be unsuitable and unsafe. Your supervisor and experienced users can advise you about this.

Write notes on each appliance – how easy or difficult it was to use, how it performs on different surfaces, where it is not safe to use it. Keep the notes for future reference when you are advising individuals, and add to the notes as you gain experience by seeing individuals using the appliances.

Keys to good practice

✓ You should check the condition of all mobility aids on a regular basis.
✓ It is important that, if you notice any signs of damage or wear, you immediately stop a person from using it. Report the fault at once and make arrangements for a replacement or repair.

REMEMBER

A mobility aid which fails during use, when somebody is relying on it, is far more dangerous and useless than no mobility aid at all.

Walking stick

Measuring a walking stick

To measure a stick correctly you need to ask the person to hold it in the hand which is opposite to his or her 'bad side', if he/she has one. If the weakness or pain is not located in a particular side of the body but is more general, for instance spinal problems, the person should use the stick on the side of the body which he or she would normally use most, i.e. the right-hand side for right-handers, the left-hand for left-handed people.

You should ensure that the person's hand is at the same height as the top of his or her thigh when it is resting on the stick handle. The elbow should be slightly bent, but make sure that the shoulders are level and that one side is not pushed higher.

● With an adjustable metal stick, you will be able to measure fairly easily by sliding the inner part of the stick up and down until the correct height is reached. The metal button will then snap into place in the guide holes.
● With a wooden walking stick, you will need to measure the correct height and then the person responsible should saw the stick to the proper length, making sure that the rubber ferrule is firmly attached to the bottom of the stick.

- It is important that you check that the ferrule is in good condition because, if it becomes worn or the suction ridges have become smooth, the stick is likely to slip when leaned on.

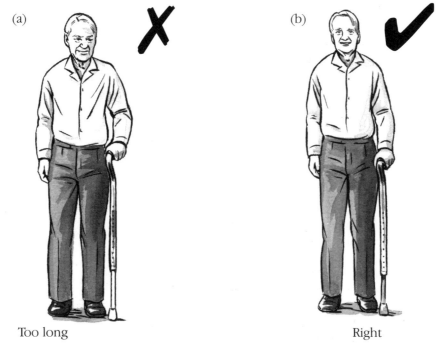

(a) Too long

(b) Right

Each individual needs to be measured for a walking stick.

Using a walking stick

Depending on how much support a person needs, there are two generally recommended ways of using a walking stick.

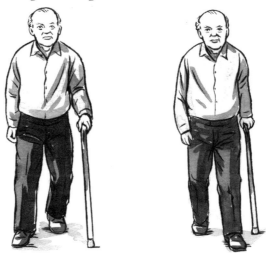

Walking correctly with a walking stick.

- For a person who needs a considerable degree of support, move the stick forward, slightly to one side. Then take a step with the opposite foot, going no further forward than the level of the stick, then take a step with the foot on the same side as the stick. This should go past the position of the stick. Then move the stick again so that it is in front of you. This sequence is repeated.

- For a person who needs less support, for example if he or she is just using a stick because of lack of confidence or is just generally a little unsteady on his or her feet: move the stick and the opposite leg forward at the same time. Then move the leg on the stick side forward past the stick. Repeat the sequence.

You may find that there is a natural progression in people who are improving their mobility and that, as they get better, they will automatically begin to move their leg and the stick at the same time. They should be encouraged to do so.

If you need to provide physical support for somebody who is walking with a stick, you should give it from behind and you should support with one hand on each side of the pelvis, just below the person's waist.

If you find that you need to offer this kind of help on a regular basis, you should consider suggesting an increase in the kind of walking support the person is offered. It is far better for him or her to have a more supportive walking aid than to rely on help from a care worker.

You may need to provide support for a person using a stick.

Quadruped or tripod

A quadruped should only be used for a person who has considerable difficulty in walking on one particular leg, either because of hip or knee degeneration or a stroke. It is not an appropriate aid for somebody who is generally unsteady.

Measuring a quadruped or tripod is exactly the same procedure as measuring a walking stick. Quadrupeds are made from metal and are adjustable.

You should check that the three or four small ferrules, which are on the suction feet, are safe and not worn.

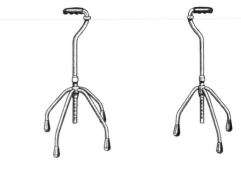

A quadruped and a tripod.

Using a quadruped

- The quadruped should be held in the opposite hand to the person's 'bad side'.
- Move the quadruped forward, take a step with the opposite foot. Then take a step with the foot on the same side as the quadruped so that it is either at the same level or slightly in front of the quadruped, and then repeat.

If you find that someone's condition is improving and he or she has started to put the quadruped and the opposite leg forward together, rather than after each other, then he or she should be moved on to a walking stick, as the support offered by a quadruped is no longer needed.

Walking correctly with a quadruped.

REMEMBER

If you need to give assistance to someone using a quadruped, tripod or walking stick, you should do it from behind. There is a risk that if you offer physical help on the person's 'free' arm you could cause a shoulder injury. Help from behind steadies the person and provides the feeling of security. It also enables you to have a firm grip.

Walking frame

The decision to provide an individual with a walking frame needs to be taken when he or she has reached the stage of needing considerable support from one or two care workers and is no longer steady on a walking stick or quadruped.

Measuring a walking frame

Walking frames are measured in the same way as walking sticks. They are usually adjustable in height between 28 and 36 inches (710 and 910 mm), although they do come in different sizes with a range of 3–4 inches (80–100 mm) alteration within each frame.

- To reach the correct height, the person should stand against the frame, holding it and leaning slightly forward. The feet should be level with the back legs of the frame and the arms only slightly bent (a).
- If a walking frame is too small you will see a service user hunched forward at the frame (b).
- If the elbows are very bent and the shoulders are hunched up, the frame is too tall (c).
- You will also need to check that the ferrules are in good condition on each leg.

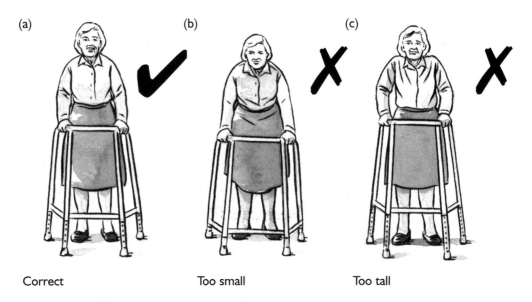

(a) Correct ✔

(b) Too small ✗

(c) Too tall ✗

Measuring a walking frame.

Using a walking frame

It is important that a person follows the proper pattern of walking in order to get the maximum benefit from a walking frame. If there are difficulties, or if the person uses a frame in the wrong way, it can be quite dangerous and may cause a fall or other injuries.

- Put the frame forward so that the person can lean on it with arms almost at full stretch. He or she should then take a step forward – if he or she has a 'bad' side, step first with that leg; it not, then either leg.
- The next step should be taken with the other leg walking past the first leg. Repeat the sequence.
- It is essential that you ensure that the frame has all four feet on the ground at any point when the person is taking a step.

Offer additional assistance if it is needed. It should be offered from behind the person, as giving assistance under one arm is not possible when a person is using a walking frame.

A walking frame with wheels on the front legs is also available. This means that the walking pattern is not interrupted in the way it is with an ordinary walking frame. This is very useful for people who are too confused to be

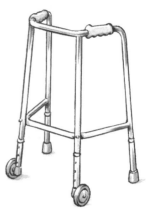

A wheeled walking frame.

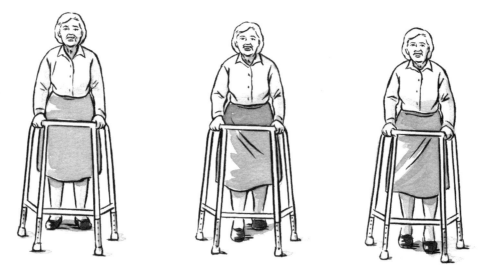

Walking correctly with a walking frame.

able to cope with learning the walking pattern for an ordinary walking frame, and is also useful for people who have particular arm or shoulder problems, which mean they cannot lift a frame. The assessment of the suitable height for a frame with wheels is carried out in exactly the same way as for an ordinary walking frame.

REMEMBER

You may need to spend some considerable time on supporting service users so that they can use walking aids properly.

Check it out

Investigate the way walking aids are cleaned and checked for safety in your workplace. Record your findings and any recommendations for improvement.

Wheelchair

Where an assessment has been made that a person requires a wheelchair, he or she is entitled to have a wheelchair of his or her own which will be correctly measured and assessed by a physiotherapist. Wheelchairs come in a range of sizes and styles. They include chairs which have to be pushed, chairs which people can propel themselves and electric wheelchairs. Many younger people with disabilities have very decided views about the types of wheelchair they will use, the amount of equipment and additions that they have on their wheelchairs, the colours they are and the speed at which they travel around in them!

Sports wheelchair (there are specialist chairs for all types of sports).

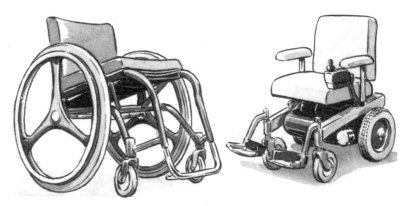

Street wheelchair.

Electric wheelchair.

> **REMEMBER**
>
> When you are teaching somebody to use a wheelchair, it is important that you encourage him or her to self-propel the wheelchair whenever possible. This gives a far higher degree of independence and allows the person to go where he or she wants – or where access will allow.

Mobility scooter

Mobility scooter.

Many people who want to be able to get out and about, but have mobility problems when outdoors, can use powered scooters to get around. Most large shopping centres have a 'shopmobility' centre where powered scooters can be borrowed or rented to make shopping easier. Similarly, many theme parks and large public attractions offer scooter facilities. Scooters can be very useful in supporting service users in maintaining their independence and their ability to make local journeys without assistance.

Keys to good practice

✓ All wheelchairs should be fitted with appropriate cushions (for example, a Roho cushion) to minimise the risk of pressure sores for people who are confined to a wheelchair for long periods of time.

✓ If you work in a residential or hospital setting you may have wheelchairs which you use for pushing people around in. These have small wheels and people cannot self-propel them. They should only be used for people who are ill, or incapable of propelling themselves anywhere.

✓ It is very important that you do not 'take over' a person's right to be in charge of his or her own mobility simply because it is quicker and easier for you to wheel the person to his or her next destination.

The use of wheelchairs should not be seen as negative. Many people with disabilities have described how getting a wheelchair has increased their mobility to such a great extent that their lives have been significantly improved. They progressed from slow painful movements with walking sticks, where everything was a tremendous effort, to suddenly being able to move themselves around at will. The biggest problems experienced by wheelchair users are the result of other people's attitudes to them and the limited access available to most buildings.

A wheelchair user is only limited by society.

How to monitor and record progress

It is essential that you regularly check the progress of anyone who is using any type of mobility aid. You should never assume that any condition will remain static – just because somebody was walking well with a frame or a stick when it was given to him or her does not mean that it is now the most appropriate mobility aid for the person to use.

TEST YOURSELF

1 Name three different types of mobility aid.

2 Explain why mobility aids are important.

3 Describe how a service user should be measured for a walking stick.

4 Why is it necessary regularly to review a person's progress with a mobility aid?

5 What parts of the body does a mobility aid assist and support?

REMEMBER

Mobility aids can make a significant difference to the quality of life that a service user experiences. A mobility aid can often be a way of allowing a person to maintain (or regain) his or her independence and freedom to choose actions and destinations.

Z6 UNIT TEST

1 You have a service user who is paraplegic following a motorbike accident. He can move his body from the waist and has full use of his hands and arms. He is young, but feels that his life is over. He spends his days watching TV, and does not think that he can do anything. He is not keen to see his old friends because he thinks they just feel sorry for him.

    a List at least three ways in which exercise would help your service user.
    b Where would you go for advice about an exercise programme?
    c What sort of exercises do you think may be included? Why?
    d What considerations would be important when he is choosing and learning to use a wheelchair?
    e How would you encourage him?

2 You are working in a day centre for older people and a group of service users come to you, saying that they want a programme of exercises they could do to music each day.

    a Who would you discuss the request with?
    b Do you think the users should be encouraged in their aim? Why?
    c What would be the benefits for them if the programme were used regularly?
    d What would you need to take into account if you were organising the session?
    e Write a list of the equipment you would need.

Contribute to the movement and handling of individuals to maximise their physical comfort

This unit is primarily concerned with those individuals with whom you work who are most dependent upon your assistance. The level of assistance they need can vary from needing help to get out of a chair to being completely dependent on others to move them, to turn them over and to alter their position in any way, for example if they are unconscious or paralysed. When individuals require this degree of care it is essential that they are moved and handled in the most sensitive and safe way. This is also vital for you as a worker – the commonest causes of people being unable to continue to work in health or care are that they suffer injuries, usually back injuries, from lifting and moving individuals. It is possible to minimise the risk to both you and the individuals for whom you provide care by following the correct procedures and using the right equipment.

The first element is about preparing individuals for being moved. In the second element you will need to learn about how to carry out the move and to ensure that you know the way to carry it out correctly and safely, and offer all the support which is needed to the individual. The final element deals with pressure sores, which are painful, debilitating and a serious potential risk of infection for an individual. Understanding the causes of pressure sores and methods of avoiding them is very important – they take so long to heal that steps should be taken to prevent them, as far as possible.

Element Z7.1 | Prepare individuals and environments for moving and handling

What you need to learn
- How to assess risks
- How to encourage independence

How to assess risks

As you may remember from Chapter 3 (Unit CU1) your employer has a responsibility under health and safety legislation to examine and assess all procedures which take place in your working environment involving risk. All risks must be noted, assessed and steps taken to minimise them as far as possible. Your employer is required to provide adequate equipment for such tasks as moving and handling individuals who require assistance.

Ideally every workplace should have, or have access to, a Back Care Advisor (BCA). These are people who have training in manual handling and are able to provide expert advice to managers, manual handling supervisors and to members of staff who are involved in manual handling.

You must ensure that you follow the information provided by the BCA for your workplace, and take every opportunity to attend information and education events to make sure you are up to date on manual handling techniques and policies.

Check it out

Find out who is the BCA for your workplace, and ask him or her when the next education sessions are planned.

The risk assessments your employer carries out are, however, general risks for your work environment. Each time you move or lift any individual, you too must make an assessment of the risks involved in carrying out that particular manoeuvre. Even if you have moved this individual every day for the past six months, you should still assess the risks on each occasion before you put anything into practice. No two lifts are ever the same – there are always some factors that are different. These factors could be to do with the individual and his or her mood or health on that particular day, they could be about the environment, or they could be about you and your current physical condition.

You should run through the same checklist each time before you carry out any activity which involves you in physically moving a person from one place to another. A suggested checklist is shown opposite. You may need to adapt it to fit your own place of work and the circumstances in which you work.

This system is best remembered as TILE – Task, Individual, Load, Environment. You should carry out a TILE assessment each time you move a service user.

Checklist

1	Is individual weight-bearing?	Yes	☐
		No	☐
2	Is individual unsteady?	Yes	☐
		No	☐
3	What is the general level of mobility?	Good	☐
		Poor	☐
4	(a) What is the individual's weight?	_____	
	(b) What is the individual's height?	_____	
	(c) How many people does this lift require?	_____	
	(Work this out on the scale devised by your workplace.)		
5	What lifting equipment is required?	Hoist	☐
		Sling	☐
		Trapeze	☐
		Transfer board	☐
6	Is equipment available?	Yes	☐
		No	☐
7	If not, is there a safe alternative?	Yes	☐
		No	☐
8	Are the required number of people available?	Yes	☐
		No	☐
9	What is the purpose of the move?		
	_____		
10	Can this be achieved?	Yes	☐
		No	☐

A checklist for assessing risks before moving an individual.

You also need to consider carefully the environment when you are assessing risk. You should take into account all of the following factors:

- Is the floor surface safe? Are there wet or slippery patches?
- Are you wearing appropriate clothing – low-heeled shoes, tunic or dress which has enough room to stretch and reach?
- Is the immediate area clear of items that may cause a trip or a fall, or items which could cause injury following a fall?
- Is all the equipment, both to carry out the lift and in the place to which the individual is to be moved, ready?
- Does the individual have privacy and can his or her dignity be maintained during the move?
- Is there anyone you could ask for help, for example a porter or member of the ambulance service?

Working with the individual to be moved

The individual who is going to be moved is the key person to be actively involved, as far as possible, in decisions about the best way to carry out the move. Unless the person concerned is unconscious or semi-conscious or so confused as to be unable to contribute to any discussion about the best way to proceed, then it is essential that you discuss with the person the way that he or she would feel most comfortable with. Many people who have a long-standing disability will be very experienced in how to deal with it. They are the best people to ask for advice as they know the most effective ways for them to be moved, avoiding pain and discomfort as far as possible.

Check it out

Your workplace probably uses an assessment form similar to the one on the next page. Find the one your workplace uses and make sure you know how to fill it in. It may be similar to the checklist on page 249.

ASSESSMENT FORM FOR PATIENTS WHO REQUIRE
MANUAL HANDLING

Name: _Mr K_   Weight: _8 stone 8 lbs_

                                                    Height: _5' 3"_

Any relevant physical disabilities: _Congenital foot deformity_

Patient's mental ability and comprehension: _Sometimes aggressive_
when being dealt with

History of falls?   Yes   No

                                 [ ]   [✓]

Any equipment used by patient   _The hoist must be used at all_
                                         timed when moving and
                                         handling due to his inability
                                         to bear weight.

Handling constraints

    Skin   _Dry_

    Pain   _occasionally on movement._

    Infusions   _-_

    Catheters, etc.   _-_

    Other   _-_

Abilities in following situations

    Walking   _Unable - needs wheelchair to mobilise_

    Standing   _Unable to bear weight - needs hoist_

    Toiletting   _Use toiletting sling and hoist_

    Transferring in/out of bed   _Use of hoist and quick fit deluxe sling_

    Transferring in/out bath   _Use of ambulift bathchair_

TO BE COMPLETED WITHIN 24 HOURS OF ADMISSION AND THE RELEVANT
INFORMATION WRITTEN INTO THE CARE PLAN. UPDATE THE ASSESSMENT
FORM AND CARE PLAN AS NECESSARY.

Assessor's signature

Grade _Officer in charge_

Date _1.5.03_

A risk assessment form for manual handling.

! REMEMBER

Your first port of call for advice on how to carry out a movement, after you have checked out the safety aspect and the risk factors, should be the individual himself or herself.

Once you have carried out all of the necessary assessments, you should explain carefully to the individual exactly what you intend to do and what his or her role is in contributing to the effectiveness and safety of the move. This will vary according to the person's ability, but nonetheless most individuals will be able to participate to some extent. Even where individuals are unconscious or appear to have no understanding of what is going on, you should still explain exactly what you are doing and why you are doing it and what the effects will be. We have a limited understanding of what a state of unconsciousness means to the person experiencing it. Every individual has the same right to be treated with dignity and respect and to have procedures explained rather than simply having things done to him or her by care workers who believe that 'they know best'. Each stage of the proposed move should be explained in detail before it is carried out, and it is essential to obtain the individual's consent before you move or handle him or her in any way. If you move an individual without his or her consent this could be construed as an assault. So you should always be sure that you are carrying out the individual's wishes before you commence any move.

Keys to good practice

✓ Assess risks to the individual and to yourself before starting any move.
✓ Ask the individual about the best way of moving, or assisting, him or her.
✓ Explain the procedure at each stage, even where it may not be obvious that you are understood.
✓ Explain how the equipment operates.
✓ Check that you have the agreement of the person you are moving.
✓ Stop immediately if the individual does not wish you to continue – you may not move a person without his or her consent.

Your clothing

The type of clothing you wear when you are moving individuals is very important. It can make the difference between carrying out a procedure safely and doing it with difficulty and possible risk of injury. Footwear should be supportive and flat, with soles that grip firmly.

Recent recommendations in respect of uniforms are that dresses should have a pleat in the skirt and a similar pleat in the sleeves. These are to allow space so that you do not find that your own movements are restricted by your clothing, possibly forcing you to move in an awkward way. It may be necessary, for example, to place one knee on a bed. This is impossible if you are wearing a straight skirt, or at least very difficult to manage at the same time as maintaining dignity – yours, not the service user's!

If you are in a situation where you do a great deal of moving and handling, it is a good idea to wear trousers with a tunic top, which also has plenty of room in the sleeves and shoulders to allow free movement. Your employer should have carried out a risk assessment and ensured that the clothing that is provided for you to wear is appropriate and complies with current best practice and requirements in terms of moving and handling.

Equipment

In your work you may use many different types of equipment, including several types of lifting and moving equipment. It is important that you check every time you use a piece of equipment that it is safe and that it is fit for use for that particular individual.

If you do find equipment has become worn, damaged or appears to be unsafe in any way, you should immediately stop using it, take it out of service and report it to your supervisor. You must do this even if it means having to change your handling assessment for the individual you were about to move. Under no circumstances is it acceptable to take a risk with equipment which may be faulty. It is better that the individual waits a little longer for a move or is moved in an alternative way rather than being exposed to risks from potentially unsafe equipment.

Make sure that you have read the instruction manual for each piece of equipment you use. It should give you a safety checklist – make sure you follow it.

Work clothing should allow for free movement when handling individuals.

Check it out

Find out the procedure in your workplace for reporting faulty equipment. Check whether there is a file or a book where you need to record the fault. You may only need to make a verbal report, or you may have to enter the details of the fault into a computer. Make sure that you know what the correct procedure is.

How to encourage independence

There are many ways in which an individual can assist and co-operate with care workers who are handling or moving him or her. It is important that this is encouraged and that individuals are not made to feel as though they are simply being transported from place to place like 'a piece of meat'. Co-operation from the individual is invaluable, both for maintaining his or her own independence and for assisting those who have to carry out the move. For example, you may be transferring an individual from a bed to a wheelchair. The first part of the process – getting to the edge of the bed and sitting on it – may well be possible for the individual to accomplish if he or she follows a correct set of instructions, rather than having to be moved by carers.

Any independence which can be achieved is vitally important in terms of the individual's self-esteem and sense of well-being. A person may be able to transfer himself or herself from a wheelchair to a chair, to a car seat or into bed, either by the use of transfer boards or by simply being able to use sufficient upper body strength to slide across from chair to wheelchair, and vice versa, once the wheelchair arm is removed.

You may be able to use self-help techniques when an individual needs a bed pan. Rather than having to lift the person manually, he or she can be encouraged, with some simple instructions, to bend the knees and raise the bottom to allow the bed pan to be slid underneath him or her (see page 261).

Techniques like this involve the active co-operation of the individual. Obviously they are not suitable for use where individuals are unable to co-operate, either because of their state of consciousness or because they have almost total paralysis. Some individuals may not be able to co-operate for emotional reasons – they may lack the confidence to make any moves for themselves because of fear of falling or fear of pain or discomfort. Where the plan of care has identified that the individual is capable of co-operation in moving and handling, this should be gently encouraged and the reasons for his or her reluctance to co-operate should be explored with the individual.

Good preparation is the key to a successful move or transfer. Where the individual and the worker are working together, there is likely to be the maximum safety and minimum risk, pain and discomfort.

TEST YOURSELF

1 Name three factors you would take into account when assessing the risk of carrying out a move.

2 In what sort of circumstances would you consider asking an individual to move himself or herself across the bed?

3 What type of clothing is most suitable for carrying out lifting?

4 What steps should you take if you have concerns about the safety of equipment?

Element Z7.2 Assist individuals to move from one position to another

What you need to learn

● Equipment for moving and handling
● Methods for manual moving and handling
● Recording and passing on information

Equipment for moving and handling

There is a wide range of equipment available and technological advances are being made continuously in the field of medical equipment. Regardless of the individual products and improvements which may be made to them, lifting and handling equipment broadly falls into the following categories:

● hoists, slings and other equipment, which move the full weight of an individual
● equipment designed to assist in a move and to take some of the weight of an individual, such as transfer boards

- equipment designed to assist the individual to help himself or herself, such as lifting handles positioned above a bed to allow individuals to pull themselves up. This category also includes grab handles, raised toilet seats, and lifting seat chairs.

Depending on the setting in which you work, you may have to use some or all of the equipment shown below. If you work with individuals in their own homes, your access to equipment may be more limited, although there is now an extensive range of equipment that can be used very effectively within an individual's own home, often removing the need for residential care.

Using equipment

Each piece of equipment will have an instruction manual. You must read this and be sure that you follow the instructions for its use. There are some general points about how to use particular types of equipment, but you must know how to use the particular equipment in your workplace.

Hoists

- Make sure that you use the correct sling for the hoist and for the weight of the service user.
- Most slings are colour-coded. Check that you have the right one for the weight of the service user.

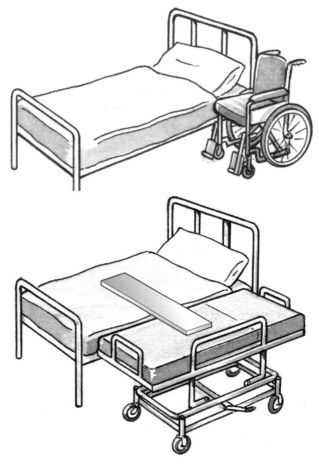
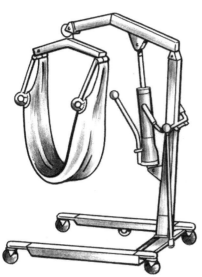

Equipment for moving and handling.

- Ensure that the seams on the hoist are facing outwards, away from the service user, as they can be rough and can easily damage the skin.
- Only attempt to manoeuvre a hoist using the steering handles – do not try to move it with the jib, as it can overbalance.
- Place the sling around or under the service user. Lower the bed to its lowest position. Then lift the service user. It is only necessary to have a small clearance from the bed or chair – there is no need to raise the service user a great distance

You cannot learn to use a hoist safely by reading a book – you must familiarise yourself with the hoists in your workplace and ask to be shown how to operate them.

Transfer boards/sheets

These require at least two people standing on opposite sides of the bed. They allow people to be moved from bed to trolley and vice versa. They can be used regardless of the level of consciousness of the individual.

They all work on the same principles. They are made of friction-free material which is placed half under the person and half under the sheet he or she is lying on. One worker then pulls and the other pushes. The sheet, complete with person, then slides easily from one to the other. There are several types available: 'Pat-slide', 'Easy-glide' and 'Easy-slide' are amongst the most common.

Slideboards

The slideboard is a small board placed between a bed and a chair or wheelchair. It is designed for use by service users who are able to be quite active in the transfer and only require assistance. The board allows the service user to slide from bed to chair, and vice versa, with some assistance in steadying and some encouragement.

Turn discs

These are used to swivel service users, in either a sitting or standing position, and can be useful for service users who are able to stand. They are particularly useful for getting in and out of vehicles.

Turn disc.

Transfer board.

Monkey pole or lifting handle

This is a handle which is fixed above a bed, and swings from a metal frame. It is designed to allow people to assist themselves. They have to pull on the bar to lift the upper part of the body off the bed. This can enable people to help themselves to sit up, turn over and change position without having to call for assistance.

When you are assessing how to assist a person to move and which equipment to use, you need to consider:

● the potential risks
● what the person can do to help himself or herself to move, and what he or she cannot do – remember that it is important to encourage as much independence as possible
● what the person knows from experience to be the best method, or the method he or she prefers.

If the person's preference conflicts with safe practice, you should tactfully explain this, pointing out the potential risks and suggesting the best method. Reassure the person, if necessary. If there is still a problem, you will need to tell your supervisor immediately.

REMEMBER
You should never move anyone without his or her agreement.

Handling belts

These enable you to assist a service user to rise from a chair, or provide a steadying hand, by holding onto the handles on the belt. It gives you a firm grip without risking bruising the service user or slipping and causing an injury to either of you.

Handling belt.

Check it out

Investigate the equipment available in your workplace for moving and handling. Make sure you know where different items are kept and how they work. Make notes to refer to when necessary.

Methods for manual moving and handling

There are very few situations in which manual lifting should be carried out. Unless it is an emergency or a life-threatening situation, there should be no need to move anyone without the correct equipment. It is important that service users are encouraged to assist in their own transfers and movements.

This means that even shoulder lifts (like the Australian lift) are no longer considered to be safe. There is no safe weight limit for lifting, so the only workplaces where lifting should now take place are units caring for babies and small children. Even there, it is important to ensure that risk assessments are carried out to avoid the likelihood of injury, as height differences between the carer and the child, or the surface involved, present other safety issues.

Care workers in a hospital or residential setting should never have to lift or move service users without the necessary equipment. This is sometimes more of a problem in community settings, where it may not be easy to use equipment in the service user's home, or the equipment may not be available.

The Disability Rights Commission has highlighted the issues in relation to the human rights of people with disabilities. They argue that if disabled people are unable to live in the way they wish because of a 'no lifting' policy – for example, some people have had to remain in bed because no equipment was available to move them, or they did not wish to be moved using equipment – then the agency refusing to provide the care is in breach of both the Human Rights Act and the Disability Discrimination Act.

Guidance from the Health and Safety Executive – 'Handling Home Care', 2002 – states that while all risk assessments must be undertaken and equipment used wherever possible, 'no lifting' policies are likely to be incompatible with service users' rights.

The NHS 'Back to Work' guidance also states that 'no lifting' is a misleading term as it is often used to mean that lifting most, or all, of a service user's weight should not be undertaken. In no circumstances, however, should the service user or carer be put at risk.

Check it out

Find copies of the Health and Safety Executive and NHS guidelines in your workplace. Check out what they say about moving service users. Find out if your workplace has its own policy, and see how it compares. Does your workplace have copies of information from the Disability Rights Commission? If not, you could obtain it. It may raise some useful points for discussion with your supervisor and colleagues.

If you need to move someone manually in order to change his or her position or to provide assistance, you should follow the principles of effective manual moving and handling:

- The procedures should be well-planned and assessed in advance. Technique rather than strength is what is important.
- The procedure should be comfortable and safe for the individual – creating confidence that being moved is not something to be anxious about and that he or she can relax and co-operate with the procedure.

- The procedure should be safe for the workers carrying it out. A worker who is injured during a badly planned or executed transfer or move is likely in turn to injure the individual he or she is attempting to move. Similarly, an individual who is injured during a move is likely to cause an injury to those who are moving him or her.

> ! **REMEMBER**
> The interests and safety of the individual and the workers are so closely linked that you must consider them both together.

Team work

Most moving and transfer procedures, whether manual or assisted, are carried out by more than one person. If you are to work successfully as part of a team, you need to follow some simple rules:

- Decide who is going to 'shout', or lead the manoeuvre.
- That person will check that everyone is ready.
- He or she will say '1-2-3 lift' or '1-2-3 move' or (depending on familiarity with American TV) 'on my count 1-2-3'.
- Everyone must follow the count of the person who shouts.

Transfer

If you are assisting an individual to transfer from a bed or chair to a wheelchair, this can be done with one person providing assistance to steady the person as he or she uses the transfer board, providing that there are no complicating factors such as an individual who is particularly heavy or tall or who has serious disabilities. In that case, they should be moved using a hoist or a turntable.

Rolling or turning

If you need to roll or turn someone who is unable to assist, either because of paralysis, unconsciousness, serious illness or confusion, you should:

- follow the care plan
- always carry this out with at least two workers
- roll the person using a transfer sheet or board, or use the bottom sheet to roll the person onto his or her side (make sure the sheet is dry and intact!)
- support the person with pillows or packing.

When the person needs to be turned again, remove the pillows, lower him or her onto the back and repeat the other way.

Overcoming 'pyjama-induced paralysis'

One of the key factors in a safe handling policy is to encourage people to help themselves. There is a great temptation for people to believe that they can do far less than they are capable of. This is often encouraged by staff who find it quicker and easier to do things rather than wait for people to help themselves.

If you encourage individuals to make their own way out of bed, for example, then they would need to follow the simple set of instructions shown in the diagram below.

1   Roll towards the edge of the bed

2   Swing your legs over the side of the bed whilst continuing to lie the top half of your body on the bed.

3   Push with your hands and sit upright.

Instructions for getting out of bed.

You may wish to encourage an individual to roll over in the bed, rather than having to be manually rolled by a care worker. This could be necessary to allow changing of bedding, a bed bath or to change clothes. The instructions for achieving this are quite simple, and can be carried out by all but the most severely ill or disabled individuals, as shown in the diagram on the next page.

1 Turn to face the direction in which you are rolling

2 Bend the leg of the other side and keep your foot flat on the bed

3 Reach across your body with the opposite arm. This uses the counter weight of moving the arm across the upper body to assist with the movement of achieving a roll.

Instructions for rolling over in bed.

If you need to get someone to raise his or her bottom from the bed in order to give a bedpan, or to prepare for rolling or turning, then you should ask the person to follow the instructions below.

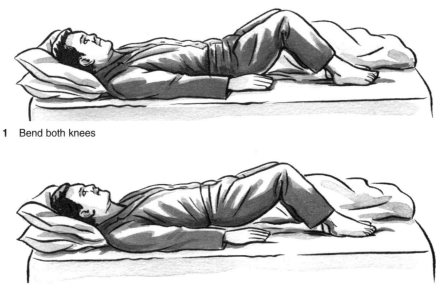

1 Bend both knees

2 Keep your feet flat on the bed and push up on your feet and hands, so that your bottom is raised.

Recording and passing on information

Information about the most effective ways of moving someone, or techniques which have proved effective in encouraging a person to assist himself or herself, should be recorded in the plan of care.

The plan of care should contain information on the moving needs of each individual, and it is vital that these are followed. However, you may notice a change in behaviour or response. This could be:

- a person finding movement more painful
- a loss of confidence in a particular technique
- an improvement in how much assistance a person can give
- a changed reaction following being moved.

Any of these changes, or anything else you notice, are significant and must be reported to your supervisor. Any changes may be indications of overall changes in the person's condition and should never be ignored.

The information you record should be:

- clear
- easily understood
- a good description of the person's needs.

Date	No.	PATIENT'S NURSING NEEDS/PROBLEMS AND CAUSES OF PROBLEMS (N.B. Physiological, Psychological, Social and Family Problems)	Objectives	Nursing Instructions	Review On/By	Date Resolved
1.5.03	8	Mobility:			8.5.03	
					15.5.03	
		Due to suffering from	To prevent	a) Encourage Mr. K to be as	22.5.03	
		a congenital foot	complications of	independent as possible.	29.5.03	
		deformity, Mr. K	immobility and	b) Always give clear, concise	5.6.03	
		is unable to bear weight	maintain Mr. K's	instructions when moving and	12.6.03	
		and needs the hoist	safety as far	handling to gain client's full	19.6.03	
		to be used when	as is reasonably	co-operation.	26.6.03	
		moving and handling	practicable.	c) The hoist must be used at all	3.7.03	
				times with either the Quickfit	10.7.03	
				deluxe sling or the toileting sling –	17.7.03	
				depending upon circumstances.	24.7.03	
				d) Ensure safe practice maintained	31.7.03	
				when moving and handling client.	7.8.03	
				e) Observe for any problems and		
				reassess appropriately.		
				f) Review problem weekly.		

An example of notes on an individual's mobility in his plan of care.

CASE STUDY

Shireen is the carer for Mrs G, who is 80. Shireen needs to move Mrs G from a bed into a chair. Mrs G is only able to assist a little as she has very painful joints and is unable to bear weight. She weighs 16 stones (101.6 kg).

1 What would you expect to see in Mrs G's care plan in respect of moving procedure? Give reasons.
2 What factors should Shireen take into account before starting to move Mrs G?
3 What should Shireen say to her?

When you are carrying out a moving procedure, it may be necessary to move items of furniture so that you can work safely. Remember that this also requires assessment: How heavy is the furniture? Is it on wheels? How many times will I need to move it? Whether you are working in a care setting or in an individual's own home, it is important that furniture is returned to its original position afterwards, so the individual can easily locate personal items in their usual places and feel reassured by the familiar surroundings.

TEST YOURSELF

1   What are the three categories of lifting and handling equipment?

2   Describe how the following are used:
    a   a hoist
    b   a transfer board or sheet
    c   a slideboard
    d   a monkey pole.

3   What are the three principles of effective manual handling?

4   Describe the procedures for:
    a   rolling or turning
    b   transfer.

5   Why should information and changes regarding mobility be recorded and passed on?

Element Z7.3

Assist individuals to prevent and minimise the adverse effects of pressure

What you need to learn
- How pressure sores can happen
- How to prevent pressure sores
- How to treat pressure sores

How pressure sores can happen

Pressure sores are the result of an interruption to the blood supply, which causes the tissue in that particular area to break down. The interruption to the blood supply is caused by various types of pressure, exerted in different ways, but the effect is the same – it causes the tissue in the affected area to die and to degenerate into a sore. Every one of us would get pressure sores if we were not able to move regularly each night whilst we were asleep. For individuals who are unable to change their own position regularly, whether that is lying down or sitting in a wheelchair, the pressure can result in a sore. There are some areas which are particularly vulnerable:

- back of the head
- sacrum (the bottom of the back)
- backs of legs and calves
- shoulders
- buttocks
- heels.

The diagram on page 264 shows the most common sites of pressure sores.

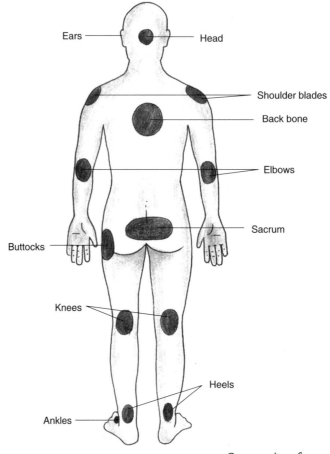

Common sites of pressure sores.

Compression

There are several ways in which pressure sores are caused, but one of the commonest is compression, where the weight of a part of the skeleton presses through the flesh and skin against a relatively hard surface, such as a bed or a chair. This compression causes the blood supply to be cut off to that area of tissue, which then dies and degenerates into a sore. This is commonly seen in people who are confined to a chair or a wheelchair. These sores develop on the buttocks because of the weight of their skeleton on their buttocks and against the chair. It also happens where people are confined to bed and are not able to move their position regularly and here other pressure points, such as shoulder blades, elbows, the back of the head and the heels, are all likely to suffer sores as a result of compression.

Shearing force

Sacrum pressure points

Heel

Shearing.

Shearing

Another way in which pressure sores can be caused is called shearing. This is when an individual is left in a half-lying, propped-up position in bed and the downward pressure, which gradually slides him or her down in bed, drags the skin across the surface of the bed and grazes it, damaging the small blood vessels (see the diagram on page 264). This can also happen if you 'drag' the service user up the bed or chair, instead of ensuring that he or she is properly lifted. These pressure sores are commonly seen on the sacrum (bottom of the back) and the heels.

Friction

Pressure sores can also be caused by friction when two areas rub against each other. This can often be seen with skin folds, rumpled nightclothes or when crumbs or other debris are left in the bed, or when there is a wet area around the buttocks and sacrum caused by incontinence.

Assessing risk of pressure sores

There has been considerable research into the care of pressure areas and several different assessment scales have been developed to judge the people who are most likely to be at risk from pressure sores and for whom preventive action can be taken at an early stage. The commonest assessment score is called the Norton Score (shown below). The lower the score a person has, the greater the chance of developing sores. However, a risk assessment score should only be used in conjunction with the judgement of an experienced and qualified professional as there are many other factors to be taken into account when determining the level of risk for any individual.

The Norton Score for pressure sore risk assessment

Physical condition		Mental state		Activity		Mobility		Incontinent	
Good	4	Alert	4	Ambulant	4	Full	4	Not	4
Fair	3	Apathetic	3	Walks with help	3	Slightly limited	3	Occasionally	3
Poor	2	Confused	2	Chair-bound	2	Very limited	2	Usually urine	2
Very bad	1	Stuporous	1	Bedfast	1	Immobile	1	Double	1

How to prevent pressure sores

It is always better to work on preventing pressure sores, and maintaining healthy, intact skin, rather than having to treat them once they have already developed. The best way to ensure that pressure sores do not develop is to keep people as active as possible, so that they are less likely to remain in one position. It is also important for individuals who are confined to bed or a chair to be assessed for a special mattress or cushion (such as a Roho cushion), which is designed to distribute weight more evenly so that the downward pressure from the skeleton is evenly spread and does not concentrate pressure in one area.

You should also ensure that individuals eat a good balanced diet with a significant protein content, as protein is required for cell renewal – this is a significant way of reducing the risk of tissue breakdown and the development of pressure sores.

It is vital to ensure that service users who are incontinent are never left sitting in wet clothes or incontinence pads which have become soaked. The effect of wet, urine-soaked clothing on skin is to render it very likely to develop sores in the pressure areas.

Some individuals are comfortable with an artificial sheepskin under their shoulders or their buttocks or to sit on one in their wheelchair. However, these are not shown to have any beneficial effect on reducing the likelihood of developing pressure sores and can present hygiene problems as they are quite difficult to launder effectively. Increasingly, they are now being replaced by the more technologically advanced forms of mattresses and cushions which use a combination of specially devised air pockets or, in some cases, water to spread the pressure more evenly across areas of the body.

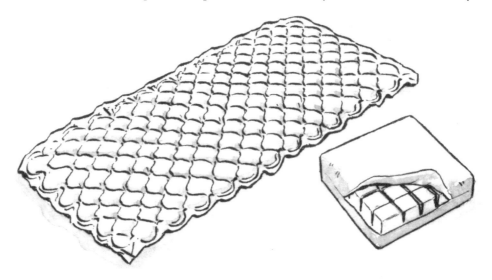

Aids to prevent pressure sores.

Reporting and recording

Just as the plans for moving and handling should be in a person's care plan, so should information on any pressure area care. There should be notes about any sore places which may be developing, and any changes in the skin, such as reddening or grazes, must be reported at once. Skin becomes very fragile as people get older, and it can be easily injured. It is these apparently minor skin injuries which often develop into sores that can take months to heal.

Keys to good practice

✓ Move people regularly.
✓ Turn an unconscious or paralysed person every two hours.
✓ Use aids such as a Roho cushion, a special mattress or fleece pads.
✓ Check that the person's diet contains adequate protein.
✓ Change wet clothes and bedclothes immediately.
✓ Report any changes you notice in a person's skin.

Try to sit in a propped-up position without moving for as long as possible without altering your position. You will find that before very long you will begin to feel uncomfortable, and after a fairly short period of time it is painful to remain without moving. Imagine how that feels for somebody who is totally unable to move.

How to treat pressure sores

Pressure sore treatments are constantly being developed and improved, so you should seek advice from a qualified medical or nursing practitioner about the latest developments. Current practice is to use dressings which will allow moist healing of the sore. At one time it was believed that pressure sores should be dried and were best allowed to heal in their dry state. There is now little argument that all wounds including pressure sores heal far better in a warm, moist environment.

A professional will assess and recommend treatent for pressure sores. There are various dressings available which adhere very closely to the skin and will allow oxygen through but no moisture, enabling the wound to retain any moisture to assist healing. As long as a wound is not infected, these types of dressings, such as Op-site, appear to achieve quite good results.

DID YOU KNOW?

The benefits of moist wound healing were first demonstrated almost 30 years ago. However, in a recent study carried out in a large hospital, less than 50 per cent of the people questioned knew about the procedure.

An individual's care plan will identify the treatment regime which needs to be used for his or her particular pressure sores, and the treatment will be supervised by a qualified practitioner. Treatments today will *not* include practices such as massaging the area or washing with soap and water, which were common some years ago. There is no evidence to support the theory that massaging the area will play any part in healing the sore and, in fact, it is likely to aggravate the situation – to cause the shearing effect described earlier.

The key to effective treatment of pressure sores is to attempt, where possible, to increase the general health of the individual – people who are malnourished or debilitated because of an illness or long periods of neglect are unlikely to heal pressure sores effectively until their general state of health has been considerably improved. The care plan should include arrangements for the individual to receive, if possible, a high protein, high carbohydrate diet.

Pressure sores are extremely unpleasant, but they are *avoidable*. Good practice and good levels of care can prevent pressure sores from occurring and can speed the healing of any which existed before the individual received care.

TEST YOURSELF

1   Which areas are most likely to suffer from pressure sores?

2   Name two ways of relieving pressure sores.

3   What are the best ways of preventing an individual from developing pressure sores?

4   Which individuals are likely to be the most vulnerable to pressure sores?

Z7 UNIT TEST

True or false?

1   It is safe to lift people manually provided they are not very heavy.

2   People should be encouraged to move themselves whenever possible.

3   Workplaces can choose not to have lifting equipment.

4   Services provided in service users' homes do not have to have lifting equipment.

5   One of the major factors in the development of pressure sores is poor diet.

6   Pressure sores cannot be prevented if someone is confined to bed.

7   Pressure sores should be left open to the air to heal more quickly.

Enable clients to maintain their personal hygiene and appearance

Keeping clean and hygienic is something that most people accomplish for themselves on a daily basis without giving a great deal of thought to the processes involved or the reasons why it is necessary. However, when people become ill, disabled or in need of care they often have to rely on others to help with their personal cleanliness and freedom from unhygienic conditions. This chapter will look at bathing, showering, hair washing, shaving and general personal hygiene.

Most people regard how they look as being very important, and it has an effect on their emotional well-being, self-esteem and general confidence. People who have become ill or who need care are not always able to dress themselves or to keep up their appearance, in the way they have done in the past. Most people are able to manage at least some of the process for themselves and additional help with specially designed dressing and grooming aids can allow them to retain the maximum possible amount of independence. There may be circumstances in which people will need particular help. This chapter will give you information on some of the skills and techniques which can help you to provide this type of care.

Element Z9.1 Enable clients to maintain their personal cleanliness

What you need to learn
- How to encourage service user choice
- Why cleanliness is important
- How to ensure cleanliness
- How to deal with problems

How to encourage service user choice

Ensure that you always discuss with an individual exactly what he or she would like to achieve, both in terms of his or her personal cleanliness and the way in which that personal cleanliness is accomplished. Do not, for example, insist that someone has a shower if he or she prefers a bath, unless of course his or her physical condition makes a bath impossible, or the facilities available in your work setting limit the choices available. Try not to impose your own ideas, and do not take over by doing activities which an individual is perfectly capable of doing for himself or herself, even though this may take a little longer. It is very tempting when you are busy to insist that you will do things because you know it will be quicker. It is important that people feel they are allowed as much independence as possible, according to their conditions and levels of ability. This means that you need to consider very carefully the time you allocate to personal washing and cleaning activities, and recognise that it may take longer than just a 'quick rub over' or a 'quick dip' – you may need to allocate considerable amount of time to the task.

You must also make sure that the choice is real. It is no use discussing with someone what he or she would like to do and then not make that possible to achieve, because you are rushing the person, or because you are making it clear that you do not approve, or because the things he or she chooses to do are not in line with the policies of the care setting.

You will need to make a judgement for each service user about the time you will need to allocate and the level of assistance you will offer. The table below summarises some of the points you will need to consider.

Service user	Considerations
Older, not confused, quite active	Little support needed, may need a check from time to time. Discuss with individual the level of assistance required
Older, confused	Needs assistance, time needed for individual to carry out process, needs supervision
Service user with a physical disability	Unless recently disabled is likely to have own system of personal hygiene. Discuss help required, be guided by individual
Service user with a learning disability	May need assistance with particular tasks, depending on level of difficulty. Discuss with individual, if possible, the level of help required

Often one of the most difficult problems to tackle in this area is the individual's own values and standards in respect of personal cleanliness. This is not necessarily about religious beliefs but about personal standards which tend to be different for different generations or for people who have been brought up in different circumstances. For example, it is not unusual for many older people to be happy with a pattern of a weekly bath with a daily wash. This kind of hygiene routine is more unusual today, where most people bathe or shower daily, but if a weekly bath is the individual's choice, then it is a very difficult and sensitive area in which to attempt any changes.

You must be careful to ensure that an individual's choice is not inhibited by the prospect of losing his or her privacy or dignity. If people are bathing or showering, then their privacy must be respected. Doors or shower curtains must be closed and there should not be an expectation that they remain unclothed while other people or staff are present.

Keys to good practice

✓ Offer people a choice in their personal hygiene – and make sure it is a real choice.
✓ Do not restrict the time available if someone wants to perform tasks himself or herself.
✓ Respect privacy, even if this is inconvenient for you.
✓ Respect people's rights to decide their own routines for cleansing.
✓ Do not expect people to fit in with a routine which is decided by the care organisation.

All of these are factors which can affect whether choice is real or whether as an organisation or as a carer you are forcing choices upon people.

Make sure that you do not use jargon to describe the assistance that you are offering. Refer to the equipment you will use for cleanliness and the parts of the body that you are cleaning in terms the service user understands. It is very intimidating when people use jargon and terms which are not understood. For example:

Do not use	Use instead
Axilla	Armpits
Extremities	Fingers and toes
Genital area	Underneath, down below, private parts, or check with the service user what terms he or she uses
Abdomen	Stomach, tummy
Cleansing agent ...and so on.	Soap

You may find that people have religious beliefs related to maintaining cleanliness. You must establish these carefully and make sure that they are followed and that people have the opportunity to carry out cleaning rituals and bathing in whatever way they wish. For example:

- Muslims and Hindus will need to be provided with running water in which to wash if at all possible. Muslims need to be able to wash their hands, face and feet in running water.
- Hindus will prefer a shower to a bath and will use a bidet rather than paper to clean themselves after using the toilet.
- Sikhs and Rastafarians believe that hair should not be cut.
- Hindus and Muslims will only accept treatment or assistance from a carer of the same gender.

Why cleanliness is important

The skin is the largest organ of the body. It provides a complete covering and protection for the body, and it is the skin which is the main area to be cleaned. The skin consists of two layers: the outer layer (the epidermis) and the inner layer (the dermis).

The epidermis is constantly being renewed, as it sheds its cells and new cells are grown by the body to replace them. You will have noticed how the skin cells are shed when you undress or change bed sheets. The skin also contains glands which produce sweat and others which produce sebum, an oily substance that maintains the water-proofing of the skin.

Skin becomes dirty because of exposure to the environment, but it also collects dried sweat, dead skin cells and oily sebum from the sebaceous glands. All of these factors combine to provide a breeding ground for an assortment of bacteria. These bacteria can cause offensive odours and can lead to infections, so skin needs to be regularly washed and the bacteria removed from the skin.

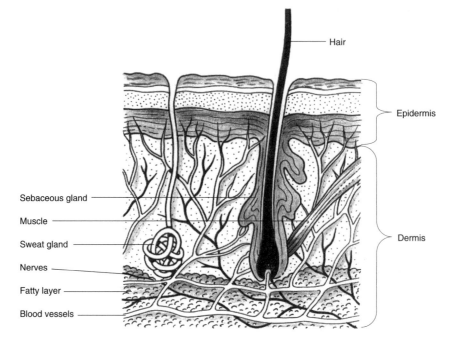

A cross-section through the skin.

Some form of cleaning should be undertaken every day. If a service user is not willing to have a daily bath or shower, then at least a daily wash would assist in the removal of accumulated dirt and waste products and will reduce the risk of the service user having an 'odour problem' which may well be remarked upon by others and can produce a difficult situation.

Personal cleanliness is also important because it improves how people feel about themselves. People tend to feel better after having a bath or a shower, so it is good for morale and a feeling of well-being. In fact baths, and how and when they are taken, can become a topic of much discussion and disagreement in many residential situations!

CASE STUDY

V has multiple sclerosis and is reasonably mobile, although she can become unsteady at times. She has so far been unwilling to use any mobility aids, and, although she has had several falls, she is happier to manage without any form of support as long as possible. She lives in a flat which she shares with two work colleagues and has a demanding job in a city bank. V has found it increasingly difficult to manage bathing and showering. As her periods of unsteadiness have increased, she has lost some confidence and so is more inclined to wash rather than have a bath or shower. This has resulted in a skin rash which is very itchy and flaky on many parts of her body. V checked this with her doctor who provided medication and a bath lotion with instructions to soak in a bath daily. When she told her doctor that she could not get into and out of the bath, he arranged for a visit from the occupational therapist. V is now very concerned about how much of her independence she may lose.

1 What do you think the OT will recommend?
2 How would you reassure V?
3 What do you think should happen now?
4 Why is it important for V to bathe or shower each day?

DID YOU KNOW?

Skin is not only the largest organ in the body, it is also the heaviest. If it were possible to remove the skin of an average adult, it would weigh about 20 lb (or 9 kg).

How to ensure cleanliness

Clearly, the ideal situation is where an individual is able to take care of all his or her own personal cleanliness needs, and all the care setting needs to do is to ensure that the individual is able to access the facilities he or she needs.

If you are providing care for someone in his or her own home:

- Check that he or she is able to reach the bathing facilities.
- If the bathroom is upstairs, it may be necessary to refer the individual for special arrangements to provide access, such as a stairlift or a downstairs shower room.
- You need to consider safety aspects and refer the person for the provision of rails and grab handles, if necessary.
- Make sure that you have found out about all the equipment that is available to assist people, and that you have discussed it with the individual.

If an individual wants any type of help or assistance, you should contact your manager, who will refer the person to the occupational therapist (OT), or another appropriate professional, for an assessment and provision of the necessary equipment.

Check it out

What is the procedure for referring people for support in personal hygiene in your workplace? Find out what it is and how it operates. Obtain a catalogue of aids for bathing and cleaning. Think about the people you work with and whether any of them would benefit from additional help.

Where you are dealing with an individual in a residential or supported living setting, it is likely that bathrooms and bathing facilities will be designed to ensure the necessary ease of access.

- If it is possible for a person to care for his or her own needs, with perhaps some help in gathering together the equipment needed, then that should be encouraged.
- If help is needed, you should ensure that you offer the minimum amount of help needed to ensure safety for the person.

REMEMBER

Your personal hygiene and appearance are important too, as is your approach to the tasks you need to undertake.

- You will need to be tactful and discreet when helping people to wash and dress.

- Your workplace may have guidelines about what you should wear when helping people to wash – perhaps an overall or a plastic apron to protect your uniform, or protective gloves. Make sure you know what the rules are and follow them – they are for everyone's protection.

- Remember to tie your hair back if it is long, and not to wear rings with stones, which can spread infection. See Chapter 3 (Unit CU1) for advice on how to prevent cross-infection and how you should be dressed.

- If you need to wear any particular form of protection, such as gloves, explain this to the individual carefully and using the right communication method.

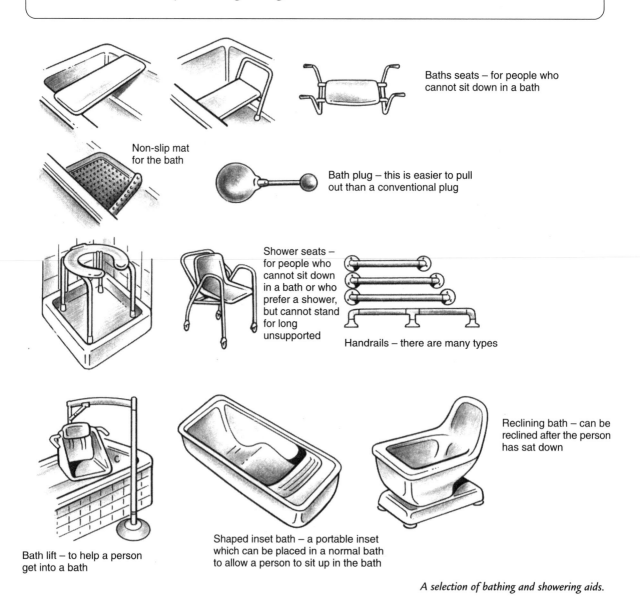

Baths seats – for people who cannot sit down in a bath

Non-slip mat for the bath

Bath plug – this is easier to pull out than a conventional plug

Shower seats – for people who cannot sit down in a bath or who prefer a shower, but cannot stand for long unsupported

Handrails – there are many types

Bath lift – to help a person get into a bath

Shaped inset bath – a portable inset which can be placed in a normal bath to allow a person to sit up in the bath

Reclining bath – can be reclined after the person has sat down

A selection of bathing and showering aids.

Bathing and showering

You will need to assess the level of help a person is likely to need. This should be discussed with the care team and detailed in his or her care plan. The most important views to take into account are those of the individual.

Don't forget that sometimes a bathing or showering aid can provide the same sort of help that a care worker could provide, but will enable the individual to maintain his or her own privacy and dignity. This may be considered preferable to having a carer present. Always make sure that you offer a mechanical aid as an alternative, if it is available. The sorts of aid which can be used are shown on page 274.

There is a wide range of aids to help people with bathing. You can see from the illustrations that they range from devices to help with removing the bath plug to mechanical hoists and baths which recline. Most care settings are likely to have a selection of these aids, although items like reclining baths are very expensive and are not necessary available in all care settings.

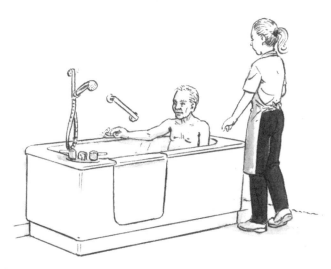

There will be situations in which it would not be safe to allow someone to bathe alone, or where a person does not feel confident and prefers to have assistance from a care worker. As in all caring situations, manual lifting and assistance should be avoided if at all possible – mechanical aids, like bath chairs and slings, should be used. They should be available in your workplace and should have been assessed as being appropriate for the person you are helping.

REMEMBER

It is the responsibility of your employer to carry out risk assessments for all individuals who require assistance with personal hygiene. Your employer must ensure that the necessary equipment is available to enable you to assist the individual safely. However, it is your responsibility to use it!

Keys to good practice

✓ The preparations for bathing are just as important as the bathing itself.
✓ Make sure that you have gathered together all of the items that you will require for a bath – towel, talcum powder, soap, flannel and so on. There is nothing worse for an individual than having to sit undressed while you dash off to find something you have forgotten, like the toenail clippers.

- ✓ Each person should have his or her own set of equipment for bathing and if everything is kept in one bag, it should be easy to make sure that you have not forgotten anything.
- ✓ Bathing a service user also gives you a good opportunity to notice any significant changes, either in their skin or in other parts of their body. You will be able to observe any changes in the skin which could be an indication of a developing pressure sore, or a mole or growth which appears to be developing and may require medical attention.
- ✓ You should immediately report any changes in the skin, including growths, moles, rashes, broken skin or insect bites.
- ✓ Make sure the service user is thoroughly dried, with assistance if necessary.
- ✓ Offer assistance with dressing.
- ✓ Assist the individual to the room he or she wishes to go to and ensure that he or she is comfortable.
- ✓ Clean the bathroom, and make sure that it is left tidy and hygienic for the next person to use.

Showering

Showering can be a very valuable way of keeping clean. Standing or sitting in a shower is much easier for some individuals than climbing in and out of a bath. It is also compatible with the religious views of some people and the personal preferences of others who like to clean themselves in running water rather than static water. Some service users are able to shower themselves with the assistance of a shower seat or a plastic chair placed in the shower. Others are happy to use a shower provided that there are protective grab handles and a non-slip surface to stand on.

Keys to good practice

- ✓ Collect together all the equipment needed for the shower, exactly as you would for bathing.
- ✓ Place a shower seat in the shower, if necessary.
- ✓ Turn on the water and check that the temperature is comfortable.
- ✓ Ensure that the individual is able to sit on the seat in the shower, if necessary.
- ✓ Check that he or she is able to reach all of the areas that require washing, such as the genitals, the feet, the backs of the legs and the back.
- ✓ The person may be glad of assistance or may prefer to shower alone, simply calling you when he or she is finished and requires further supervision to leave the shower.
- ✓ If you are going to leave someone to shower alone, make sure that you explain to him or her how to adjust the water temperature. Ensure that there is a call buzzer within easy reach in case of problems.
- ✓ After the shower, make sure that the individual is thoroughly dry, providing assistance if requested.
- ✓ Assist the person to the room he or she requests and ensure that he or she is comfortable.
- ✓ Tidy the shower room and leave it clean and hygienic.

Washing

If you work with someone who is unable to get out of bed, either permanently or temporarily because of an illness, there may be occasions when bathing or showering is not needed or wanted, but a wash would be welcome and would help to freshen the person up.

Keys to good practice

✓ Hands and face can be washed with a bowl of warm water, soap and a face flannel. This can be offered several times during the day, particularly after meals.

✓ You should also provide a bowl of water and soap, flannel and towel for an individual to wash his or her hands after using the bed pan or a commode.

✓ If you are offering a more extensive wash, perhaps of the arms, under arms and upper torso, many service users may be able to do this for themselves, or you could offer to help.

✓ Ensure that a person has sufficient privacy to wash.

✓ Do not leave a bowl with dirty washing water and utensils lying around. Make sure it is cleared away immediately after use.

✓ Some people may prefer to wash at the wash basin, if there is one in the room.

✓ You will need to establish whether the individual needs any assistance, particularly with washing the back and feet.

✓ Some people may need assistance to stand up to have a strip wash, whereas others may be confident that they can manage alone, in which case you should simply return when they have finished.

✓ Tidy up and leave the washbasin clean and hygienic.

Check it out

Make a list of the people you provide care for, and note the procedure each one uses for personal hygiene. Then consider the reasons for each service user:

● Is it because of personal preference?

● Is it because of physical ability?

● Is it because of access problems?

● Is it because of the policies of the organisation or restrictions on staff time?

Bed bathing

If you have someone who is completely confined to bed, you will need to give a bed bath. This is far more extensive than a simple wash and is not something that an individual can carry out alone.

✓ You will need to collect together all of the items that you require in advance. You cannot leave someone stripped and half-washed while you go to find something you have forgotten.

✓ During a bed bath you should ensure that the person does not become chilled. You may need to close any open windows in the room. You also need to ensure that at no time does the person lie in bed totally uncovered.

✓ You will need a deep bowl for water. You will also need soap, two flannels and two towels – one of each for the face and the body area.

✓ You will need special disposable wipes for washing the genital area. If your workplace does not have these, you will need an additional flannel and towel for the genital area.

✓ Remember to collect together a nail brush, hair brush and nail scissors.

✓ You will also need to have clean linen for the bed and a clean nightdress or pyjamas, as well as sufficient disposal bags for soiled linen and clothing, and disposal bags for the soiled wipes, in appropriate containers.

How to bed bath

- Start by explaining the procedure to the individual and ask if he or she needs to use a commode or bed pan before you begin.
- Make sure that the person consents to being bathed. Do not attempt to bed bath somebody against his or her will.
- Ensure that there is privacy before carrying out the bed bath and that the individual feels reassured.
- Ensure that the person is comfortable. For example, lying flat may be the easiest position for many people for bed bathing, but for someone who is breathless or has a chest condition lying flat can be uncomfortable, so he or she might be better propped upright on pillows.
- Ensure you have all the necessary equipment to hand: bowl, two flannels, two towels and soap.
- Fill the bowl three-quarters full with hand-hot water.
- Strip the top bed clothes and undress the service user, leaving him or her covered with a sheet or a blanket.
- Spread the bath towel over the service user's chest. Then follow the procedure outlined below.

1 Wash, rinse and dry the face, ears and neck with one of the flannels. Remember to check whether or not the individual wants soap used on his or her face – some people find it very drying.

2 Change to the body flannel and wash, rinse and dry each hand in turn, and clean the finger nails.

3 Wash, rinse and dry each arm paying particular attention to the underarms, making sure that they are thoroughly dried.

4 Wash the chest and abdomen. Be very careful to dry the area underneath the breasts for women, and any stomach creases where moisture can build up, cause soreness and encourage the development of fungal infections.

5 Change the water and then continue washing each leg. Place the large bath towel under each leg when you are washing and rinsing.

6 Wash each foot in turn, and then ensure that you have dried everything thoroughly, particularly between the toes where fungal infections develop easily if they are left damp.

7 Roll the person in order to wash his or her back. If you are the only worker present it is important that you roll the person towards you, which reduces the risk of a fall from the bed.

8 When you have finished washing the whole of the service user's body, change to a different flannel or to special wipes, and wash and clean the genital and anal area thoroughly. If you are using disposable wipes, they should be discarded into an appropriate disposal bag.

1 Head and face
4 Chest and abdomen
3 Arms
7 Back
8 Genital area
2 Hands
5 Legs
6 Feet

- Fold the sheet as you wash each part of the body so that only the part you are washing is exposed and the rest of the body is covered by the sheet.
- Make sure that you have taken all the necessary steps to dry the service user thoroughly. This is a good opportunity to check for the development of pressure sores and to ensure that you have taken the necessary preventive measures. If you notice any changes to the skin, you should report them immediately.

Extra tasks

- If the individual is unable to get out of bed, take the opportunity to change the bottom sheet whilst he or she is rolled onto one side. Then remake the bed with fresh bed linen. If the individual is able to get out of bed, this is a good time to offer a clean nightdress or pyjamas, and assist him or her to sit in the chair whilst you remake the bed.
- Check whether fingernails or toenails need to be clipped. If it is a straightforward job, you should carry this out. If the toenails are particularly hard, they should be left for a chiropodist. You should report this to your supervisor, who will arrange for a chiropodist to visit.

Check it out

Find out the arrangements for chiropody in your workplace. Make sure you know what steps to take to refer a service user to a chiropodist. Find out:

- who you need to speak to
- whether you have to make a written report
- who is responsible for contacting the chiropodist
- how long it takes.

Shaving

Shaving is very important for most men. They usually find it uncomfortable and irritating to have stubble on their faces. If an individual is not able to shave himself, you will have to arrange to carry this out. Ask him what kind of help he needs. He may be able to carry out the shaving himself if you put the soap on his face. Where you need to carry out the whole procedure of shaving, you should remember that it is not straightforward and is not the same for every individual. You will need to establish whether the service user shaves with a safety razor or with an electric razor.

A safety razor.   *An electric razor.*

If a service user tells you that he shaves with a cut-throat razor, this is probably better left to a visiting barber!

I always shave with this!

Keys to good practice

Safety razor
✓ Check with the individual which direction he normally shaves in. This makes a difference to how easy it is to shave and to whether or not you are likely to pull any hairs or to make the skin sore.
✓ Make a lather on the chin and cheeks either with a traditional shaving brush or with a hand-rub shaving soap. These are normally available in tubes.
✓ Take long firm strokes with the razor in the direction that he has indicated. Make sure that you rinse the razor frequently as it will become clogged with soap and bristles.
✓ When you have finished shaving, rinse the individual's face and dry it thoroughly.
✓ Ask him if he likes aftershave, and if there is any particular one that he has and uses regularly.
✓ Make sure that you clear away all of the equipment when you have finished.
✓ Ensure that any used blades are disposed of in the 'sharps' box.

Electric razor

✓ First, ensure that it is clean by flipping the top and dusting or blowing out any accumulated stubble.

✓ Shave in the direction that the service user has told you his beard grows.

✓ Do not scrub an electric razor backwards and forwards across the face – just allow the razor to move in the same direction as the stubble growth.

✓ Aftershave lotion should be applied if the individual wishes.

✓ Remove all of the equipment and tidy up afterwards.

Check it out

If you have never shaved anyone before, try shaving a friend or colleague. Even if you shave yourself every day, it is very different shaving someone else! If you cannot find a colleague or friend brave enough to let you try, blow up a balloon, cover it in shaving soap and shave away. If you burst the balloon – you need more practice!

Mouth care

Mouth care (oral hygiene) is extremely important for everyone because bacteria will multiply in a mouth that is not regularly cleaned, and this will lead to infections and mouth disease. Many individuals are able to maintain their own mouth care, perhaps with a little assistance. However, you will need to carry out mouth care for people who are seriously ill or who have special needs.

Much mouth care occurs naturally because, as long as people maintain a sufficient intake of fluids, the saliva in the mouth carries out a great deal of cleaning. However, various illnesses and conditions, as well as the natural ageing process, can change the way in which the mouth works. Saliva production can be reduced and people may suffer from dry and crusted mouths, and infections, such as thrush (a fungal infection), sore tongue or ulcerated gums or cheeks may develop. A reduction in saliva production also increases the incidence of bad breath (halitosis).

DID YOU KNOW?

The average person produces around 1 litre ($1\frac{3}{4}$ pints) of saliva each day.

Oral hygiene involves:

- cleaning teeth or dentures
- cleaning between teeth to ensure the removal of all food particles
- cleaning of gums and soft parts of the mouth
- checking for problems.

Most people will be able to clean and floss their teeth, clean their dentures, ensure the general cleanliness of their own mouths and deal with minor problems, such as ulcers or cracked and sore lips, without any assistance. However, if you do need to assist you should follow the procedure outlined below.

1   Provide the individual with a bowl of water or assist him or her to a washbasin.
2   Offer to put toothpaste on the toothbrush, if necessary.
3   Assist with brushing only if required. If you do need to assist, you should brush gently but firmly, ensuring that all teeth are brushed on all surfaces. Brushing should be done for at least one minute.
4   Give the individual a glass of water to rinse the toothpaste out of his or her mouth.
5   Offer the individual dental floss to clean between his or her teeth. Be prepared to assist with flossing if required.
6   Note whether any parts of the person's mouth are painful or if there are any sore places.
7   Make sure that anything you have noticed is reported.
8   Offer the person a mouthwash.

If you are caring for service users with a very high degree of dependency then you may need to carry out regular mouth care for them.

Keys to good practice

✓ Mouth care can be done either with a small, soft toothbrush or, more usually, with swabs which are used to clean around the teeth, gums, palate and inside of the cheeks.
✓ Use the swabs to remove any food particles and clean all the surfaces of the mouth.
✓ You can obtain liquid toothpaste, which is probably the easiest sort to use.
✓ A diluted solution of sodium bicarbonate (one teaspoon in 500 ml of warm water) is commonly used for mouth care, particularly where the mouth is dry and crusted, but it can leave a very unpleasant aftertaste and is better followed by swabbing out with a more pleasant-tasting mouthwash.
✓ After you have finished cleaning and moistening the person's mouth, protect his or her lips with lip salve or Vaseline.
✓ Remember that all of the equipment that you use should be maintained for that individual only and should be clearly labelled and kept together.

Eye care

When people are fit and well, their eyes are kept moist and clean naturally by fluid which fills the eye and drains into the nose. However, when people are ill their eyes can often become dry, irritated and sore, and you may need to bathe them to soothe them and to remove and treat any infection.

Keys to good practice

✓ Before you begin cleaning a person's eyes, make sure that you have cottonwool swabs and a suitable bag in which to dispose of them, a bowl of clean water or saline, a paper towel and eye drops, if the person uses them. To bathe somebody's eyes you will need to:
1   Make him or her comfortable and explain what you are going to do.
2   Ensure that he or she is in agreement and wants you to carry this out.
3   Ideally, the person should lie flat, with you behind his or her head. However, this may not be possible and you may need to work with the person's head leaning slightly backwards with the shoulders supported.

4 Wash your hands to ensure that they are clean, and take universal precautions (see Chapter 3, Unit CU1).
5 Arrange the paper towel under the person's face, usually tucked into the clothing just below the chin. Dip a swab into the water or saline, squeeze it gently and swab the eye once, working from the nose to the outside. This should be done in a single movement.
6 Throw the swab away.
7 Repeat this procedure on both eyes until the eyes are clean and clear of any crusting or infection. Dry the skin around the eyes with clean dry swabs.
✓ Remember to use each swab once only, as it is easy to cross-infect from one eye to the other or to introduce infections into the eye.

Hair washing

Washing the hair of someone who is confined to bed can be extremely difficult. If the person is able to have a bath or a shower, then washing the hair is not a problem, but for those who are restricted to bed and only have a bed bath, you need to be able wash their hair.

Keys to good practice

✓ The most effective way to wash hair is with an inflatable hair wash tray which allows you to wash the hair and drain the water away without the service user having to move from the bed. This is very important for people who are suffering from back injuries or other forms of paralysis.
✓ The same effect can be achieved by removing the bedhead and placing a bucket on the floor at the back of the bed.
✓ Protect the bed with a plastic sheet.
✓ Use a jug to pour water gently over the service user's hair. This will either drain into the inflatable tray or over the plastic sheet into the bucket.
✓ Check with the individual that the water is a comfortable temperature.
✓ Shampoo the hair, making sure that the shampoo does not get into the person's eyes. Then rinse with clear, warm water.
✓ Dry the hair with a towel. Then comb through gently, style and dry with a hairdryer.

Inflatable hair wash tray

Shoulder hair wash tray

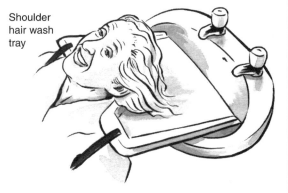

The side walls are formed by two separately inflatable chambers. Water drains out through a tube which can be clamped off.

Most useful for wheelchair users as it allows a basin wash without having to get out of the chair. Padded flaps hold steady on the shoulders, and a recessed edge cradles the neck.

How to deal with problems

The main problem you will probably come across in the area of personal cleanliness is when someone refuses to be bathed or washed, or refuses to wash or bath himself or herself as often as necessary in order to keep clean. This situation can often cause problems when the person is living in a residential or hospital setting and there are other people who object to the odour that can come from somebody who fails to wash regularly. This is a case where tact and gentle persuasion is likely to be the most effective solution – an explanation of the reasons why keeping clean is important, followed by some fairly firm but friendly advice. It may be best to suggest that the individual begins fairly slowly, rather than with a full bath. He or she should be offered the option of a wash, and then gradually encouraged over time to take a bath or a shower. If you are faced with this sort of situation, you will need to use all your communication skills. You could try this approach:

Carer: 'Would you like me to arrange some help for you to have a bath or a shower?'

Service user: 'No.'

Carer: 'That's fine. Do you think you'll manage on your own?'

Service user: 'I don't want a bath.'

Carer: 'Well, it is very important that you do have a bath or shower regularly, otherwise you could get all sorts of skin problems – and you would start to be a bit smelly.'

Service user: 'I don't smell – are you saying I smell?'

Carer: 'You will do if you don't get clean. What would you rather do – have a bath or a shower, or maybe you'd prefer a good wash?'

Service user: 'I don't mind a wash, but I'm not getting under one of those showers.'

Carer: 'Great – do you need any help with getting a wash?'

Try to find out, tactfully, if there is a reason for the person's reluctance to wash. Does he or she experience discomfort when washing, for example? You may be able to offer a solution to this problem. A person's reluctance to wash may also be a symptom of a general change in his or her condition.

You also need to be aware of people's religious views in respect of bathing and cleanliness, and take care to observe any special requirements. Make sure that you ask about religious beliefs about washing and bathing, if you are not sure.

If you experience any problems in getting someone in or out of the bath or shower you must summon help immediately. This is a potentially dangerous situation and one you should not attempt to sort out on your own. You could end up injuring either the individual or yourself quite badly. It is always better to summon help.

What and when to report

● Any problems in providing people with help for their personal cleanliness must be reported to your supervisor and recorded clearly in the person's notes.

- Any changes you notice in a person's body or skin could be very significant and should be immediately reported and recorded.

If you are able to get the balance right between allowing the individual independence, choice and dignity and, at the same time, offering assistance in an acceptable way, you will perform an invaluable role in promoting that person's physical and emotional well-being.

TEST YOURSELF

1 Describe three different ways of getting a person into and out of a bath or shower.

2 Why is it important to keep the skin clean?

3 Name the substances that collect on the skin if it is not regularly cleaned.

4 Is it possible to wash the hair of someone who is confined to bed? If so, how?

5 What is the key thing to remember when bathing someone's eyes?

6 How would you prepare for a bed bath?

Element Z9.2   Support clients in personal grooming and dressing

What you need to learn

- How to ensure choice
- How to offer support
- How to deal with problems

How to ensure choice

I'm so glad I can choose my own clothes.

To make sure that individuals really do have a choice in how they look and how they dress, you have to be sure that they are able to discuss the kind of clothes that they want, and the sort of colours, styles and fabrics that they like to wear. It is important that people are not simply told what to wear or made to wear clothes which are convenient for the care setting. Individuals in a residential setting could be in danger of having less choice than those who are in their own homes or in a day centre.

Wherever possible you should encourage individuals to wear the style of clothes that they enjoy and find comfortable – whether the style is formal or informal, whether they like bright colours or dark colours, whether they like flowers, spots or stripes, you should try wherever possible to meet their requirements. The way people look and the clothes they choose to wear are probably the single biggest statement of their individual personality – you must never attempt to undermine their ability to be themselves.

You should also ensure that people are able to choose the kind of make-up, perfumes or aftershaves that they would like to use. Try to provide them with the kinds of product that they have always used or would like to try.

It is important, however, that people's choices should be informed choices and that you explain to them any changed factors in their lives that need to be taken into account. For example, someone who has become incontinent may need to rethink the kind of fabric that his or her clothes are made from – it may be necessary to consider buying clothes in fabrics which can be easily laundered. If someone has developed a sensitive skin condition, he or she may have to think about using particular types of make-up, perfume or aftershave.

The use of a prosthesis (an artificial breast, arm or leg, hair piece or wig) may mean that the person has to change his or her style of clothing. Someone who previously liked low-cut dresses and blouses may have to try a different style if she is wearing a prosthesis in place of a breast which has been removed. Someone with an artificial arm may want to wear clothes with long sleeves, and so on.

Helping people get dressed

There are many aids which allow people to dress themselves. Several are shown below. They can make the difference between the person having to ask for help and being totally independent. Managing zips and pulling on shoes, stockings and tights can be

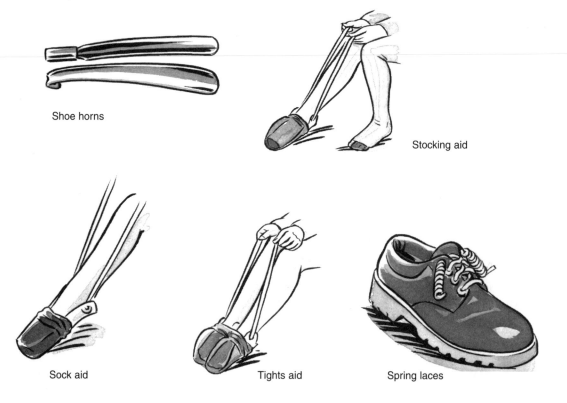

Shoe horns

Stocking aid

Sock aid

Tights aid

Spring laces

Aids for hair grooming

very difficult with limited movement or weak hands or arm muscles. A well-designed dressing aid can make it perfectly possible for a person to dress himself or herself without relying on help from a carer.

Similarly, specially designed combs and brushes allow individuals to continue grooming their own hair. Many will prefer this, rather than having to ask for help.

How to offer support

Dressing

To offer support in dressing an individual, follow the keys to good practice outlined below.

Keys to good practice

✓ If a person does need help in dressing and undressing, the first thing you must do is to ensure that he or she has privacy and that dignity is maintained.

✓ Ensure that you are dressing the person in clothes which he or she has chosen to wear and not clothes that you have chosen. It is demoralising and demeaning not to be able to choose the clothes you wear, and it is one of the key features of 'institutionalised' people that they lose freedom of choice over clothes.

✓ Make sure that you do not fall into the trap of choosing clothes on the person's behalf because you think that they will be appropriate.

✓ Follow the advice given in the diagrams below and on the next page.

Putting on a shirt or jacket
Slip your hand through the sleeve from the cuff and hold the person's hand. Pull the sleeve up and round the shoulder. Remember, if the person has a 'bad side', start with that arm.

Putting on trousers
With the person lying on the bed, pull the trousers over his or her feet. Pull them up as far as possible. Ask the person to lift his or her buttocks off the bed while you ease the trousers up to the waist. Fasten them.

Putting on a sweater

If the person's arms both function, slip the sweater over the head first, then help the arms into the sleeves.

If the person is lying down, slip the arms into the sweater first, then ease the neck opening over the head.

Supports, prostheses and orthoses

Once you have established with an individual which clothes he or she wishes to wear, you must also take into account any supports, prostheses or orthoses which are being used, and make sure that they are fitted comfortably.

Types of support, prosthesis and orthosis

Supports	Prostheses	Orthoses
Hearing aids Glasses Voice synthesisers	Artificial limbs Artificial breasts Wigs Dentures	Surgical stockings Callipers Surgical collar Truss/support

The table above lists some of the most common aids and appliances you are likely to come across when assisting people to dress, although there are many others and you will need to be sure about the needs of individual people. They are all very significant in terms of an individual's well-being, both physical and emotional. They will have been prescribed and will be part of the plan of care.

It is important that you ensure that aids or appliances are used properly and that the person is wearing them correctly, that they sit well and are comfortable and that they do not rub or chafe. If you do notice that any prosthesis or orthosis is causing irritation or soreness, you must report this immediately to your supervisor and ensure arrangements are made for the adjustments needed.

Check it out

Make a list of individuals you deal with in your workplace. Note any supports, prostheses or orthoses each of them has. Check what the process is in your workplace for recording them for each person, and for recording their whereabouts when they are not in use.

Grooming

Grooming is just as important as dressing. If an individual is not able to carry out grooming for himself or herself, you will need to offer help. The main areas of grooming where you may need to assist are likely to be:

- hair care
- make-up
- manicure.

Hair care

The way that hair is styled and groomed is very individual and most people have very strong feelings about how they like their hair to be done. If you work in a residential, day-care or hospital setting, visiting hairdressers may be available on a regular basis. If you are visiting and supporting individuals in their own homes, you may be able to arrange for a mobile hairdresser to visit periodically in order to cut and perm or colour their hair.

In between hairdressers' visits, keeping hair washed and nicely groomed and styled is extremely important in terms of a person's emotional well-being. You should ensure that you wash and dry and style the hair, as far as possible, in the way that the person wishes you to.

Make-up

You will need to discuss with the individual the type of make-up that she uses and establish what sort of help may be needed to apply it. You will need to:

- establish the type of make-up the person wishes to use, for example foundation, powder, lipstick, etc.
- check with the plan of care that there is no reason why the use of make-up could be a problem, for instance, skin, mouth or eye infections
- establish whether the person has the make-up or whether she needs assistance to purchase it
- discuss colours, and try to arrange for the person to sample some different types and colours of make-up
- check with a service user which perfume or cologne he or she prefers to use – the use of perfume or cologne is a very personal matter
- ensure that each service user has her own make-up and that it is not shared – this reduces the risk of cross-infection.

Check it out

Find out whether there are any arrangements for people in your workplace to try out make-up, or for a beauty therapist to visit. Check whether there are any arrangements with local beauty salons or cosmetic companies to offer their products. If there are not, you may want to discuss with your manager whether this would be possible to arrange.

Manicure

The day-to-day care of the nails will be partly undertaken during normal bathing, when you should use a nail brush to keep the nails clean. You should ensure that fingernails are regularly cut or filed to a rounded shape, to the shape of the finger. Some women may like to have a manicure and you should offer the use of nail varnish.

File a nail to the shape of the finger   Cut toenails straight across using clippers   Offer nail varnish

Nail care.

Toenails can be difficult to cut, particularly in older people where they can become very hard and almost impossible to cut with normal nail clippers. Where it is possible to cut toenails, they should be cut in a straight line and never rounded, because this can encourage ingrowing toenails.

If there are difficulties in cutting nails, you will need to arrange for a chiropodist to visit. He or she will have the proper equipment to deal with the individual in a professional way.

You can be alerted to some medical conditions by the condition of a person's nails. For example, some types of anaemia can cause nails to grow into a concave shape, when they turn up at the ends, and some types of illness can cause ridging on the nails.

If you notice anything unusual, you should report it immediately and record it, as it may be an indication of a condition that needs medical attention.

Other considerations

Make sure that you always take into account people's personal beliefs and preferences in the question of hair, dress and personal grooming. These are just as important as in the area of personal cleanliness. For example, Sikhs and Rastafarians believe that hair should never be cut or shaved. Many Orthodox Jewish women wear wigs. Always ensure that you ask the individual, or seek advice from members of the family or others if it is not possible to ask the person directly.

How to deal with problems

You may be faced with an individual who refuses to use the prosthesis or orthosis which has been prescribed, because he or she thinks that it is ugly or uncomfortable or does not feel that it is providing him or her with any effective assistance. If gentle persuasion fails to convince the person of the value of it, and if you have checked that it is not because it is uncomfortable or ill-fitting, then you should report this immediately so that it can be discussed with the professional who prescribed it.

You may also be faced with a situation where a person wants to wear clothes which are unsuitable given the nature of his or her condition. For example, you may find somebody who insists on wearing clothes which can only be dry cleaned, even though he or she is incontinent. The only thing you can do in this situation is to try to persuade the person by explaining the difficulties that this will present, but finally (if he or she can afford the dry cleaning bills!) it is the person's choice and you cannot impose your views.

Ultimately, the way people look, both in terms of their appearance and their clothing, is very much a matter of individual taste, preferences and beliefs – it is a very personal expression of their identities. You can only offer assistance, not direction, and you should encourage individuals to take as many of their own decisions as they can.

TEST YOURSELF

1   Name three types of dressing aid.

2   What factors would you consider when advising on suitable clothing?

3   What would you discuss with an individual when choosing make-up for her?

4   At what stage would you call in a chiropodist?

5   In what order would you dress somebody who has two arms functioning well?

6   Name three types of prosthesis which you need to take into account when somebody is dressing.

Z9 UNIT TEST

1   You have to help an older woman get ready for grandson's wedding. She has poor mobility, but can get around with a walking frame. She likes to look smart and always has her hair done. Think about what you would need to do.

   a   What aspects would you need to discuss with her in advance?
   b   What would she need assistance with before the day itself?
   c   What would you do on the day?
   d   What would you do first on the day?
   e   How do you think she will want to look?
   f   Why is it important for her to feel she looks good?

2   You have just admitted a service user with mental health problems to your hostel. He has been living rough for the past six weeks, and you are asked to assist him with personal hygiene.

   a   What would you do first?
   b   Why?
   c   Why is it important to try to get him clean?
   d   How do you think he may be feeling?
   e   Make a list of the personal cleansing and grooming tasks which are likely to be needed.
   f   How would you try to persuade him to co-operate?

Enable clients to access and use toilet facilities

In our society using the toilet to dispose of body waste is something which is carried out in private. Being continent, that is, being able to retain body waste until we are in an appropriate place to dispose of it, is an essential part of being acceptable within our society. People who have difficulty in conforming to this accepted way of behaving, because they are unable to access toilet facilities before they become incontinent, are likely to suffer a high degree of humiliation, low self-esteem and embarrassment. There is a very important role to be played in ensuring that people are able to access toilet facilities appropriately when they need them.

People who need help to use toilet facilities are often faced with a very difficult situation. They may be aware that they need assistance but find it embarrassing to ask. As a care worker you should be able to encourage them to ask for assistance and to offer it in a way which removes any embarrassment.

Waste products from the human body are excellent indicators of what is happening internally. In much the same way as gauges and dip sticks are used to measure the internal workings of a car, we can use measurements and observations of human body waste to examine what is happening within the body. Body waste also needs to be disposed of in a safe and hygienic way. It is, by its very nature of being a waste product, composed of potentially infectious materials and can easily cause contamination and cross-infection if not dealt with appropriately.

Element Z11.1 Enable clients to access toilet facilities

What you need to learn
- How to ensure the service user is offered choice
- How to maintain the service user's dignity

How to ensure the service user is offered choice

One of the key areas in maintaining independence is to give individuals choice in all areas of their care. This applies no less to toilet facilities than to anything else. It is, of course, a difficult area to discuss and you may find it far from easy to talk to people about their use of toilet facilities and about their body waste. They may well be embarrassed by the discussion, but it will be made worse if you show that you are also embarrassed.

Try to think about toileting and body waste as a necessary physical process to be undergone in the same way as any other aspect of care. Try not be influenced by any embarrassment about discussing this type of private and personal matter directly with someone. If you are able to treat it in a general, matter-of-fact way, the individual is likely to find it much easier to respond to you.

It is also useful to try to establish whether the person has any preference as to the gender of the worker who will provide any assistance needed. It may become clear that the individual would prefer to hold a discussion on the matter with a worker of the same gender. This is not always possible in every work setting and, if it is not, it will have to be explained to the person. However, if it is possible for a worker of the same gender to talk with an individual at his or her request, that is a choice which should be offered.

To ensure that an individual is provided with the maximum possible choice, certain areas will need to be discussed and established with him or her. You will need to discuss:

- getting to the toilet
- adjusting clothing once he or she has reached the toilet facilities
- being able to get on to the toilet facility
- the type of toilet facility that he or she would prefer to use.

Getting to the toilet

The question of accessing the toilet facilities will need to be looked at in terms of:

- the person's mobility
- the frequency with which he or she needs to use the toilet
- the urgency with which he or she usually needs to use the toilet.

For example, somebody who has poor mobility may still be able to reach the toilet independently. But somebody who suffers from urgency – an urgent need to empty the bladder – and is not able to 'hold on', may become incontinent as a result of poor mobility, simply because he or she is not able to reach toilet facilities in time. Similarly, frequency – a condition where someone often needs to empty his or her bladder – can present problems for someone with mobility problems. It is one thing to undertake a painful, slow walk to the toilet every two or three hours, but it is quite another to do it every half hour!

REMEMBER
The aim, as in all service user care, is to ensure that people are as independent as possible. However, in these circumstances you will need to balance somebody's independence in terms of going to the toilet with his or her level of ability and the likelihood that difficulty in reaching the toilet could cause incontinence. Such an outcome may be considered by the person to be far worse than being given a helping hand to reach toilet facilities in time.

DID YOU KNOW?
The capacity of the average bladder is about 1 pint (500 ml). Most people produce about 3 pints (1.5 litres) of urine every day.

Adjusting clothing

The other area which can present difficulties for people with limited mobility is being able to adjust their clothing once they reach a toilet facility. Being able to undo trouser flies, adjust buttons, or reach to remove underclothes may be extremely difficult for people who have poor or limited use of their arms or who are unsteady and need to be supported with both hands.

Help with accessing the toilet

You may find that you need to offer assistance to an individual who needs help to get on and off the toilet. He or she may have difficulty in sitting or in rising from a seat without help. If a person needs help to get in and out of a chair, then it is possible that he or she will need similar help with a toilet – but may find it much more difficult to ask, or to accept the help.

Different types of toilet facility

When you are discussing toilet facilities with people, you will need to ask them about the type of facility they prefer to use. This may be dictated by their condition.

- If they cannot get out of bed, they will be limited to using a bed pan and urinal.
- If they can move from bed, they may prefer a commode.
- Those who can reach a toilet with or without assistance may prefer that option.

Do not forget to discuss a person's needs in terms of cleaning himself or herself after using the toilet.

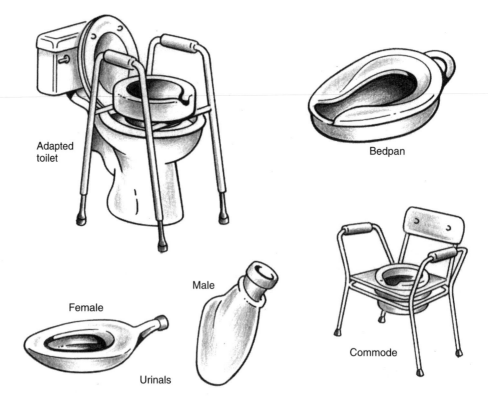

Adapted toilet

Bedpan

Female

Male

Urinals

Commode

Some types of toilet facility.

Using the right language

It is important to establish what language and terms an individual uses to refer to all matters connected with the use of toilet facilities and his or her own body waste. There will be many different ones, although there are some widely known and understood terms, such as 'spending a penny', 'having a tinkle', 'going for a wee', and a great many other euphemisms. It is important that you establish exactly what a person means so that you can avoid misunderstandings. A misunderstanding is much more likely to happen with people who are from a different culture, or even from a different part of the same country where different expressions may be used.

People are also likely to have different ways of describing toilet facilities. They may refer to 'a lavatory', 'a loo', 'the bathroom' or 'the john', again depending on the area of the country or their own background or culture. You should ask the individual and be quite clear that you understand exactly what he or she means by particular references. If you are unsure, you should ask the family if the person is unable to make it clear to you. You will also need to establish with an individual directly or by asking his or her family if there are any particular religious or cultural beliefs associated with using toilet facilities.

Check it out

Write down as many different expressions as you can think of for going to the toilet. Think of as many different words as possible to describe the toilet. Note down the ones in use in your workplace. Notice if everyone uses the same words, or whether individuals have their own expressions.

CASE STUDY

Mr J had just arrived in residential care. He had recently had prostate surgery and found that he needed to be able to get to the toilet quickly. He was concerned that he may not know where the toilets were in his new surroundings and was becoming very worried. His key worker, Julie, was very kind and pleasant, but he didn't feel that he could explain his worries to her. When she asked if there was anything else he wanted to ask, Mr J said 'Yes', then 'Er no – it's alright'. Julie guessed that there may be something he was too embarrassed to discuss with her. She offered to ask one of the male care workers to come and talk to him, and Mr J seemed relieved.

Leroy asked Mr J if he had any questions, and he then explained his worries about needing the toilet urgently and not being able to get there. Leroy spent time showing him where the toilets were and promised that he would make sure there was a urine bottle in his room each night until he felt more confident. Mr J was much happier and continued to settle in very well.

1   What may have happened if Mr J had not been able to speak to Leroy?
2   Was Julie right to ask Leroy to step in, or should she have reassured Mr J herself?
3   Is there anything else which may have helped Mr J?

Making choices happen

Once you have established the level of help and assistance that a person is going to need, you must then set about considering how you can adapt the environment as far as possible to increase the level of independence that he or she is able to exercise. You may want to think about:

● providing a mobility aid
● providing a room nearer the toilet facilities
● arranging a regular toiletting visit.

How to maintain the service user's dignity

When you talk to colleagues and individuals about the basic information that you need in respect of using toilets, the discussions should be held in private, and not in full hearing of other residents, visitors or workers. These are generally not matters that people are happy to discuss in front of others and so every effort should be made to maintain privacy. The type of privacy you are able to offer may well be limited by the kind of setting in which you work. If the best level of privacy available is a curtain drawn around a hospital bed, then you should at the very least provide this. If a person has his or her own room or if there is a quiet area where you can go to talk, so much the better. Obviously, if you are discussing these matters in a person's own home, there should be no difficulties in ensuring privacy.

If you do need to provide assistance, after having reached that decision jointly with the person, you should offer it quietly and without any public announcements, whenever it is required. It is not acceptable to walk into a lounge full of residents and say: 'Oh, Mary, you are ready for your trip to the loo then!' Whilst this may be well meant, it can be humiliating in the extreme for a person to have a public announcement in this way.

You will need to establish when you talk to an individual what indication he or she will give you when help is required. He or she may simply call you over, or if help is only needed once he or she is actually in the toilet, it may be a case of pressing a buzzer and getting assistance when it is needed.

The curtain around the hospital bed is far from ideal, but is the best way of ensuring privacy in this situation.

If a person is not able to go to toilet facilities, but needs to use a commode or bed pan, again it is important that privacy is maintained. The curtain around the hospital bed is far from ideal, but it is the best that can be provided in some circumstances.

How to help a person to use a bedpan

1 Wash your hands and use gloves.

2 Ensure as much privacy as possible.

3 Ask the person to raise his or her buttocks off the bed by raising the knees with feet flat on the bed and lifting the hips.

4 If the person is unable to raise himself or herself, roll him or her away from you, put the bedpan on the bed and roll the person back onto the pan.

   Important: If you roll the person, THERE SHOULD BE ANOTHER WORKER at the other side of the bed. If you are alone, you must raise the bed rails on the far side of the bed. If there are no bed rails, do not roll the person alone.

5 Assist the person to sit up and cover him or her with a sheet.

6 Leave him or her alone to use the bedpan, making sure that the buzzer is within reach for when it is needed.

7 If the person has not buzzed after ten minutes, check that he or she is alright and does not require help.

8 Remove the bedpan and cover it.

9 Wash or clean the person, if required.

10 Provide a bowl of water, soap and flannel to allow the person to wash his or her hands.

11 Dispose of the waste after checking and measuring, if necessary.

12 Wash your hands.

How to help a person to use a commode

1 Wash your hands and use gloves.

2 Make sure there is a clean bedpan in the commode.

3 Assist the person out of bed and onto the commode.

4 Leave the call buzzer within reach.

5 Leave the person alone to use the commode.

6 When he or she has finished, assist with cleaning or washing, if necessary.

7 Dispose of cleaning materials in sluice or toilet.

8 Assist the person back into bed or a chair.

9 Remove the bedpan and cover it.

10 Dispose of the waste after checking and measuring, if necessary.

11 Wash your hands.

Privacy

The toilet door should always be closed so that the individual can be completely private. Toilet doors should have locks in case individuals wish to lock them, but there must be a safety unlocking mechanism on the outside of the door. All toilets for residents' use must have a means of calling for help in an emergency. This is clearly essential, as a person could remain undiscovered for some time, if he or she was taken ill or had an accident inside a locked toilet cubicle.

Keys to good practice

✓ Hold discussions in private.
✓ Agree the level of help needed.
✓ Agree how the person will indicate when he or she needs help.
✓ Ensure privacy for an individual using the toilet – do not interrupt him or her, or allow anyone else to do so.
✓ Offer help quietly and unobtrusively.

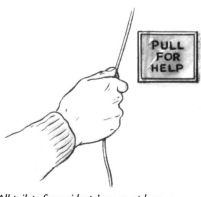

All toilets for residents' use must have a means of calling for help in an emergency.

Menstruation

It is important to maintain the privacy and dignity of female service users who are menstruating (having periods) and require assistance to dispose of sanitary towels or tampons. As with toilet facilities, these discussions should be held privately with the individual concerned and her preferences in respect of disposal should be established.

As long as her wishes in disposing of used sanitary protection are not in conflict with the policies of the care setting, for example wishing to flush away sanitary towels in an ordinary toilet (which is likely to cause major plumbing difficulties), they should be complied with as far as possible. The disposal of sanitary protection and the offer of help should be made discreetly and privately in order to avoid any embarrassment for the woman concerned. It is an area which many women find difficult to deal with publicly, especially in mixed gender care settings.

Keys to good practice

If you are talking to a woman about menstruation and sanitary protection, you should observe the same considerations as when talking about using the toilet. You need to find out about:

✓ the type of sanitary protection she prefers
✓ the nature of her periods – heavy, light, sudden, regular, irregular, etc.
✓ how often she likes to change her sanitary protection
✓ what level of assistance she needs
✓ her preferences for disposal.

ment Z11.2 | Assist clients to use toilet facilities

What you need to learn

● How to assist service users to clean themselves
● How to check for abnormal body waste
● How to leave the environment clean after use

How to assist service users to clean themselves

Helping service users to clean themselves after using the toilet is another area of assistance which will require discussion with the individual concerned. If you are providing assistance in terms of accessing the toilet, you may be able to observe just what a person is able to achieve in terms of cleaning appropriately.

Many service users need help to wipe themselves after using the toilet, particularly if they have limited arm and shoulder movement or spinal problems. The bodily twists and turns involved in effectively cleaning the anal and genital areas after using the toilet are quite difficult to achieve if you have either muscular or joint problems in the upper body. Some people may be able to clean themselves if they are supported whilst they do so. The questions you will need to ask are:

● Are you able to clean yourself, or do you need help?
● What sort of help do you need – support whilst you clean yourself? Or someone to clean you?
● Do you clean with toilet paper?
● Do you need a bidet or other facility with running water?
● Do you use wipes?
● Are your requirements different depending on whether you have emptied bowels or bladder?
● Do you need help with cleaning menstrual blood?

Bidets

A bidet is an extremely useful way of cleaning after using the toilet, if it is installed at the right height. Bidets can be difficult for people to use if they are too low. However, a bidet can be helpful for meeting the religious requirements of people who need to clean themselves in running rather than static water. You may need to offer assistance with:

- getting on and off the bidet
- washing the anal and genital areas
- drying.

Bedpans/urinals

A person using a bed pan may find it difficult to clean himself or herself, whether using wipes or ordinary toilet paper, and you will need to discuss with the person whether he or she will need your assistance. A person using a bedpan may need help with:

- getting on and off the bedpan
- cleaning or washing the genital and anal areas
- drying.

Commodes

A person who is able to get out of bed, but cannot manage the walk to the toilet, may be able to use a commode. As with the other options, he or she may need help with:

- getting on and off the commode
- cleaning or washing the genital and anal areas
- drying.

Treatment of catheter bags and stoma care are not covered by this unit but are dealt with elsewhere within the care standards.

Keys to good practice

✓ Establish the level and type of help a person needs.
✓ Wear an apron and gloves.
✓ Wash or wipe the genital and anal areas gently.
✓ If washing, use clear water. Do not use soap.
✓ If using wipes or paper, make sure the area is clean and free from faeces.
✓ Wipe from front to back – never from back to front.
✓ After cleaning, dispose of the cleaning materials in a sluice or toilet.
✓ Wash your hands.
✓ Make sure that you always assist the person to wash his or her hands after using the toilet, regardless of the facility used.

How to check for abnormal body waste

The waste from bodies is a good indicator of any health problems which may be developing. It can often be an early indicator of illnesses or potentially serious conditions. Because of this, it is important that you establish with a person his or her normal pattern of body waste, so that you can identify anything which would cause concern. You will need to ask about:

- normal frequency of emptying bladder
- normal frequency of opening the bowels
- what are the normal faeces like? Are they small and hard, or loose?
- what is the normal quantity and colour of the urine?

Abnormalities can indicate many potential illnesses, and they can range from the common and easily treatable conditions to serious conditions. It is important that you always report any changes in a person's normal pattern of waste to your supervisor (see the table below). They should also be recorded in the person's chart.

Changes you may see and should report

Change	Action
Faeces change from soft to small and hard	Constipation – needs to be reported
Faeces change in colour from brown to pale yellow	Could indicate conditions which require urgent medical attention
Loose or liquid faeces	Diarrhoea – should be reported
Dark, concentrated urine	May mean an inadequate fluid intake – should be reported
Cloudy or offensive smelling urine	Could indicate an infection – should be reported
Blood in urine or faeces	May indicate a condition which requires medical attention – should be reported

Checking for changes

It is relatively easy to check for changes in a person's body waste if you provide him or her with assistance to use toilet facilities, or if he or she is using a bed pan or a commode when you will be disposing of the contents. It is more difficult where a person is fully independent and takes himself or herself to the toilet, flushes and cleans afterwards. In this situation, you will not have the opportunity to monitor any changes and all you can do is to make the person aware that such changes can be significant and that he or she should report any changes.

Check it out

Find out about the system in your workplace for checking body waste and reporting changes. Check out the system for recording body waste and where the information goes.

DID YOU KNOW?

The flushing toilet that we use today was developed by a man called Thomas Crapper. It was considered a vast improvement on previous water closets, which used static water or earth and became very unpleasant!

How to leave the environment clean after use

If you are assisting a person to use toilet facilities, or to use a bed pan or a commode, it is important that you clean and tidy the environment afterwards. If the person is using ordinary toilet facilities, this will involve checking that all of the waste has been flushed away, and that there is no residue left in the toilet pan. You should wipe the seat if there has been any spillage and ensure that the person has washed his or her hands. There are appropriate cleaning fluids that can be used to carry out these procedures and they should all be available in your workplace.

It is important that toilets and commodes are left clean after use so that they will be pleasant for the next person to use. It is also important for the dignity of the individual that he or she knows there is no residue left from the disposing of his or her own waste. The smell created by the disposal of body waste should be dealt with by the use of ventilation and air fresheners where appropriate. However, these should be used with discretion in the presence of the individual, who may feel humiliated by a very obvious use of sprays.

On some occasions, particularly when people are unwell, their body waste may be very offensive in odour. On these occasions, a general cleaning with disinfectants, ventilation and air fresheners may have to be used in combination to combat any remaining odour.

> ## REMEMBER
>
> Throughout the process of assisting service users in the use of toilet facilities, you should be taking universal precautions, i.e. wearing gloves and apron.

CASE STUDY

On a gynaecological ward, a woman was recovering from major surgery and requested to use the commode. She had been severely constipated and had been given an enema which was in the process of working. Just at the point when the commode was brought and the curtains were drawn around her bed, the evening meal was served to the other women in the ward. She heard through the curtains comments being made by the other women. 'This is awful. I can't eat this. I feel sick with the smell.' 'Poor thing, she can't help it, but I can't eat my tea'. She was left feeling extremely humiliated and spent the rest of the evening crying quietly in her bed.

1   How could this situation have been avoided?
2   What do you think should have happened?
3   Should the other women have kept quiet?
4   Can you think of a similar situation which could occur in your workplace?

TEST YOURSELF

1   What are the main points to remember when helping someone use a bedpan?

2   What are the techniques for washing or cleaning a service user after using the toilet?

3   Name three different changes you may notice in a service user's body waste.

4   How would you check the body waste of someone who was independently accessing toilet facilities?

5   Why is it important to check body waste?

What you need to learn

- How to record body waste
- How to collect and dispose of body waste
- How to maintain hygiene

How to record body waste

You may be asked to record four types of body waste:

- urine
- faeces
- vomit
- blood.

Urine

You may be asked to record someone's urine output in order to maintain a fluid balance chart. There are many conditions in which a medical practitioner will attempt to establish how well the body is maintaining its fluid balance, i.e. expelling an appropriate amount of urine in relation to the amount of fluid taken in. Where this type of examination is taking place, you will be asked to keep a record of the drinks a service user is having and the amount of urine he or she is passing. This information is kept on a fluid balance chart. This will mean that you will have to ask him or her to urinate into a bed pan or other suitable container. This container can be provided in the toilet so that it can be used there, and you will then need to pour the urine into a measuring device and record in millilitres (ml), how much has been passed. This is also a good opportunity to record and examine the nature of the urine – you may be asked to describe its colour and whether its smell is offensive or normal.

Faeces

Many care settings will record how often service users have their bowels open. This is important to ensure that they are not constipated or that they are not developing an infection which involves frequency or loose stools. Unless there is a particular reason for retaining the faeces, it is normally sufficient to record that bowels have been opened, either by asking an independent service user to inform you or by recording it where you have provided the assistance.

Vomit

Vomits may need to be recorded depending on the person's circumstances. If the medical practitioner has asked you to record the volume of vomit or nature and contents of the vomit, it should be collected in a bowl and then its description and quantity recorded in the notes.

Blood

In some situations, it may be necessary to record blood loss. For example, on a maternity or gynaecological ward, blood loss may need to be recorded, although the estimating of the amount is likely to be carried out by a qualified health professional, such as a nurse or midwife. The range of blood loss can be from spotting to haemorrhage, and an important role for you is to report immediately any significant change in a person's blood loss. In other situations you may be asked to record the level of blood loss from a wound site, possibly following surgery. Again, it is important to report any significant change immediately.

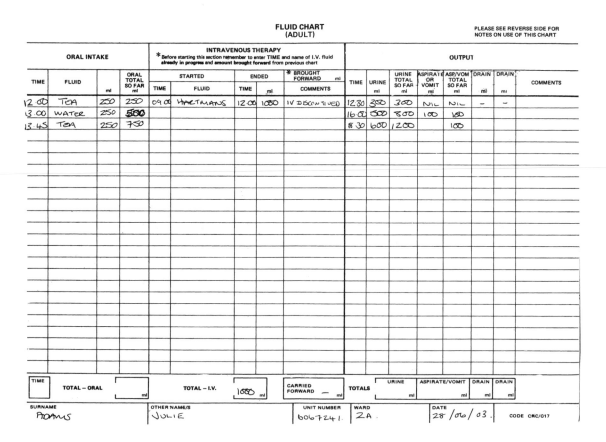

An example of a fluid balance chart.

Check it out

Make sure you know the procedure for checking and measuring body waste in your workplace. Is it carried out in a particular place? Do you have special equipment? Where do you have to record the measurements? If you cannot find this information in the procedures for your workplace, ask your supervisor.

How to collect and dispose of body waste

The commonest way of collecting body waste is in a toilet and the commonest way of disposing of it is simply to flush it away. There may be situations where it is necessary to collect body waste in a bed pan or a commode. This could be because of the needs of the person, i.e. he or she is unable to reach a toilet, or because of the need to retain the person's body waste for further examination.

- If you are dealing with body waste in a bed pan or a commode and it is for straightforward disposal, it should be covered and taken to the manual sluice or to the toilet in line with the procedures laid down for your workplace.
- If the body waste is required for further medical examination, it should be covered and left in an appropriate place, such as the sluice. The person who has requested this to be carried out should be informed that it has been done, and given the location of the waste.

A similar procedure should be carried out for vomit:

- It should be collected in a bowl and disposed of in the sluice, unless it is needed for medical examination.
- People who feel sick should be given a bowl and, where possible, vomit should be collected in the bowl.

If dressings are blood soaked, they should be disposed of appropriately in clinical waste containers.

You must be very careful to follow the correct procedures for disposing of clinical waste, such as used dressings. Your workplace will have laid down a very clear set of procedures.

Menstrual blood on sanitary towels can be disposed of in a special container designed for disposal of soiled sanitary wear. Alternatively, they can disposed of along with other clinical waste.

Soiled linen which has urine, faeces, vomit or blood on it must be dealt with through the special arrangements in your workplace for the disposal of soiled linen. This is likely to consist of a disposal bag in a particular colour, usually red, which goes directly into a washing machine.

REMEMBER
Always wear gloves and wash your hands after dealing with body waste of any kind.

How to maintain hygiene

In Chapter 3 (Unit CU1) you covered in detail the appropriate containers which must be used for clinical waste. Each workplace will have these containers and you should ensure that you follow the correct practice. It is important always to wear gloves and an apron to reduce to risk of cross-infection whenever you are dealing with body waste and its disposal. You should never leave containers uncovered. If they are awaiting examination, ensure they are removed to an appropriate place. It is never acceptable to leave a container of body waste next to a person's bed or in an environment where people have general access.

If there has been a spillage of body waste, perhaps an accident where somebody has been incontinent or has vomited onto the floor, you must clean it appropriately, ensuring that you use the right types of cleaning fluid – those which contain disinfectant – to deal with the spillage. The utensils which have been used to clean it should either be disposed of or thoroughly washed and disinfected. You should ensure that you wear gloves at all times when dealing with spillages of body waste.

Although the question of dealing with body waste can be embarrassing and not always pleasant, if it is dealt with kindly, professionally and with humour, life can be made much easier for both individuals and care workers.

Z11 UNIT TEST

1 What are the expectations of our society about body waste?

2 How would you discuss normal patterns of body waste with a service user?

3 How might someone feel about being incontinent?

4 What factors do you need to take into account when discussing body waste and service users' preferences?

5 What kinds of assistance may a service user who has difficulty walking need when using a toilet?

6 What are the ways that you can collect and dispose of body waste?

7 What steps do you need to take to maintain hygiene when cleaning areas used for disposal of body waste?

8 How do you deal with a spillage?

Enable clients to achieve physical comfort

Dealing with people in pain is never easy. Faced with someone who is suffering, it is natural that you would want to do everything in your power to help and to relieve the suffering. This chapter will give you the opportunity to look at the nature of pain and the steps that you can take towards relieving suffering. You will need to understand how the various approaches to pain can affect the well-being of the individual who is suffering, and how cultural influences affect the way that people experience pain. You will also look at various ways of dealing with pain, ranging from alternative therapy to traditional western medicine.

Rest and sleep are important for everyone. This is universally recognised – there are well-worn sayings that everybody accepts, such as 'It will all seem better in the morning', 'Sleep on it', 'It won't seem so bad after a good night's sleep', and so on. For many people who are receiving care it is difficult to achieve proper rest and sleep for many reasons. It is important that you, as a care worker, understand the importance of ensuring that the people you care for are adequately rested and are able to sleep.

Element Z19.1 Assist in minimising client pain and discomfort

What you need to learn
- What pain is
- How to help people to express their pain
- How to respond to individuals who are in pain
- Ways of dealing with pain

What pain is

Pain is basically whatever the person who is suffering it perceives it to be. Physical pain can be experienced as a result of disease or injury or some other form of bodily distress. Childbirth, for example, is not associated with injury, disease or stress but can nevertheless be an extremely painful experience. Pain is caused by the transmission of the sensation of pain from the site of the injury, disease or stress along a pain pathway. It is transmitted through sensory nerve endings along nerve fibres to the top of the spinal cord and into the brain. There are thought to be different routes for pain pathways for acute pain, caused by an immediate injury, disease, inflammation or illness, and for chronic pain, which is long-standing and continuous. The sensations associated with these types of pain are often described very differently. Acute pain may be described as a stabbing or pricking sensation, whereas chronic pain is more likely to be described as a burning sensation and is perhaps quite difficult to locate in one particular spot.

Emotions play a considerable part in the experience of pain. If someone is afraid or tense or has no knowledge of what is wrong, he or she is likely to experience more pain than someone who is relaxed, and knows exactly what the cause of his or her pain is. Sometimes the fear of pain can not only make pain worse but can cause additional pain by anticipation. This is commonly seen in a person who has an illness or injury in which movement is extremely painful, and he or she reacts in anticipation of being moved. There is also compelling evidence that people who have had limbs removed can continue to feel pain in the limb long after it has been removed. The evidence shows that experiencing pain is a lot more common in a limb which had been painful prior to removal, and would suggest that the pain pathways somehow still continue to function even after the cause has been removed.

Historically there have been many different interpretations of pain, which to a large extent have affected how we view pain today:

● *Pain as a punishment* In the past, pain or illness was often seen as a kind of judgement of somebody who had been wicked. This goes back as far as biblical stories about plagues of boils and the suffering of Job.
● *Pain as a warning* There is a school of thought which believes that pain is an important indication that there is something amiss, that pain has a purpose and that it is designed as a warning. This view still has influence today. Some care and medical practitioners believe that giving pain relief masks the symptoms, and so it is often better to allow people to continue to suffer until a firm diagnosis of their condition has been made. However, most diagnoses today are confirmed by test results or x-rays rather than purely on a patient reporting his or her symptoms.
● *'All in the mind'* As early as the fourth century BC the philosopher Aristotle believed that pain was purely an emotional experience and that it was connected with the heart and not the brain. This view is still influential today – forms of relaxation are found to be extremely beneficial in providing control for pain, both acute and chronic.
● One of the most widely held perceptions of pain today is that it is an *interaction between various factors*, both physical and emotional. It appears logical that both the mind and the body are involved in the experience of pain, and this understanding has given rise to some of the theories of pain control that are used in modern medicine.

DID YOU KNOW?

A recent survey carried out by the Pain Research Institute found that 7 per cent of the general population suffered from chronic pain – but 22 per cent of the population over 65. It also found that more than 70 per cent of people who take painkillers for chronic pain are still in pain.

How to help people to express their pain

Because of people's beliefs, values and culture they may not find it easy to say that they are in pain. This can result from a feeling that they do not want to make a fuss, be a nuisance or bother anyone. Many think it is somehow 'wet' or 'babyish' to complain and that they should accept pain without complaining.

It is important that you create as many opportunities as possible for people to express their pain and that you contribute towards creating an atmosphere where people know it is acceptable to say that they are in pain and they want something done about it. You can help by:

- noticing when somebody seems tense or drawn
- noticing facial expressions, if someone is wincing or looking distressed
- observing if somebody is fidgeting or trying to move around to get more comfortable
- noticing when somebody seems quiet or distracted
- checking if someone is flushed or sweating or seems to be breathing rapidly.

All of these are signals which should prompt you to ask a person if he or she is in pain and if any help or relief is needed. Even in the absence of any obvious signals, it is important to check regularly and ask if any of the people that you care for are in pain or in discomfort or need any assistance.

> ## ! REMEMBER
> Your work is invaluable in reassuring people that expressing pain and discomfort is not only acceptable but preferable to suffering in silence.

You will need to be particularly aware of possible pain when you are providing care for people who are not able to communicate directly with you, including:

- people who do not use English as a first language
- people with speech or hearing difficulties
- people with a severe learning disability or multiple disabilities
- people who are extremely confused.

In all of these cases you may need to look for indications of distress and be able to react to those rather than waiting for the individuals to communicate directly in some way. If a person who is very confused is in pain, this can be difficult to detect because he or she may not be able to find appropriate words to communicate with you.

You will need to be especially vigilant if you provide care for anyone who comes into these categories.

How to respond to individuals who are in pain

Clearly the most natural response to anyone who is in pain is sympathy. This may seem obvious but it is always worth restating that one of the most supportive responses to anyone in pain is sympathy and some 'TLC' – tender loving care.

Find out the guidelines in your workplace for responding to service users' pain. Check the procedure to be followed. Find out the forms of pain relief which can be provided, and those which have to be referred for a medical opinion. Make sure that you know what you can do to help, and what you need to refer to your supervisor.

A person's plan of care will include a strategy for dealing with any pain that he or she experiences. This strategy will have been carefully planned by the whole team if the person you are caring for suffers from a condition which is known to involve pain.

Alternatively, somebody may be suffering pain as a result of an accident or injury which is a sudden occurrence, and you may need to respond before a plan of care has been drawn up. If this is the case, it is important that you offer sympathy and support, and immediately refer the individual to your team manager or supervisor who can arrange for a medical assessment to take place and appropriate pain relief to be prescribed.

REMEMBER

Pain is whatever the person experiencing it believes it to be.

Responses to pain are almost as varied as the individuals involved. Background, culture and beliefs have a great deal of influence on how we respond both to our own pain and to others who are experiencing pain. If you have been brought up with the view that you should 'get on with it' or 'not make a fuss', then you may find it difficult not to become exasperated with somebody who constantly complains about the level of pain that he or she is experiencing. There may be a temptation to remind the person that there are 'plenty worse off than you' or that 'if you take your mind off it and think about something else you will feel a lot better.'

None of those responses is likely to be helpful to somebody who is suffering pain. None of them is an acceptable response from a care worker.

CASE STUDY

Miss L is 87, and she has very advanced Alzheimer's disease. She has no apparent awareness of her surroundings and no longer speaks. She is cared for on a psycho-geriatric ward in her local hospital. Miss L is very thin and fragile, and spends her days mainly sitting in a chair in the lounge. One day, staff noticed that she was eating even less than usual and seemed to be short of breath and quite agitated. It was decided to x-ray her to see if there were problems with a chest disease. When the x-rays were examined it was clear that Miss L had a broken rib.

The cause of the break was not known, but it was clear that Miss L must have been in pain for several days before it was noticed and any action taken. She calmed down and returned to her usual behaviour once she was given pain relief for her rib.

1 What steps should have been taken to notice Miss L's behaviour?
2 How do you think she must have been feeling?
3 What could have happened if no one had noticed?

Being sympathetic does not mean that you cannot offer suggestions and be constructive in advising an individual about steps he or she can take personally to minimise pain. Sympathy is about more than just patting somebody's hand and agreeing that it must be awful; it includes offering practical help and ideas to improve things. It is also important that you ask the individual what help and support he or she would like you to give. It may be that he or she knows from previous experience that a hot water bottle, a change of position, a cushion or a walk around the garden will help to minimise the pain. Make sure that you ask the individual before you impose any of your own suggestions.

The effect of pain on other people

One of the most difficult situations to deal with is when an individual is upsetting others with his or her expression of pain. If somebody is moaning or crying out, other people can become very distressed. If it is happening at night, it can disturb the sleep of others. In situations where others know that they too may experience similar severe pain at some point in their illness, open expressions of pain may give rise to a great deal of fear and distress.

This is a difficult and delicate situation to handle. The one thing that you must never do is to say to the person who is in pain, 'Be quiet, you are upsetting everybody else'. However, you may need to consider moving the person to a place where he or she will be less disruptive or, if that is not possible, having a quiet word with other people to explain that the person is in pain and that he or she cannot help crying out. If the individual is requesting additional pain relief, it would be appropriate to make an early referral in order to give him or her some rest and relief from the pain.

Keys to good practice

✓ Respond to pain at the level the person feels it, not what you think it is.
✓ Be alert for signs of pain, even though people may not complain.
✓ Respond quickly to requests for pain relief.
✓ Reassure people who are frightened and ensure that they are given information by someone who is qualified to do so.
✓ Ask people what methods of pain relief work best for them.
✓ Deal tactfully with situations where one person's response to pain is distressing for other people.

Ways of dealing with pain

One of the most influential theories about pain is the 'gate control theory'. Put simply, the theory is that all pain sensations pass through an area at the top of the spinal cord at the base of the brain which is called the substantial gelatinosa. This organ acts as a 'gate' which can be opened or closed to pain depending on external stimulus, such as pain relief or distraction of attention.

Pain messages pass through a set of fibres through the substantial gelatinosa and into the brain. The gate theory says that other fibres can also be stimulated by events such as particular medications, vibration, temperature changes, electrical impulses, massage, and so on. When the other impulses being passed along the fibres are greater than the pain impulses, the gate will stay 'shut' and the pain will not be experienced. Where the pain impulses are greater than the other stimuli, the gate will remain 'open' and pain will be felt.

b The pain impulses are not impeded from passing through the gate

a The other stimuli passing through the 'gate' are stronger than the pain impulses

Gate control theory.

Gate control theory has created a different approach to dealing with pain in general, and has led to a greater acceptance of methods other than offering straightforward analgesic medication (pain killers) to relieve pain. There is now a recognition that pain can be adequately dealt with in other ways. The types of response to pain which are known to be effective are:

- drugs
- physical methods
- self-help methods
- alternative therapies.

Drugs

Drugs used for pain relief are classified as:

- analgesics (aspirin, paracetamol, etc.)
- opiates (morphine, heroin)
- anti-inflammatories (ibuprofen)
- anaesthetic spinal block (epidural).

Drugs which are supplied on medical prescription for the relief of pain are likely to be analgesics or, in more extreme cases of severe or prolonged pain, they may be opiates.

DID YOU KNOW?

Legally, within the UK, drugs can be administered only by a registered general nurse or midwife and prescribed by a medical practitioner, a dentist or a vet!

Check it out

Find out the procedure for the administration of drugs in your workplace. A registered general nurse or midwife must be the person who administers the drugs, and a second person must check the drugs prior to handing them out.

If additional pain relief is requested, referrals must be made to your supervisor and through him or her to a medical practitioner who is able to prescribe additional drugs if necessary.

Physical methods

Physical methods of pain relief include:

- massage (superficial or pressure)
- vibration
- ice application (with massage)
- superficial heat or cold
- transcutaneous electrical nerve stimulation (TENS)
- transcutaneous spinal electroanalgesia (TSE)
- repositioning.

Self-help methods

Self-help methods of pain relief that have been found to be effective include:

- moving or walking about, if this is possible
- imagining oneself in a pleasant place and in comfort
- taking a warm bath
- taking some recommended exercise
- finding a task to distract from the pain
- having a conversation.

Sometimes even the simplest of methods can be effective in responding to and dealing with pain. It may be sufficient just to alter somebody's position or to provide him or her with a hot water bottle or an ice pack. Sometimes a distraction, like getting him or her involved in an activity or talking to him or her, can help.

Many individuals who have long-term problems will have developed their own strategies for dealing with pain and you should make sure that you know what they are and what part you can play in making them effective. Self-management is always the most effective method of dealing with pain and discomfort because it gives the individual the maximum amount of control. People who feel out of control, and who do not having any information, experience a greater degree of pain than people who feel that they are in control and have a strategy that works for them to minimise their pain.

You should note down in the plan of care each individual's preferred way of dealing with discomfort and make sure that you are able to offer him or her the assistance needed. Sometimes it can be a case of simply positioning a limb or feet on a pillow, raising the feet a little or helping the person to get up and move around, and this can make all the difference.

Alternative therapies

Often people get relief from having a massage or from using aromatherapy oils. The practice of reflexology is often a useful way of relieving pain, and many agencies and care settings have experts who visit on a regular basis to offer services like this.

The so called 'alternative therapies' are increasingly being accepted by practitioners of mainstream western medicine as having an invaluable role to play in the reduction of pain and the improvement of general well-being. Alternative therapies include:

- **aromatherapy**, the use of natural oils
- **homeopathic medicine**, which works by treating the illness or disease with minute quantities of naturally occurring substances which would cause the illness if taken in larger amounts – these may not be used in some care settings
- **reflexology** – specialised foot massage which stimulates particular areas of the feet which are said to be linked to parts of the body
- **acupuncture** – like the other treatments, this must be administered by an expert – it uses ancient Chinese medical knowledge about specific points in the body which respond to being stimulated by very fine needles, and is now being increasingly recognised by western medicine and becoming available from the National Health Service in many places
- **yoga and meditation** – work essentially on the emotional component of pain. Meditation works by dealing with the mental response to pain, whereas yoga combines both mind and body in an exercise and relaxation programme. Relaxation can often be a key to relieving discomfort and to helping people cope. Pain is increased by muscles which are tense, so when people are able to relax and to find a relaxation technique that they can practise for themselves when necessary, this can be extremely beneficial.

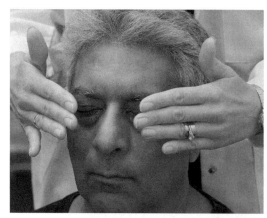

A massage often brings relief from pain.

Alternative therapies should be used only where care professionals are in agreement that they may be used with a particular individual.

Some individuals may prefer to use homely remedies which have been used in their family for many years. This could be something like a 'hot toddy' which will have to be mixed in a particular way. Others may prefer to use alcohol, or they may want to use illicit drugs, such as cannabis, which is known to provide relief in some conditions. Requests for these forms of pain relief should be referred to your supervisor in the first instance.

CASE STUDY

G is 37 and has multiple sclerosis. He is currently living in a specialised unit as he is no longer able to care for himself. He hopes to be in the unit for only a short time until his medication and treatment regime is stable, then he plans to employ personal assistants using the direct payment scheme and live in an adapted bungalow.

In the meantime he is causing concern among the staff of the unit because he is a regular cannabis user. He finds that cannabis is effective in relieving pain and discomfort, and says he intends to continue to use it.

The staff hold a review along with G and his key worker to discuss the situation and how to respond.

1   What would you do in this situation?
2   Is G right to relieve his pain by illegal means if necessary?
3   Can the unit support him in this?

Most methods of pain relief are not curative, i.e. they are not treatments or cures for any particular illness, disease or injury, but they are palliative – they provide relief from the symptoms without curing the illness or disease itself. These palliative treatments may be offered alongside something which is designed to cure a particular condition. For instance, an infected wound may be treated with antibiotics to clear the infection and with pain killers to deal with the pain caused by the infection. In other situations, the cause of the pain may not be curable, but it can certainly be relieved and strategies developed to help people to cope with it. This would be the case where people have diseases like arthritis, terminal cancer, osteoporosis or other long-standing, chronic conditions, which can cause ongoing, serious pain.

Measuring pain

One of the important factors that you need to establish when somebody is experiencing pain is how much pain he or she is feeling. This is difficult because every individual experiences pain at a different level and it is not possible to have an objective measure of pain.

You need to be very clear that pain is about what a particular individual experiences and cannot be measured against pain which you suffer or anybody else may suffer. You cannot measure one person's suffering against another's because each is a very individual experience.

Several methods have been developed to try to measure pain, but one of the most effective is to ask the person to describe it to you on a scale of 1–10 – 1 being mild discomfort and 10 being the most excruciating pain he or she has ever felt. This will at least give you some idea of the level of discomfort the person is feeling and the sort of assistance he or she is likely to need.

Remember that this is not about comparing like with like. If one person with arthritis only puts his or her pain at 3 and somebody else puts his or hers at 7, you cannot say that the person who rated his or her pain at 7 is a 'moaning minny' and that the one who put his or hers at 3 is a 'wonderful, brave soul'. It is about individual experience and you need to react to the level at which that individual describes his or her pain.

Check it out

Draw a scale going from 1 to 10. It will probably look like a ruler or a thermometer. Try to remember an occasion when you have experienced pain and rate it on a scale of 1–10. Note it on the scale you have drawn, then think of another occasion in which the pain was less, or more, than the first time. Rate it and note that down too. Try to think about the reasons for the difference. Was it just the sensation of pain, or were there other reasons? Did you know more about what was wrong? Were you given pain relief? Were you with people you knew and trusted?

TEST YOURSELF

1   Name three factors that influence how people respond to pain.

2   What are the most straightforward ways of relieving someone's pain?

3   Name three types of medication that can be taken for pain.

4   Name two ways of dealing with pain other than medication.

5   Explain gate control theory.

6   Why might two care workers react differently to the same person complaining of the same pain?

7   What factors are likely to make discomfort worse?

8   What factors are likely to help relieve pain and discomfort?

Element Z19.2 | Assist in providing conditions to meet clients' need for rest

What you need to learn
- Why rest and sleep are important
- What happens during sleep
- What are the barriers to rest and sleep?
- How to assist rest and sleep

Why rest and sleep are important

The effects of sleep

A great deal of research has been carried out into sleep, but none of it has yet established exactly what purpose sleep serves. There are many theories, but none have been proven. Some theories suggest that sleep is for the repair and renewal of the body, while other theories say it is for allowing our brains to organise and file all the things which have happened during the day and get the information into some kind of order. Some say that it is about escaping from the world and a chance to recharge our batteries. Research has been carried out into what happens when people are deprived of sleep and there is a wealth of information available on this subject. One researcher made a famous comment that 'the effect of sleep deprivation is to make the subject fall asleep!'

Researchers have managed to keep volunteers awake for between 100 and 200 hours at a stretch, but after that time they tend to fall asleep anyway, regardless of what steps are taken to keep them awake. So it would seem clear that sleep is very necessary and that ultimately the body will ensure that it does sleep.

The physical effects of sleep deprivation are quite slight:

- slight changes in temperature
- insignificant changes in heart and breathing rate.

Most people deprived of sleep are still able to carry out physical tasks without any serious change in their ability to do so.

Emotional changes are more noticeable. People tend to become:

- irritable or anti-social
- very depressed
- suspicious almost to the point of paranoia
- very poor at carrying out mental tasks.

Memory also seems to be affected by lack of sleep. People's ability to recall things they learned before being deprived of sleep seems to be quite seriously affected.

How much sleep do we need?

The length of time people sleep varies and is dependent on several factors.

The age of the person involved has a significant effect on the length of time that he or she requires to sleep. For instance, babies sleep for 14–16 hours a day, while older people may need only five or six hours at night, with several short naps during the day. Most people sleep for an average of eight hours.

DID YOU KNOW?

The Sleep Research Centre has found that people can sleep more than they need to. The research showed that this extra sleep was not beneficial and, like 'over-eating', it is possible to 'over-sleep'.

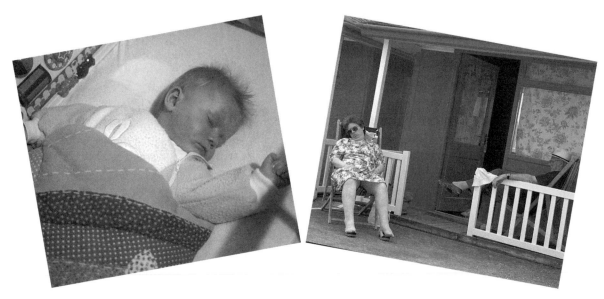

The amount of sleep people need varies with age.

Research has identified two specific groups of sleepers, called long sleepers and short sleepers. Long sleepers sleep for nine hours or more a night, while short sleepers sleep for only five or six hours. There does not seem to be any significant difference between these two groups in their well-being or health.

What happens during sleep

Sleep has four stages:

- **Stage 1:** This is called non-rapid eye movement or NREM sleep. It happens when you have just dropped off to sleep, when you are easily woken.
- **Stage 2:** This is a relaxed sleep but you can still be woken easily. This is NREM sleep.
- **Stage 3:** This is the stage of complete relaxation, your pulse rate is beginning to drop. This is rapid eye movement or REM sleep. It is the stage of complete relaxation when snoring stops, blood flow to the brain increases and the temperature of the brain rises. This is the stage at which people dream. Their eyes dart underneath their eyelids intermittently, breathing is irregular and people tend to move around.
- **Stage 4:** This is deep sleep when it is difficult to be woken and when sleep walking and bed wetting can occur. This stage is also NREM sleep.

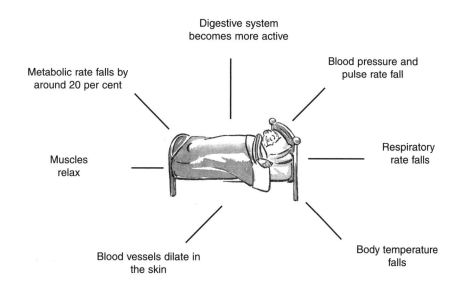

Digestive system becomes more active

Metabolic rate falls by around 20 per cent

Blood pressure and pulse rate fall

Muscles relax

Respiratory rate falls

Blood vessels dilate in the skin

Body temperature falls

What happens to the body during sleep.

Dreams and illness

Research has been carried out into the types of dream people have when they have particular illnesses. Interestingly, dreams appear to be related to particular types of illness (see the table below).

How illnesses and dreams are related

Type of illness	Type of dream
Cardiac	Death/dying (men), separation (women)
Brain injury	Lost resources (money, food, etc.)
Migraine	Terror
Strokes or other neurological damage	Loss of recall, strange dreams in which it is hard to see
Drugs and withdrawal	Loss of recall, vivid or bizarre dreams
Narcolepsy (sleeping sickness)	Vivid or bizarre dreams
Severe organic disease, such as cancer	The ability to dream is lost

Patterns of sleep

The normal pattern of sleep follows natural body rhythms:

- at night people sleep
- during the daytime people work
- evenings are for play.

Shift work disturbs the natural rhythm. Shift workers often find that their health and general feeling of well-being are affected by this changed pattern, which could be:

- night for working
- morning for sleeping
- afternoon for play.

The pattern will vary depending on the timing of shifts.

Other known interruptions to normal sleep patterns are caused by jet lag or by illness when sleep may be disturbed.

Shift work disturbs natural sleep patterns.

Check it out

Make a note for a week of your own sleeping habits. If you are deprived of sleep, note down your reactions. If you work shifts, try to keep a record of how you feel on different shift patterns. Note the things which change your sleeping habits, perhaps worry or anxiety, the hour at which you eat, alcohol consumption, shift work, the demands of children and so on. See what you can find out about yourself and sleep.

What are the barriers to rest and sleep?

A range of factors which can make it difficult for people to sleep. These broadly fall into three categories:

- physical factors:
  - pain or discomfort
  - lack of exercise
  - disturbed body clock
  - feeling hot or cold
  - illness
  - overeating
  - consuming too many stimulants, such as caffeine, alcohol, etc.

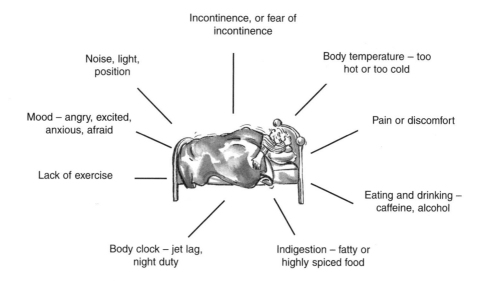

Incontinence, or fear of incontinence

Noise, light, position

Body temperature – too hot or too cold

Mood – angry, excited, anxious, afraid

Pain or discomfort

Lack of exercise

Eating and drinking – caffeine, alcohol

Body clock – jet lag, night duty

Indigestion – fatty or highly spiced food

- emotional factors:
  - worry
  - anxiety
  - distress
  - fear of incontinence
  - fear of disturbing dreams
  - fear in a strange place

- environmental factors:
  - noise
  - external temperature
  - uncomfortable bed or bedding
  - light.

How to assist rest and sleep

You have an important role in helping people both to sleep and to rest. You will need to know how best to support people to sleep well at night and to have rest at times during the day.

How to help people to sleep at night

- Reassure the person and make sure that there is nothing that he or she is anxious or worried about.
- Encourage the individual to carry out some relaxation exercises which will put him or her in a better mental and physical state to drift off to sleep gently.
- Offer a warm drink, preferably a milky drink without any caffeine or stimulants.
- Offer a hot water bottle if the person feels cold.
- Ensure that the individual is comfortable.
- Offer to adjust the person's position or the pillows or to make the bed more comfortable, if required.
- Offer to take the individual to the toilet or to provide a bed pan, if necessary. Often a full bladder or bowel will prevent people from going to sleep.

The environment in which the individual is sleeping is just as important as the care of the individual.

- Try to ensure that noise is kept to a minimum and that squeaking trolleys or noisy shoes, loud laughter or talking amongst the staff are avoided.
- The lights should be dimmed.
- Rooms and sleeping areas should be warm but ventilated.

There is much that can be done during the day which will help to ensure sleep at night. If an individual takes physical exercise, as far as possible coupled with mental stimulation, then he or she is far more likely to achieve satisfactory rest that somebody who has been in an environment with nothing to do either physically or mentally during the day.

Pain or discomfort will obviously be a hindrance to sleep, so it is important that you establish that the individual has adequate pain relief to enable him or her to rest. If he or she needs to be turned during the night, ensure that this is done as comfortably and quickly as possible with minimum disturbance.

A noisy environment can hinder sleep.

Rest during the day

Rest at other times of the day is also important. When planning care, thought should be given to times in the day when individuals are able to have a period of rest. Rest periods should be, as far as possible, uninterrupted by treatments, procedures, observations or activities, so that individuals can rest and relax. Often this period may fit in best immediately after lunch – an early afternoon nap is often welcome.

Rest may not involve sleeping. Reading, relaxing or just being quiet and undisturbed may be equally useful.

Keys to good practice

✓ Everyone who is receiving care should have a plan of that care drawn up by the care team. It is important that plans for rest and sleep are included in the care plan.

✓ Establish what each individual's normal pattern of sleep and rest is by talking to him or her, and by observation.

✓ Any indications of change in an individual's normal sleeping or resting pattern should be recorded and concerns passed on immediately to your supervisor or manager.

✓ Make sure that you talk to the individual concerned about changes in their sleep patterns. Try to establish what the cause may be.

REMEMBER

Everyone benefits from rest and sleep. It is an important part of your job that you do everything in your power to ensure that the people in your care get the maximum possible benefit from resting, relaxing and sleeping.

Check it out

Find out if your workplace has a policy on rest and sleep. Is there a specific time of the day for resting? Are there particular procedures to ensure a restful environment? Are the people you care for able to choose how much or how little they rest and sleep, or is your workplace organised around set times?

Z19 UNIT TEST

1 Describe some of the ways in which people might express their pain without speaking about it.

2 What are analgesics?

3 What is the aim of palliative care?

4 Describe the possible effects on other people in care if an individual is loudly expressing distress over pain.

5 If you were asked to devise a relaxing afternoon activity for a group of people with painful arthritis, what factors would you consider, and why?

6 List five ways in which you could provide your service users with a restful environment.

7 Describe the different stages of sleep.

8 List some possible physical barriers to achieving proper sleep.

Glossary

Abuse	Treating someone or something in a way that causes harm. Abuse may be directed at oneself (self-harm) at others or at things. It may be emotional, financial, physical, psychological or sexual.
Assumption	An acceptance that something is true although there is no real proof of it.
Care setting	The context for health and social care services. These include hospitals, residential settings, day-care facilities, clinics and domiciliary settings.
Care team	All those with a formal or informal responsibility for care, whether paid or unpaid. The care team includes the service user/patient.
Carer	A person who is delivering care in an informal capacity. A carer is someone who is responsible for supporting an individual through the provision of some form of care, be it physical, emotional or financial. The carer is usually a partner, relative or friend.
Clinical procedures	Clinical activities in which health care workers may be involved.
Communicate	Share information, ideas, views and emotions with people by speaking, writing, body language or through the use of equipment.
Consent	An agreement to do something or allow it to be done. 'Informed consent' means that a person has been given the relevant information to decide whether the course of action is the right one.
Discrimination	The practice of treating one person or group of people less fairly or well than other people or groups.
Diversity	The fact that there are many different people, beliefs and things which occur naturally.
Enable	To act in such a way that others will be able to do something through the provision of resources, information, encouragement or help.
Environment	The surroundings in which services are delivered, particularly the intangible aspects.
Equal opportunities	Offering services without discrimination as to race, sex, religion, disability, etc. which aim at ensuring everyone has equal access and equal treatment.
Ethics	Moral principles about right and wrong behaviour. An ethic of a particular kind is an ideal or moral belief that influences the behaviour, attitudes and philosophy of a group of people.
Facilitate	To make something easier or more likely to happen.

Group	A set of people who are considered together because they have something in common.
Health and social well-being	All aspects of social, physical, intellectual, communication and emotional/psychological health.
Individual	Any person who may be the focus of the activity concerned. This may be the person who is in receipt of the services but also may be other workers, managers or others in the vicinity.
Infringement of rights	An action or situation that interferes with someone's rights and freedom.
Key worker	The person who has the main responsibility for relating to a service user and is the main point of contact.
Manager	The person with direct managerial responsibility for the worker in the sense of allocating, co-ordinating and evaluating her/his work.
Materials and equipment	All types of supplies, consumables, sundries, instruments, equipment and machines. These may be clinical or non-clinical. 'Materials' is used to refer to items which have a short life or single use. 'Equipment' refers to items which may be used many times.
Package of care	The set of measures brought together to meet a person's needs.
Plan of care	An outline of an individual's present and future needs and the ways in which these needs will be met.
Policy	Protocols, procedures and requirements to which the worker must adhere. Policies may be set at international, national, local or agency level.
Practice guidelines	Recognised good practice within agencies, including codes of good practice and recognised methods of working.
Records	Electronic, written, diagrammatic, photographic or other information kept about an individual while in receipt of services.
Referral	The act of forwarding a case or issue to a person who is authorised or better qualified to deal with it. Referrals may be between workers in the same agency or across agencies.
Stereotype	A particular fixed general image believed to represent a particular type of person or thing. If you stereotype people you form a fixed idea of them so that you assume they will behave in a particular way.
Team leader	A person who is heading a team of workers to achieve common outcomes.
Values	The moral principles and beliefs that are considered important.
Visitors	Someone who goes to see a person or place who does not usually work there, live there or attend there.

Index